IN FLANDERS
FLOODED
FIELDS

IN FLANDERS FLOODED FIELDS

Before Ypres there was Yser

by

Paul Van Pul

Pen & Sword
MILITARY

First published in Great Britain in 2006 by
Pen & Sword Military
an imprint of
Pen & Sword Books Ltd
47 Church Street
Barnsley
South Yorkshire
S70 2AS

ISBN 1 84415 492 0

A CIP catalogue record for this book is
available from the British Library

Typeset in Sabon by
Phoenix Typesetting, Auldgirth, Dumfriesshire

Printed and bound in England by
Biddles Ltd, King's Lynn

Pen & Sword Books Ltd incorporates the Imprints of Pen & Sword Aviation, Pen &
Sword Maritime, Pen & Sword Military, Wharncliffe Local History, Pen & Sword
Select, Pen & Sword Military Classics and Leo Cooper.

For a complete list of Pen & Sword titles please contact
PEN & SWORD BOOKS LIMITED
47 Church Street, Barnsley, South Yorkshire, S70 2AS, England
E-mail: enquiries@pen-and-sword.co.uk
Website: www.pen-and-sword.co.uk

*Plerosque Belgas esse ortos a Germanis, Rhenumque antiquitus traductos propter
loci fertilitatem ibi consedisse Gallosque, qui ea loca incolerent, expulisse solosque
esse, . . . , Teutonos Cimbrosque intra suos fines ingredi prohibuerint; qua ex re fieri,
uti earum rerum memoria magnam sibi auctoritatem magnosque spiritus in re militari
sumerent.*

Commentarii De Bello Gallico, II, 4.

Most of the Belgae had sprung from the Germans, and a long while ago had been led
across the Rhine and had settled there on account of the productivity of the soil, and
had driven out the Gauls who inhabited those regions. They were the only people
who, in the memory of our fathers, when all Gaul was ravaged, had prevented the
Teutoni and the Cimbri from entering their territory; and in consequence of the
recollection of this achievement they assumed great authority and great airs in
military matters.

Transl. J. Pearl, p.54.

Contents

List of Maps

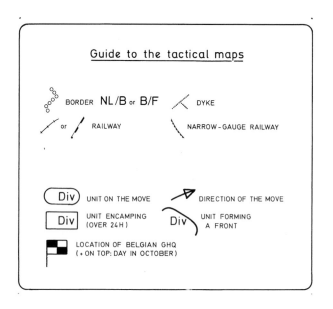

Foreword

The episode of the Great War described in the following pages was fought on Flemish soil – in Flanders' Fields. Despite the fact that the majority of the Belgian population was from Flemish origin and spoke the Flemish dialects[1], the Belgian establishment then was still unilingual Francophone. As an example we can quote the fact that from junior high school on, only one language was tolerated in the classroom and on the playground: French. One of the results was that most of the localities and physical features in Flanders had a French designation that appeared on all official documents. As such many are still known today in the English language.

During the same war, and for a variety of reasons, a Flemish Movement developed in which the Flemish soldiers, who formed the backbone of the front-line fighting forces, came up for equal language rights against the Francophone – and military – establishment.

One of the many and earlier results of this drive for Flemish emancipation was that all toponyms in Flanders reverted to their Dutch spelling. However, as this is a book in the English language we prefer to use the place-names as they were used and written at the time of the battle. Whoever does any reading or research on this tumultuous period in Western European history, be it in French or English, will inevitably run into the same – but now outmoded – spelling.

Since then the Kingdom of the Belgians has come a long way and evolved into a federal state with three official languages: Dutch, French and German.

To visualize the events recounted we included twenty-nine dedicated maps, spread throughout the book. But still, to the uninitiated, the names of places, hydraulic structures, canals and rivers might be daunting. To the layperson it is indeed confusing when the Nieuport Lock is in Furnes and the Furnes Lock in . . . Nieuport! We have therefore included in the map-index the present-day names in brackets. This will also assist readers who one day might want to check out the battlefield on a modern-day map, or even better, visit the various places that once were so gallantly defended by the three western armies against the invading enemy.

In October 1914 Flanders was still experiencing a war of movement. The tactical situation changed hour by hour. So-called 'action pictures' are therefore rather uncommon. Everyone was still too busy advancing or retreating. These few pictures later found their way into official archives and only recently most of these institutions have started to charge for the use and publication of the pictures in their care.

Because of this potential extra financial burden we have limited the photographic material in this book to pictures that were voluntarily provided to us without charge. As such the pictures in this book have either never been published before or were once published many years ago. Where possible we got written or verbal permission to use the illustrations. Our special thanks go to all who helped us with this task.

In order to make the book enjoyable for people less familiar with military jargon, abbreviations have been kept to a minimum. Most were only used with the maps and in the bibliography. A list can also be found at the start of this book.

NOTE
1. The official language in Flanders and the Netherlands is one and the same: Dutch. The Flemish dialects were formerly known as 'Dietsch' and in that sense have also close ties with Low German or *Plattdeutsch*.

Acknowledgements

The following account is the first in-detail, English study of the run-up to and the subsequent military floods during the first phase of the First Battle of Ypres, in Belgium better know as The Battle for the Yser river. It covers the events during the month of October 1914[1] in the western part of Belgium. This work was conducted without financial assistance from public or private sponsors. Only the spontaneous and unselfish cooperation of tens of individuals and institutions, in and outside Belgium, allowed us to realize this book.

It would take pages to mention and thank everyone who contributed to the result. Allow us though to name a few without whom this project would simply have been impossible. Our thanks to all for their continuing help, advice, encouragement and support.

From the first hour there were Renée Beever and Mick Laurijssens, soon followed by Staff Colonel Maurice Paulissen, then Head of the Centre for Historical Documents of the Belgian Army in Brussels and his Chief Historian Jeroen Huygelier. Also in Brussels we immensely appreciate the help of Hervé Thys, son of the late Colonel Engineer Robert Thys, who opened the family archive for us.

In Nieuport we are very grateful to many people, especially the now Honorary Citizens Jules and Bertha Callenaere-Dehouck and City Curator Walter Lelièvre.

Finally it was our special friend Leo Van Riel and his extensive knowledge of graphic computer work that proved to be indispensable in getting the many maps printer-ready.

NOTE
1. This book was first published in Dutch in 2004 under the title: *Oktober 1914. Het koninkrijk gered door de zee. [October 1914. The kingdom rescued by the sea.]*

Glossary

AKP	Archives of the Royal Palace, Brussels
Bde	Brigade
BEF	British Expeditionary Force
Br N Div	British Naval Division
Btn	Battalion
Cav	Cavalry
CA	Belgian Cavalry Division
DAB	French Army Detachment in Belgium (French: *Détachement d'armée de Belgique*)
Div	Division
EFRA	Expeditionary Force for the Relief of Antwerp
EMA	(French) Army Staff (French: *Etat major de l'armée*)
FM	French Marine Fusileers
Ers	Reserve (German: *Ersatz*)
Fr	French
Ge	German
GHQ	General Headquarters
Gp	Group
HLN	Flemish newspaper: *Het Laatste Nieuws*
KLM-MRA	Royal Museum of the Army, Brussels.
LFL	Flemish newspaper: *La Flandre Liberale*
LO	Liaison Officer
Res	Reserve
Rgt	Regiment
RIT	French Territorial Regiment
SGR/CHD	Centre for Historical Documents of the Belgian Army, Evere-Brussels (now SGRS S/A).

Introduction
Flanders' Flood

The young German soldiers were bewildered. This morning they had fiercely attacked and captured a trivial settlement dominated by a church and a windmill just across a slightly elevated railway track. Before daybreak their commander had said this would be the last significant hurdle to take in their persistent drive to capture the first French Channel Port, Dunkirk.

Now, while this not unpleasant autumn day was drawing to an end, they were urgently being recalled. Obviously they were not fleeing from the enemy guns, but because of a more powerful, secretive enemy that was quietly turning the naked, flat land behind them into an inland sea. Hurrying nervously, they ran between the scattered remains of brick houses and wooden sheds back to the railway track.

Before heading into the murky water one of the infantrymen noticed a nameplate on the rural station on the right hand side of the road: *Ramscappelle* it read.

Only yesterday they had all felt upbeat, strong and especially unbeatable. Now a vast mass of icy, brownish water drove them back like *Ramsch*; inferior merchandise, junk being returned to its masters.

After a forced march of half an hour, with the muddy water soaking their boots and socks, they passed a homestead surrounded by a large, square moat. At the entrance a placard read: 'Great Hemme Farm'. The buildings were on somewhat higher ground and part of the moat itself was still visible. By now the water was slowly creeping up their legs and chilling them to the bone.

Not far away to the left, several horse-drawn carriages were struggling to find their way through the landscape-turned-lake. Suddenly the horses lost ground and the wagons and animals disappeared in a treacherous, invisible waterway. The frightened coachmen managed to jump off the wagons and wrestle themselves onto firm ground, leaving their equipment and horses and fleeing in panic to the safety of the river levee in the distance.

The Germans would never make it back to their homestead before Christmas as they had promised their loved ones.

This is the comprehensive story, for the first time ever in the English language, of one of the few successful, large-scale retreats in military history. It is the remarkable tale of the conscript army of a small country, led by a devoted monarch. Almost succumbing under the beating of the mighty German siege artillery inside one of the most elaborate fortresses in the world, it managed to escape. Marching out to the coast it met with the relief force and at the very last minute, its exhausted young men turned and made a stand behind a small winding river. Nevertheless the enemy still seemed overwhelming.

Then a handful of officers and men, guided by two middle-aged, simple civilians, turned the region into an inland sea. They succeeded in checking the brutal invader, not by fire, but by water.

Both sides often used abandoned farm buildings in the inundated polder as reinforced listening posts.
Nieuport 1914-1918, R. Thys, 1922.

For King and Country

In 1830, after the Belgian francophone uprising against Dutch rule in Brussels and the subsequent declaration of independence, the national congress voted to install a monarch at the head of its institutions. One of the members of the congress would call it: 'A king by vote'.

As such the Belgian head of state, unlike in other countries with a monarchy, is officially known as 'The King of the Belgians': – the king of the Belgian *people* – not the country.

Article 68 of the Constitution declared the king as being the commander-in-chief of the armed forces. Moreover it appeared that the members of the national congress were not interested in foreign policy and would leave this up to their new head of state as the same article also stated that 'the king could declare war, conclude peace and enter into alliances'.

Here again is a fundamental difference with other monarchies. In times of crises, Belgian monarchs have always distinguished themselves by taking active control of the army in the defence of the country and its people.

This had happened in 1831 with King Leopold I, immediately after independence of the country from the Netherlands and again in 1914 with King Albert [1].

The thirty-nine year old king, rather shy and reserved took his inaugural oath to the Constitution very seriously as most people found out and appreciated only later. As such, when on 4 August 1914, the German Imperial armies dragged the small kingdom into an essentially Franco-Prussian feud, King Albert personally headed his army to defend the integrity and independence of his nation.

Bound by a constitutional pledge of perpetual neutrality by the European powers of the day – Russia, Great Britain, France and Germany – the king steered a political and military course that aimed at getting the German armies out of the country, without in any way favouring the French 'cause'. This irritated many Belgian politicians and a large part of the military establishment who saw a swift and close cooperation with the French (army) as a necessity to free the country from the invader. But the king knew his history lessons well and feared a post-war Belgium under French dominance as much as a German victory.

This difference in opinion on the basic policy to follow, created tensions between the king and his personal advisers on one side and people in his High Command and some politicians on the other.

Another article in the Constitution that would cause friction at the highest level was Article 64. This article said that no act by the king could be law unless a minister, who thereby took full responsibility, countersigned it. In normal circumstances this basic law would not cause any legal problem but when, in times of war, the king – as proscribed in Article 68 – would be 'in the field' it was not always evident that there would be a government minister close at hand to approve of every royal tactical or even strategic decision, let alone countersign!

In those days the position of Prime Minister did not exist yet. The king himself was supposed to preside over the cabinet meetings, which he often did. Instead one minister was unofficially appointed as 'Chief of the Cabinet', a post which he held in conjunction with his ordinary cabinet post.

In the period we describe, the Minister of War, Baron – later Count – Charles de Broqueville, fulfilled the role of chief of the cabinet.

Being intuitive, rather inclined towards close cooperation with France, this brilliant but also loyal politician often differed in opinion from his soft-spoken, intelligent monarch on the political course to follow and the military action to be taken. Both men nevertheless knew that they needed each other in order to defeat this national tragedy.

It is in a large measure thanks to their skilful interaction throughout the Great War that Belgium emerged as a mature and respected nation on the world stage at the end of this horrendous armed conflict.

The policies King Albert followed and the strategic decisions he took were mainly inspired by two men: first his lifelong mentor, General Harry Jungbluth, who had been

Charles de Broqueville, born in Postel (The Kempen region east of Antwerp) in 1860; in 1914 Minister of War, Chief of the Cabinet and Prime Minister. In large part thanks to the pragmatic and clever interaction between the king and this shrewd but loyal politician Belgium survived the Great War intact.
Onze Helden, R. Lyr, 1922.

The former royal palace on the Meir in Antwerp. On 6 September 1914, during a meeting of the recently established War Council, Minister de Broqueville succeeded in sacking three of the king's senior officers and replaced them with his own protégé, Colonel Maximilien Wielemans. *Author's photo archive.*

recalled for active duty on 6 September 1914 to head the Military House of the king, and secondly Captain Commandant Émile Galet, his aide-de-camp and former fellow at the Royal Military Academy.

During a 'palace revolution' on 6 September 1914 in Antwerp, the Minister for War had managed to have the royalist Lieutenant General Antoine de Selliers de Moranville, Chief of Staff, and his Deputy Chief, Louis de Ryckel, removed in favour of his own confidant Colonel Maximilien Wielemans. Due to his rank Wielemans became Deputy Chief while the post of chief of staff was left vacant for the time being.

With hindsight Wielemans' character proved to be a rather frail counterweight to the king's eminent personal military advisers but there were undoubtedly enough pro-French feelings around at High Command and in the military cabinet of the minister to compensate for this personal weakness.

It is in Antwerp that our story starts.

NOTE
1. Albert of Belgium (1875–1934), since 1909 third king of the Belgians. Although Albert II (1934 –), grandson of King Albert (I), was sworn in as sixth king of the Belgians on 9 August 1993, we refer in the text to the man often cited as the *King-Soldier* as King Albert, for simplicity's sake dropping the roman numeral one.

Chapter I

Farewell to a Fine Fortress

Throughout the centuries mankind has developed an economically acceptable strategy to defend itself against a brutal invader. Remnants of this policy can be found in various forms all over the world. As there was never enough manpower available to defend a whole territory, leaders always prepared certain well located 'fortified places'. In case of an attack the population would retreat into these enclosures and leave the remainder of the land to the tyranny of the enemy. This practice of constructing strongholds – fortress building – culminated in a mathematical form of art practised by military engineers like the Frenchman Sébastien Le Prestre de Vauban (1633-1707) and later, in Belgium, by Captain Henri Alexis Brialmont (1821-1903).

Although even before the time of Christ, people lived on the banks of the Scheldt River near where now 'Het Steen' (The Stone Fortress) stands, the first semi-circular earthen bulwark, not 200m in diameter, can only be traced back to 980 A.D. With the continuous expansion of the city subsequent new walls were built. The 'Spanish Ramparts', built in the sixteenth century, are certainly the most depicted on old cartographical maps of the City of Antwerp.

In 1859 the city had again spread far outside its fortifications and it was decided to flatten the Spanish walls. The Belgian government nevertheless wanted to keep Antwerp as a fortified place and ordered the construction of no less than two, later three, wider rings of fortresses around the economic heart of the country. So in 1914 the 'Fortified Place of Antwerp' was definitely one of the most impressive and elaborate fortified positions in the world.

General Henri Alexis Brialmont, engineer and chief architect of the ring of fortresses around Antwerp in the nineteenth century.
Onze Helden, R. Lyr, 1922.

1

The outermost ring of forts, some 18km from the city centre, was the most modern and had been built following the late-nineteenth century development of heavier and more far-reaching field guns. This row of concrete forts was nevertheless not continuous. Between the Fort of Breendonck and the one at Wahlem in the south, for instance, a distance of 8.5km, the low laying and wet terrain did not allow for the construction of heavy structures. A similar problem arose west of the Fort of Bornem, near the Scheldt riverbank.

So in the event of war, the engineers of the Garrison Army were to open the drainage gates to the adjacent rivers and flood these vulnerable polders, including areas north and east of the city.

The second row of older, closely spaced forts, 6 to 7km from the town hall, consisted of heavy masonry structures and had been built in conjunction with the inner, continuous fortifications following the plans of the then Lieutenant General Brialmont in 1860.

As planned, when the Imperial German Armies invaded Belgium in August 1914, the military engineers started to prepare these fortifications for the defence of the city. Older conscripts that made up the garrison army manned the forts and by the end of September large tracts of polders along the Rupel and Nèthe rivers were ready to be inundated.

Liège and Namur had also been provided with a belt of fortifications at the end of the nineteenth century. As it was assumed that a large, modern army would not be able to make its way along the narrow, winding forest roads of the Ardennes, the prevailing minds of the day saw an aggressor from the east (i.e. Germany) inevitably pass through the city of Liège while an initial attack from the south (France) would be directed against the city of Namur on the confluence of the Meuse and Sambre rivers. So by either one of these cities the Belgian Army would have to make a stand to hold up its honour and defend its guaranteed neutrality.

Fort number 3, south-east of the city. This is the oldest and only 'Brialmont' fortress in the defensive ring around Antwerp that would ever have any tactical value. Strangely enough this would be in *another* war and, on top of it, for the enemy! In 1941 the German occupier built a concrete runway on the nearby aerodrome of Deurne (see the arrows) with the eastern threshold abutting the fort. Allied pilots were forced to start or end their bombing run over the fortress which had been well equipped with AA-guns by the enemy.
Author's photo archive.

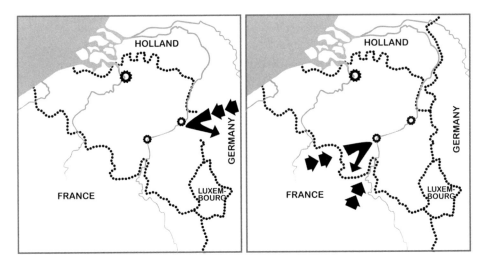

In a continental context the Belgian fortifications round Liège and Namur were the key to prevent Prussia – later Germany – and France going to war again. It did not turn out that way.

It should be no surprise that Antwerp had been chosen by the government to become the *réduit national* or National Entrenched Camp, rather than the capital, Brussels. Already Antwerp was one of the most important seaports in the world and a commercial centre second to none. Since 1860 the whole national defence policy of the country had been built around the concept of Antwerp being the operational base and national refuge for the Field Army. But, in 1914, suddenly a major problem arose.

We translate from General Émile Galet's book *S.M. Le Roi Albert*:

> As established in 1905, at the time of the enlargement of the Fortified Camp [of Antwerp] the way to act, in case of war, will be that Antwerp, as operational base for the Field Army, will become the seat of government, the bulwark that, if it falls, will be our defeat and the loss of our independence.
>
> This official standpoint was a repeat of the concept of 1859 when the original forts had been built as a reaction to the expansionist tendencies of the Second French Empire. It was evident then that, after an invasion from the south, we would stubbornly defend our territory and retreat towards Antwerp where we would make a last stand, protected in the rear by the northern [Dutch] frontier.
>
> This reasoning does not hold entirely if we assume an invasion from the *east*. In that instance Antwerp is not at the edge of the country but in the middle. If then Antwerp would be the national retreat it would mean that the army would not have utilized all the defensive lines in the country nor that it would have used all chances to be rescued before being eliminated.
>
> In the beginning of the war the cornerstone of our strategy was still the doctrine of Antwerp as ultimate refuge. It was obviously still a viable option. In case of a German attack the clause of guaranteed neutrality was still valid. It

3

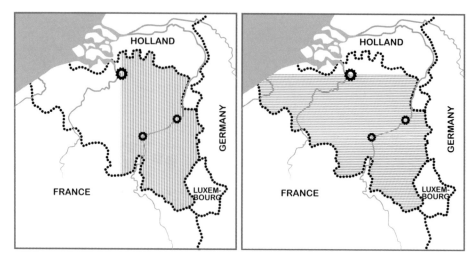

Antwerp, as a national refuge against an invader from the south (picture right) made sense.
Against an aggressor from the east (picture left) the case was rather doubtful.

was reasonable to assume that, given the expected delays for the invader to reach
the fortified place, . . . our guarantors from the west and the south would still
be able to send us reinforcements with whom we would be able to thwart the
whole enterprise.

The appropriate moment for the arrival of the allied support did not depend
on us. It was even not sure if we would get help. In fact, of the two possible
scenarios – a timely or a late arrival – it was the last one that occurred.

If, before the war, someone had predicted that it would take the French and
British armies three months before they would come to our rescue it would have
provoked indignant outcries from all sides; such a statement would have been
unthinkable. Nevertheless that was what happened. The policy of Antwerp was
therefore not always suitable.

Since 1860 Antwerp had been the cornerstone of the Belgian defence policy. The city
had one of the largest and most modern ports in the world and was the commercial
heart of the country. The region within the perimeter of the fortified place was therefore destined to be the operational base for the Field Army and, in case of emergency
it could serve as the national retreat.

Since the invasion of the country by the German Imperial Armies on 4 August 1914,
the Field Army had fought the defensive war as laid out in 1851:

The role of the Belgian Army is to fight a defensive war, that is a war where the
country will be defended stubbornly. This is understood to mean not to lose the
enemy from sight, take up position as often as possible so as to force him to
deploy and manoeuvre, to keep the enemy close by to observe his movements
and be able to seize the opportunity to take the offensive as soon as circumstances are favourable. (Galet p.369)

4

The Antwerp Roads before the war. The port enjoyed important trading relations with Germany. Foreign warships would regularly call at the city wharf, like the new German battleship *Kaiser Karl der Grosse* in 1905. These visits were not solely made as a matter of 'showing the flag', but they also allowed the officers to acquire the latest nautical information and gain practical experience navigating the winding Scheldt River.
Onze Helden, R. Lyr, 1922.

But against an overpowering enemy, the Field Army could but reluctantly, retreat towards its fortified supply base. Eleven days after the invasion the last bulwark of the Liège Fortified Place, the sentinel against an invader from the east, fell into German hands. On 20 August, not without several bloody clashes and battles, the Field Army had withdrawn within the Antwerp outer line of fortifications.

At that moment, as the hostile forces were coming from the east, most of the western part of the country was still unoccupied. But France and Great Britain, the now friendly powers, on whose goodwill the Belgians had to rely for help, had not been quite as prompt in coming to the rescue as had been anticipated.

Now the terrible prospect of a siege of the National Refuge was looming. The prediction of the Minister for War who had developed the defensive strategy in 1851 rang through the minds of many a military mind:

I am convinced that the siege [of Antwerp] will not take place unless we have been abandoned by God and the world. In that case, the whole army will be united.

Help had been promised, but when would it arrive? The Anglo-French forces were having their own share of troubles in northern France. To relieve these forces somewhat – and in the meantime draw attention to his country's difficult situation – the king

A young Winston Churchill, in 1914 as First Lord of the Admiralty.
Onze Helden, R. Lyr, 1922.

decided to launch a sortie from the almost besieged city into the German right. The raid was carried out at the end of August and involved the Field Army pushing towards Brussels and Louvain.

Another sortie, with the same objectives, was again carried out in the first half of September. Because of the restricted capabilities of the Belgian Army these attacks were limited in scope and lasted only a couple of days: the first sortie on 25 and 26 August and the second from 9 to 13 September.

King Albert launched the second sortie three days after the start of the famous Battle of the Marne. It can safely be said that this bold move by the Belgians deprived German High Command of an additional 60,000 soldiers in northern France. These men, destined for France, were instead diverted to bolster the 'observation army' in front of Antwerp.

In spite of this brave war effort by Belgium, substantial military assistance was not forthcoming. The only foreign politician with enough stature to come up with practical plans for immediate and major aid to the Belgians in Antwerp was First Lord of the Admiralty, Winston S. Churchill. At first he wanted the Dutch to open the Scheldt River for any supplies the defenders in Antwerp needed. But the Dutch government insisted on its neutral status and London lacked the political will to enforce such a policy.

The only way left for the British to supply Antwerp would be overland via the road Ostend-Ghent-Antwerp. With the Germans already advancing on Lille this would soon become a treacherous adventure. On 7 September Churchill wrote:

> You have only to look at a map to see the folly of trying to feed Antwerp by Ostend and Ghent.

Nevertheless the British had a lot more at stake in the defence of Antwerp than the French. Lord Kitchener, and indeed the rest of the cabinet in London, saw a direct threat to the whole British Empire in a capture of Antwerp by the Germans. The Belgian port was indeed sealed off from the North Sea by the Dutch territorial waters of the Westerscheldt River but, being a deep-water port, the Germans might be enticed to flout Dutch neutrality and make it a homeport for the *Heimatflotte*. The Britons had never forgotten the level-headed sally used by Napoleon Bonaparte at the end of a speech to Antwerp dignitaries on 19 July 1803:

> I will make Antwerp a pistol, pointed at Great Britain.

The entrance to the Royers Lock in Antwerp. Inaugurated in 1907 this sluice is 180m long, 22m wide with a draught of 11m at high tide. The Admiralty therefore feared that the German *Hochseeflotte* would use the Antwerp docks as a supply warehouse and operating base. Technically this fear was well founded: the *Kaiser Karl der Grosse* for instance was 125.3m long, 20.4m wide and had a draught of 8.25m.
Author's photo archive.

Antwerp did possess a vast complex of docks, including two large, brand new ones, connected to the river via a sea lock that would be able to handle the majority of German battleships.

Churchill though, with the support of Kitchener, did what he could.

One characteristic incident should be mentioned here: on 1 October Rear Admiral Henry Oliver, Director of the Intelligence Division at the Admiralty, arrived in Antwerp. With the assistance of one Belgian officer, five soldiers and a local boy scout he managed to disable thirty-eight German merchant ships then in port. As a result none of these ships put to sea for the remainder of the war.

Guns and ammunition out of naval stores were sent to Antwerp but at the end of September the Germans had their heavy artillery in place around the city and started their siege bombardment.

The British Prime Minister, Lord Asquith, wrote on 30 September:

> The Belgians are rather out of 'morale' and are alarmed at the bombardment of Antwerp which has just begun. They are sending their archives and treasures over here and talk of moving the seat of Government to Ostend.

Upon this distressing news the government in London dispatched Churchill to Antwerp to investigate the situation first hand. Meanwhile the 1,800 men strong Royal Marine

Brigade, already in Dunkirk, was ordered to Antwerp immediately as a first step, awaiting more reinforcements to be sent. Eighty-two London double-decker buses transported the men via Eecloo to Ghent. During the day of 3 October telegrams went back and forth between the British and French governments – the latter then already installed at Bordeaux – dealing with the composition of an Anglo-French Relief Force for Antwerp.

Churchill spent 4 October in Antwerp, trying to boost morale. His mere presence and unflinching attitude worked magic. So as he had apparently succeeded, he at once asked London to send the two Naval Brigades that he himself had set up in August but which were still in training. They were the only troops readily available that were not destined for the BEF.

In Winston Churchill the Belgian king had found an ally. Against the wishes of some of his Francophile ministers and generals, King Albert wanted to stay and defend Antwerp with his combined Field and Garrison Army. But all this depended on the timely arrival of sizable reinforcements and a secure link with the as yet unoccupied west of the country.

Hope of this happening was dashed however around midnight when Colonel Tom Bridges, special envoy from British Field Marshal French, pulled into Antwerp. He had travelled in one stretch with his open Rolls Royce from Fère-en Tardenois (Aisne), where the headquarters of the BEF was located, to Antwerp. Because the German armies were already threatening Lille, the dashing envoy had been obliged to skirt far westward. As such he had travelled 600km over the narrow, winding cobblestone roads of northern France and Belgium that night, a remarkable feat in those days!

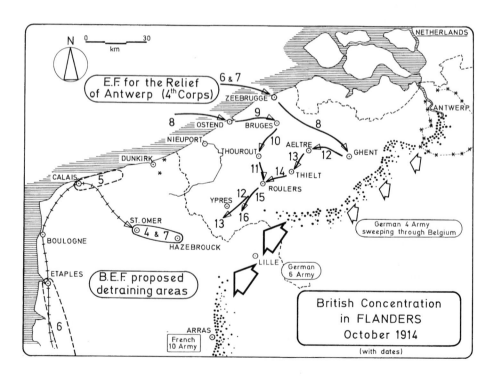

While London proclaimed that the Belgians were to hold Antwerp until reinforcements arrived, Bridges brought the disturbing news that the whole of the BEF was being transported from the Soissons area, 90km north-east of Paris, to Lille, 200km north of Paris and near the Belgian border. This would dramatically shorten the British supply lines and offer the BEF a quick evacuation route in case the German advance west suddenly accelerated.

Since the German advance was already closing in on Lille the British troops had to be transported from Soissons first west and then along the Channel coast up to Calais. From there they travelled back inland (see map opposite).

A typical example of the uncertain and rapidly changing situation are the orders for their final destination: on 4 October they were supposed to detrain between St Omer and Hazebrouck but the next day this was changed to the area Calais/Gravelines. The disembarkation was even moved back to Etaples/Abbeville on 6 October. Then, when the tactical situation seemed to improve, the orders on 7 October once again reverted to the region of St Omer/Hazebrouck.

For King Albert the future of the Fortified Place of Antwerp was thus sealed. This major British troop redeployment, six army divisions, would most likely provoke a corresponding shift of German forces. This British initiative, with grumbling French approval, would thus create a whole new theatre of operations far west of Antwerp.

With the enemy already in Brussels and now certainly bound to march west in force, suddenly the still free link between Antwerp and the coast was in grave and immediate danger. The promised Anglo-French reinforcements could, on the one hand, be prevented from reaching Antwerp while, on the other, the Belgian Army might get trapped inside the entrenched camp sooner than anticipated.

On 5 October the king's premonition was strengthened by two messages. At Schoonaerde, 20km east of Ghent, German advance units tried to force the passage of the Scheldt River. Due to fierce resistance they failed but it was inevitable that they would soon try again; this time certainly better prepared.

At 15:00 a dispatch arrived from the Belgian Mission at French General Headquarters indicating that:

On 2 October 1914, engineers of the Fortified Place of Antwerp prepare the destruction of the new bridge on the main railway line between Antwerp and Brussels over the Nèthe River.
Photo archive Thys.

Eight German cavalry divisions are trying to encircle the French left flank . . . supported by *Landwehr* infantry attacking the suburbs of Lille.

Likewise from south of Antwerp itself, the news was not encouraging. During the night the Germans had managed to get a foothold on the north bank of the Nèthe River, west of the town of Lierre. The Belgian infantry, constantly suffering from the superior German artillery, had been unable to regain control of the levee. A counter-attack launched the next night failed to throw the enemy back over the river.

In the early morning of 6 October news arrived that the enemy was bombarding three positions around Termonde – 30km south-west of the city – on the Scheldt River upstream from Antwerp. Further west still at Schoonaerde, the defenders, taken under enfilading fire, were retreating from the north bank while it was reported that the enemy was preparing bridging equipment on the opposite side. The Belgian Fourth Army Division, stretched out here along the river, informed High Command that it had no more reserves to engage. Upon this news the Deputy Chief of Staff ordered the Sixth

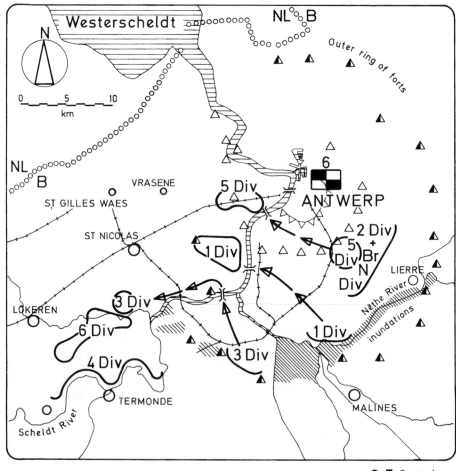

6-7 October

Army Division, which was until then holding the Antwerp outer perimeter south of the Scheldt, to cross the river and march west to reinforce the Fourth and the Cavalry Division to prevent the Germans from crossing the river.

Meanwhile the German bridgehead north of the Nèthe river near Lierre had been strengthened with a few guns. These, together with a frontal bombardment, created confusion among the retreating defenders. Soon after noon the Fifth Army Division, worn out, filtered through the Second Army Division positioned in second line north-west of Lierre. The Germans had gained a bridgehead within the fortified position.

As Churchill did not want his two newly arrived British Naval Brigades to be immediately engaged in the front line he ordered them to fall back to a position three kilometres behind the Belgian Second Army Division. With the Second already 5km away from the Nèthe River it was now certain that the whole outer defence of the entrenched camp had to be given up. Soon the Germans could bring their siege artillery to bear on the city centre itself. Only a few more days would be left before the inevitable surrender.

At 16:00, at the Royal Palace in the city, the Defence Council was called to review the situation and make new proposals. Winston Churchill attended the meeting.

Unanimously it was decided that, since the main line of defence had been broken, the entire Field Army should cross the Scheldt to the left bank that same night. To defend the second line around the city, the commander of the entrenched camp, General Deguise,[1] asked to retain ten garrison battalions, the British Naval Division and most of the Second Army Division. In peacetime the Second was garrisoned in Antwerp and its officers were well acquainted with the local conditions.

This solution satisfied the king. The defence of the national refuge on the right bank would be entrusted to the same number of British and Belgian troops; a honourable settlement. In the meantime the most exhausted divisions, the First, Third and Fifth, could cross the river and, covered by the Fourth and Sixth, would be able to recoup in relative safety.

At 20:00 the Army Orders for 7 October were issued. In it the entire operation was detailed. Each of the three divisions was to form a separate column and cross the river in a different spot. The Third Army Division was to pass on the southernmost pontoon bridge near Rupelmonde. The First was to cross near Hemixem, while the Fifth had to take the pontoon bridge near the city at Burght. General Headquarters would be installed in St Nicolas, 18km west of Antwerp, the next morning.

After having been engaged in combat for several days and, despite the night time march, the rank and file proceeded swiftly and by seven the next morning all the troops had reached their assigned encampments on the left bank of the Scheldt.

All the tribulations of the previous days passed through King Albert's mind while he spent the morning of 7 October in Antwerp. It would be hard for him to say goodbye to this jewel in the Belgian military crown; this economic powerhouse of the nation. All the army divisions, except the Second, were now on the left bank of the river. Further along the Scheldt, towards Ghent, the Fourth and Sixth Army Divisions had taken up positions to guard against any enemy intrusion across the river. The First, Third and Fifth, that had suffered most in the previous days, would be able to take a short break in the temporary camp organized on the left bank, opposite the city.

By withdrawing within the second line of forts, the perimeter of the Antwerp Fortified Place had been reduced to 17km. These eight forts – in essence the original fortifications

Intended Make-Up of the French-British

EXPEDITIONARY FORCE for the RELIEF of ANTWERP

under

Major General Sir Henry RAWLINSON

(As planned on 5 October 1914)

1	**Royal Naval Division** *(Brigadier General Sir G.Aston)* (8,000 men)	Royal Marine Bde	*Arrived in Antwerp on 4 October 1914*
		1 Naval Bde	*Arrived in Antwerp on 6 October 1914*
		2 Naval Bde	
2	**7th Division** *(Major General T. Capper)* (18,000 men) (5,500 horses)	20th Inf Bde	
		21st Inf Bde	*Disembarked in Zeebrugge on 6 and 7 October 1914*
		22nd Inf Bde	
		Northumberland Cavalry	
		Heavy Artillery	
3	**3d Cavalry Division** *(Major General J. Byng)* (4,000 men) (4,000 horses)	6th Cav Bde	*Disembarked in Ostend on 8 October 1914*
		7th Cav Bde	
		Divisional Artillery	
4	**Brigade des Fusiliers Marins** *(Rear Admiral Ronarc'h)* (8,260 men)	1 Rgt F.M.	*Arrived in Ghent on 8 October 1914*
		2 Rgt F.M.	
		Regt Zouaves	
5	87e Division d'Infanterie Territoriale *(General Roy)* (15,330 men) (380 horses)		*Never showed up in Belgium*

Forty-four per cent of this theoretic force would have comprised French troops. Ultimately only 15 per cent of them showed up as the Marine Fusiliers Brigade under Ronarc'h. With a force reduction of more than a quarter the relief operation was doomed from the start.

designed by Brialmont – were defended by the garrison troops. The interval of these forts, 10km in all, were occupied by the Belgian Second Army Division and the British Marine Division, now composed of the Royal Marine Brigade and two naval brigades.

King Albert deemed this deployment sufficient until the expected arrival of the Franco-British relief force under Major General Sir Henry Rawlinson. With these reinforcements – 53,000 men – it would be possible to return into the city and retake the outer line of forts.

But for the moment his main worry was the protection of the communications with the coast. No reinforcements could be sent in when the Germans threatened the city of Ghent, halfway between Antwerp and Ostend.

Before his return to London, Churchill and General Rawlinson, who had been appointed commander of the Anglo-French 'Expeditionary Force for the Relief of Antwerp' on 3 October, had reached an agreement with the Belgian government that Churchill described to Lord Kitchener as follows:

> That while the town endures bombardment General Paris with naval division and Belgian support will defend inner line forts to the utmost.
>
> That the rest of the Belgian Field Army shall be immediately withdrawn across the Scheldt to what they call the entrenched camp of the left bank. The Scheldt, various forts and entrenchments, and large floods protect this area, and here they hope to find time to recover and re-form. From this position they will aid to the best of their ability any relieving movement that may be possible from the west.
>
> Rawlinson will organize relieving force at Ghent and Bruges and prepare to move forward as soon as possible.

Henry Rawlinson and Churchill left Antwerp for the coast in the evening. Some 15km outside Ghent they met with Rawlinson's brother, Alfred. He was one of the thousands of well-to-do British gentlemen who had volunteered enthusiastically at the start of the war. While driving his own Hudson sports car equipped with, among other things, four spare tyres, he was now a relay runner of sorts between the various headquarters. Together the small convoy drove to Bruges from where Churchill continued to Ostend where a fast Royal Navy destroyer was waiting for him.

For a moment the king contemplated staying in Antwerp, at least until the German bombardment of the city centre began. His sheer presence would certainly bolster the morale of the troops that had been left behind. This chivalrous gesture appealed to his spouse, Queen Elisabeth, but Baron de Broqueville expressed the fear that the longer the king remained in the city the greater the chance that, in a surprise attack, he might be taken prisoner by the enemy. Such a development would, of course, be the most disastrous that could happen to the country and it had to be avoided at all cost.

Based on a few second-hand remarks some historians have maintained that the king intended to surrender in Antwerp. This seems to us – and we are not alone in this opinion – to be rather far-fetched. All indications are that this was not the case. We present our personal view in the next few lines.

As the location of the Royal Palace in the city centre was well known to the Germans it was feared that it could become a target for an aerial bombardment by German zeppelins. So, in order to secure his personal safety King Albert suggested at some point that he should move from the palace to the fortified barracks in the suburb of Berchem. There he would be in relative safety and very close to the city aerodrome at *Wilrijkse Plein* from where an aeroplane could fly him out at a moment's notice. As in those days there were still large open pastures outside the old continuous fortifications, it was even possible to land alongside the railway tracks in Berchem and pick up the monarch within walking distance of his new quarters.

There was another important factor that must have weighed heavily on the Belgian decision to 'abandon' the Fortified Place of Antwerp. After the Battle of Gravelotte in the Franco-Prussian War of 1870 Marshal Bazaine had opted for a retreat of his Army of the Rhine inside the Fortified Place of Metz instead of retreating towards Paris to join a newly formed French Army at Châlons. As such he enabled the Prussian Army to fully encircle Metz and cut him off from the rest of France. Now, forty years later, a similar scenario was about to unfold unless the Belgian Army was to retreat to the west to join the *Entente* armies.

However, there were now more urgent matters. Since General Headquarters had been moved to St Nicolas the king was without news from the High Command. In order not to paralyse the supreme command of his army it was finally decided that he would not postpone his departure.

At 12:00 the king gave his last orders to the commander of the entrenched camp. General Deguise and his troops would retreat to within the second line of forts and continue the defence from there. The king nevertheless emphasized his desire that advantage should be taken of the different possibilities of the Fortified Place in order to delay the enemy.

Around 13:30 the royal couple left the palace and drove to the pontoon bridge near *Het Steen* (The Stone), the medieval castle on the riverfront. The still remaining citizens and the thousands of refugees cramming the streets near the riverfront applauded and cheered the royal couple on their slow journey. Amidst exceptional crowding they managed to cross but it took an hour and a half to cover the remaining 18km to reach St Nicolas. The road being filled with an amalgamation of refugees, soldiers and an unbelievable assortment of carts, wagons and motorcars, it was difficult to make progress.

The air at the re-established General Headquarters was filled with anxiety. The latest intelligence reports spoke of the enemy having been sighted north of the river near Schoonaerde while fighting was going on in Termonde and Wetteren. The Fourth Army Division had tried to contain the damage but, being stretched over 30km along the river-bank, this was an almost impossible task.

Meanwhile an important German cavalry detachment had been sighted marching towards Ghent, but this time coming from Lille in the south. The enemy was clearly threatening the Belgian supply line Ostend-Ghent-Antwerp. With the Anglo-French relief force nowhere near, it was better to play it safe. The covering force near Ghent under the Belgian General Clooten had to be strengthened with part of the First Army Division, the remainder to go by rail to Ostend to protect the new base.

The Fifth Army Division, having been heavily engaged in the battle for the Nèthe River, could not be considered a fighting unit anymore. It, therefore, was ordered to march westward on a northerly route along the Dutch border.

In the evening the Army Orders for the next day were issued accordingly. While the

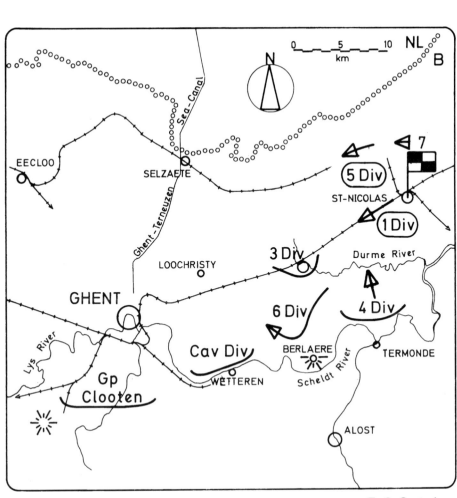

EECLOO

SELZAETE

ST-NICOLAS

5 Div

1 Div

7

NL
B

Sea-Canal

Ghent-Terneuzen

LOOCHRISTY

3 Div

Durme River

GHENT

6 Div

4 Div

Lys River

Cav Div

BERLAERE

TERMONDE

Gp
Clooten

WETTEREN

Scheldt River

ALOST

7-8 October

Third Army Division was to move to Lokeren, a town almost halfway between St Nicolas and Ghent, the Fourth and Sixth Army Divisions were to cover this withdrawal from the south. Both divisions would remain in position along the Scheldt northern bank, between the towns of Termonde and Berlaere. Further west the Cavalry Division was to destroy the bridge at Wetteren.

As a result of these orders however, the Belgian Army would be stretched out over a front of some 130km, from east of Antwerp to Ostend. The Belgians would not be able to maintain such a large deployment for long. Nevertheless, all good intentions of the Commander-in-Chief to keep the corridor between Antwerp and Ghent open would soon be dashed.

During the night of 7 to 8 October, High Command, apparently without the king's knowledge, ordered the Fourth Army Division to withdraw north to Waesmunster before daybreak, after which the Sixth Army Division would execute a similar manoeuvre, but towards Loochristy, 10km west of Lokeren. Abandoning the defence of the river east of Ghent meant giving up all hope of relieving the *Réduit National*, the Antwerp Fortified Place. Certain staff officers had evidently given up the idea of any military resistance along the winding Scheldt.

NOTE
1. Victor Deguise (1855-1925).

Chapter II

Into the Unknown

For the king and queen, lodged at the *Walburg Château* owned by the mayor of St Nicolas, Mr. van Naemen, the night was just as short as for anyone else trying to catch a few hours of sleep. At midnight the royal couple was awakened by an alarmingly loud cannon shot. It appeared as if the enemy was closing in on the town. The king got up and sent the commandant of his *gendarmerie* escort to investigate at General Headquarters. Once there staff officers informed the commandant that the explosions they heard were from German siege artillery bombarding the city of Antwerp.

As there did not seem to be any immediate danger, the royal couple went back to bed. But evidently it was difficult to fall asleep again; every fifteen minutes or so a distant salvo shook the windows. In the end, around 06:00 on Thursday morning, 8 October, both got up and started preparations to leave.

An hour later King Albert left St Nicolas for the town of Selzaete, some 25km west along the Ghent-Terneuzen Sea Canal and near the Dutch border. Upon arrival Captain Commandant Galet, who accompanied the king on the trip, descended upon the offices of the re-established General Headquarters. Here he found out, to his great dissatisfaction, about the repositioning of the two army divisions mentioned earlier. This move was certainly endangering the link between the Field Army and the defenders of the Antwerp Fortified Place. As long as Antwerp had not fallen to the German Armies, the king wanted the Field Army to

The charming Walburg Castle in the town of Saint-Nicolas where the royal couple stayed for the night on 7 October after they had left the palace in Antwerp.
Author's photo archive.

17

keep a corridor open so as to extract as many men in fighting condition as possible. Immediately officers were sent to both army divisions with the following orders: for the Fourth to halt the retreat and hold the line of the Durme river and for the Sixth to occupy the railway between Lokeren and Ghent.

At 11:00 the Commander of the Fourth Army Division still insisted on a withdrawal west but Captain Commandant Galet responded:

> It is the intention of the king that the Durme river will be held until further notice to cover the communications with the defenders in Antwerp.

As a matter of fact, a hasty retreat was indeed unnecessary: patrols by Fourth Army Division units indicated that the area between the Durme and Scheldt rivers was still free of Germans.

As the Belgian Legation in Bordeaux had announced on 3 October, the French General Paul Pau arrived in the afternoon as a special adviser from the Generalissimo to the king.

That same day the Legation in Bordeaux had also announced that the French government would send two divisions (30,000 men) to land at Ostend while the British would do the same. Later it cabled that the British had protested against the French sending Territorials – older reserve units. As we already mentioned, the British fulfilled their promise while the French reduced their commitment to a brigade of *fusiliers marins*. It must be said though that the latter would prove to be a valiant bunch.

The French General Paul Pau. He was a fatherly figure who didn't buy into the widely accepted French military vision of attack to the extreme -'*attaque a outrance*'.
Onze Helden, R. Lyr, 1922.

General Paul Pau was truly a man of the old guard. Unlike Joffre, with whom he nevertheless was on good terms, he had always been an opponent of *l'attaque à outrance* – the French 'always attack' obsession. This military theory had been feverishly preached for some time by men like Ferdinand Foch – whom we will meet later – and Louis de Grandmaison, and was enthusiastically followed by the majority of French officers.

In 1911 the French government had offered him the post of Generalissimo but he had declined. The minister of war had not been willing to accept his sole condition: his veto over the nomination of generals. As a result Joseph Joffre had been chosen for this highest military position.

One year after he had left the Military Academy of St Cyr near Paris, in the Franco-Prussian War of 1870, Pau had not only lost his right hand, but had also witnessed the downfall of the French Empire and the subsequent imprisonment of Napoleon III (Louis-Napoleon). This distressing political experience had left many Frenchmen, and especially the officers' corps, with an indelible trauma out of which the offensive spirit of the early twentieth century was born. But apparently the young Pau would have none of it.

Since Pau, throughout his career, had been shown to be an excellent organizer and had always been level-headed in tactical matters, Joffre had recalled him for active duty and had put him at the head of the newly formed Alsace Army in the second half of August.

Now at age sixty-six Pau was sent by his friend Joffre to Belgium in a disguised attempt to lead the young king of the Belgians and his army from Antwerp directly south-west into France – Armentières /Lille – and thus into the influence of the French forces.

The message from Joffre to the French Mission at Belgian Headquarters (5 October) read (our underlining):

> General Pau will go to Antwerp. He will give the king all <u>indications</u> of such a nature as to secure a <u>complete</u> cooperation between the Belgian and French armies. In particular, the Belgian forces, after leaving Antwerp, will have to receive all information to enable them to continue their efforts towards the <u>southwest</u> of Antwerp and the allied forces.

And on 9 October:

> Command in the North is organised as follows: Belgian troops, under the command of the king with <u>General Pau as adviser</u>; . . . .

Soon Joffre would find out that his delegate to the Belgian king would act more as a father towards his son. Jean Ratinaud, in *The Race to the Sea* would later describe Pau as '. . . a likeable and competent old soldier . . . more an old grandfather than a warrior' and the young lieutenant, André Tardieu – later president of the French *assemblée* – called him '. . . father Pau . . .'.

The rather shy, myopic young gentleman at the head of the Belgian Army was not as easily 'led' as Joffre had imagined.

At 15:00, in the presence of Colonel Wielemans and Captain Commandant Galet, the king met the old French general for the first time. Pau explained that the Anglo-French left was now at Hazebrouck and that the Germans had attacked this town but had been repulsed. As a result the 87th Territorial Division, destined for the relief of Antwerp, had been diverted to protect the detraining of the BEF.

What the French general did not know yet was that the 89th Territorial, originally also earmarked for Antwerp, would equally be diverted to protect the BEF near Hazebrouck. This explains why, of the four-plus promised divisions only the British 7th Infantry Division, the 3rd Cavalry division and one French brigade actually would be on hand to protect the withdrawal of the Belgian Army from Antwerp. It was the latter, the *fusiliers marins* under Ronarc'h, that were now arriving in Ghent.

Upon orders from Joffre Pau insisted that the Belgian Army should concentrate between Deynze and Thielt -two towns some 20km south-west of Ghent – with its right flank against the Lys River. According to Pau this was preferable to falling back on Bruges and Ostend where the Belgian Army risked being isolated at the coast.

For the king this was an unacceptable proposal. It would leave the Belgians in a dangerously exposed and advanced position some 40km ahead of any major Anglo-French force without any protected flank. Perhaps the French intended to have the Belgian Army close ranks with them as soon as possible, but with German units already threatening several crossings of the Lys River, taking the direction of the south-west would be near suicide. Moreover, at this point, the king did not want to sever the link with the last defenders of the Antwerp Fortified Place for a promise.

In the morning General Pau had already met with Baron de Broqueville in Ostend and had given him a similar explanation. The Belgian Minister of War was in agreement with the French general to suggest to Joffre not to deploy the French 87th Territorial west of Hazebrouck but instead to bring it forward to the (Belgian) Poperinghe area. This (at first sight) French concession would be of no use to the Belgians as the town of Poperinghe was not only 50km south-west of Deynze but, according to the king's plans, also 30km from the coast, too far to cover his exhausted army in either case anyway.

Since de Broqueville had exchanged views with the French General before the latter had even met the monarch, the Minister of War feared the king's wrath over this obvious breach of protocol. So in an effort to appease his monarch de Broqueville managed to have at least the French Marine Brigade put under the direct orders of the Belgian Commander-in-Chief.

Throughout the campaign, this undercurrent of Francophilia, not only in Belgian political circles, but also at Belgian GHQ where a majority of officers held similar pro-French views, would continue to hamper King Albert and his close advisers in developing their own 'independent' strategy. With every step they made or decision they took, they would encounter inarticulate opposition from both quarters.

Later in the day de Broqueville apparently met Antony Klobukowski, the French Ambassador to Belgium. To the latter he put the request of moving up the detraining of the 87th Territorial from Poperinghe to Roulers but to no avail: Joffre insisted on keeping the division in the Hazebrouck area to protect the detraining of the BEF. At Belgian High Command, in the late afternoon and presumably in the absence of Pau, a compromise was reached: as news arrived that German units were attacking the Third Army Division in Lokeren, Wielemans feared for the safety of the Fourth. It was therefore decided to pull the Fourth Army Division from its exposed eastern position west across the Ghent-Terneuzen Canal. Afterwards the Third and Sixth Army Divisions would follow.

In the meantime General Henry Rawlinson, informed that the Belgian Field Army had left Antwerp, worried about the fate of his Royal Naval Division still held up in the city. At 07:50 Major General Paris, Commander of the Division in the entrenched camp, had phoned Rawlinson in Bruges telling him that he could not hold out beyond the day. He had witnessed the departure of the Belgians and had experienced the deplorable state of the remainder of the defenders. As a result Rawlinson sent a cable to Colonel W.E. Fairholme, British Military Attaché to the Belgian Government, asking for rail transport for his division when they would have to evacuate the place.

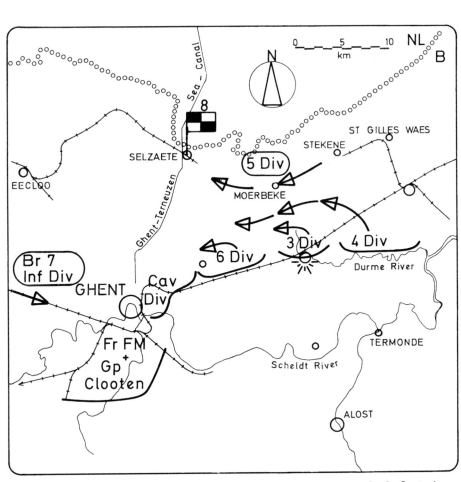

8-9 October

The arrival of his own forces was another source of anxiety for Rawlinson. His cavalry division, after landing in part in Zeebrugge, was ordered to march to Ostend and billet there. The city was covered by the British Seventh Infantry Division, which had taken up a position in an arc some 6km around the port. This way Rawlinson had his force concentrated and could await developments.

The situation was regarded as quite uncertain for, at 10:45, a message arrived from London not to unload any motor vehicles and to keep all empty transports under steam and in port until further notice. By the time Rawlinson had moved his Headquarters back to Ostend in the afternoon, the British Cabinet had decided to continue the landing operation. But the transport vessels had to stand fast in case the force had to be re-embarked in a hurry.

Finally, at 17:45, Rawlinson received definite orders: the relief operation into Antwerp was formally cancelled but instead his forces would have to protect the retreat of the Belgian Army towards the Anglo-French lines.

Communications between the retreating Belgian Field Army and the Antwerp garrison had by now ceased. The previous day in St Nicolas, the staff officers at High Command had heard the German bombardment of the city for themselves but the actual tactical situation was unknown. Decisions to be taken on the spot had been left to the Military Governor of the besieged city. He alone could assess the situation. The king, nevertheless, wanted to inform the Governor that, in case he decided to order the remainder of the field forces to leave the entrenched camp, the British troops would get priority over the Belgian Second Army Division and trains would be waiting for them at the St Gilles-Waes station to evacuate the Britons to Ostend.

A dispatch as such was prepared and sent by special military courier to Antwerp. But unknown to the king, Colonel Wielemans had added, unfortunately in a rather direct way:

> For your information, our troops are forced to evacuate Lokeren and to withdraw to the west of the canal from Ghent to Terneuzen.

If this was not a moral blow for the defenders of Antwerp, it certainly facilitated the decision by the Governor, General Deguise, to relieve the British Division and the Belgian Second Army Division from their positions and send them west.

General Paris did receive the order to withdraw by 17:00 and an hour later most of his men were marching through the darkening city streets in order to cross the river by the Burght pontoon bridge. A rather peculiar incident should be mentioned here: the 1st Naval Brigade – minus one battalion – only found out by 22:00 that the rest of the division had already gone. As such they themselves reached the Scheldt quays by 01:30 the next morning by which time the pontoon bridge had been destroyed! In the

Lieutenant General Victor Deguise. On 6 September, at the 'Palace Revolution', promoted to Military Governor of the Fortified Place of Antwerp, replacing General Arthur François Dufour. The latter had refused, among others, to give the Broqueville a copy of a confidential report about the situation that the king had asked him to prepare. Dufour reasoned that King Albert – being Commander in Chief – was his immediate superior and that therefore the Minister of War, if he really wanted a copy, should ask the king himself!
Onze Helden, R. Lyr, 1922.

end the unfortunate troops had to requisition a small steamer docked nearby and cross the river in small groups.

In Selzaete itself, the whole day, a steady, westbound stream of army convoys slowly crossed the bridge over the sea canal. To the south-east one could hear the regular thunder of the artillery, some 20km away. Finally, in the early evening the Fifth Army Division, on its northern route from Antwerp to Ostend, passed through town.

By 20:00 Captain Commandant Galet read the Daily Army Orders, as made up by High Command, to the king. Always concerned about the well being of his soldiers, the monarch made the remark that no provisions had been made concerning the protection of the retreat of the British Division and the Second Army Division. Being put on the spot, Major Maglinse, Head of Operations, replied after a while that the retreating divisions would leave several detachments guarding the approaches to the railway St Nicolas/Selzaete and that the Cavalry Division, still east of Ghent, would move closer to Antwerp to distract the enemy.

Not without difficulty, King Albert's aide-de-camp had managed to billet the royal couple at local brewer and alderman De Clercq's residence. Here the queen arrived around 21:00 in the evening.

As the population was slowly being dragged into a general panic, rumours were spreading like wildfire. Galet's sleep was interrupted abruptly after midnight when he was urgently called to the bridge over the canal. Some individual, fearful of the impending arrival of the Germans, had turned the bridge with the result that the endless stream of refugees and military convoys had ground to a nervous halt. Exasperation and congestion were growing by the minute and only the reopening of the crossing provided the necessary relief in this psychological volatile situation.

While trying to regain some sleep, Galet could but ponder about the future: this army had become an unruly amalgamation of disheartened young men, driven only by the fear of the enemy and the urge to escape. This mass had to be taken to a safe place, as soon as possible, to be rebuilt into a real organization that would be able to withstand, albeit with some help, the German steamroller.

On the Scheldt Roads in Antwerp, a grandiose hallucinating scene was developing. The crude oil tanks along the riverbank, on the southern outskirts of the city, had been hit by enemy shells and were burning ferociously. The wallowing flames projected a frightening glow on the 100,000 or so refugees massed along the quays, pushing to find their way towards one of the pontoon bridges still functioning across the wide river.

Once on the left bank the tension in the human pack dropped to make way for exhaustion. Along the paved stone road

Maglinse – here as major general after the war – was in 1914 Chief of Operations at Belgian General HQ.
Onze Helden, R. Lyr, 1922.

23

hundreds of fugitives, in a haphazard manner, lay in the adjoining fields, trying to catch some sleep. But unperturbed the troop columns kept on walking in the cool night.

Additional orders for 9 October had been issued at 00:30 by Belgian High Command:

> The Second Army Division will march with the British the following route: St-Gilles-Waes, Stekene, Moerbeke, Wachtebeke and Selzaete. The British will entrain at the station of St-Gilles-Waes.

After 15km, in the village of Vrasene, the men got two hours of rest. It was now early morning and still dark. Most men collapsed against the brick houses and wooden fences bordering the road. The few lanterns put down haphazardly on the cobblestones threw a lugubrious light on the weary faces. A small tin of sardines was passed around. With grubby hands the thin fish were quickly groped from the can and swallowed eagerly

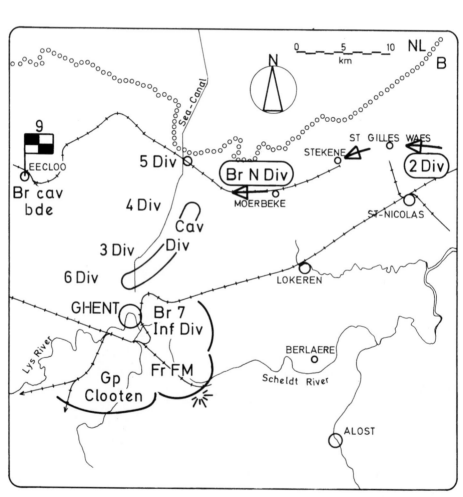

9-10 October

while the others watched carefully so as not to miss a cheat. A few still alert men dug up some potatoes, carrots and beets in the nearby fields. Coal and a couple of furnaces were requisitioned from the few remaining and frightened villagers and the cooks started to prepare food for the hungry men.

Suddenly the order was passed to 'get going' immediately. No further explanation was needed. Without another decent meal the tired men got up again and disappeared in the fading dark towards St Gilles-Waes.

Once in the open fields the rising sun peeked over the horizon and soon the morning heat burned on their backs and weakened their exhausted feet. With every step the small army shovels on their belts banged merciless against their legs. Cursing between their teeth was the only sound they could still utter. But even a weary and disillusioned soldier has a practical mind. Soon, here and there, men quietly unbuckled the hated tool and dropped it unnoticed by their officers in the roadside grass.

Not far behind a column of Royal Marines followed. Although just as drained as the Belgians these men nevertheless proved to be frugal Tommies. Ashamed of such wastage some of the British would bend over painfully and, with a sigh, pick up the gravediggers' tools abandoned by their Belgian comrades.

That same morning, some 100km to the west, in the utmost corner of the Belgian countryside, four British officers on clattering motorcycles halted at the drainage locks in the small coastal town of Nieuport and inquired where they could find the lock-keeper. After all, this junction of roads, waterways and modest fishing port on the North Sea, might gain strategic importance in case hostilities drew nearer.

A peaceful view of the 'Goose Foot' lock system in Nieuport as the British officers found it in October 1914. In the foreground, the Ypres Lock with the swing bridge to the right, left the so-called 'Greek Temple' standing between the Ypres Lock and the Spring Sluice. In the background the Café du Comte along the Bruges Canal, near the Count Lock. The Café de l'Yser would be across the bridge to the right (just outside the picture).
Historical prints collection Callenaere-Dehouck.

The officers, after courteously greeting the lockkeeper, asked in a polite manner if they could use the telegraph and telephone apparatuses in his office. The lockkeeper, in order to gather data concerning the water levels at various points in the polder, normally used this modern, electric equipment. He was the important civil servant who, based on this information and relying on his knowledge and experience, decided how to discharge the excess surface water from the intricate web of canals.

Having only a limited command of the French language, the officers underscored their words with gestures to clarify their intentions. The lockkeeper, obviously flattered by the cultivated behaviour of his visitors, gladly consented.

After being seated by the telephone they asked the operator in Nieuport for a connection with the city of Roulers. The lockkeeper, noticing their linguistic difficulties, assisted them in getting their call through. After ringing off they left but, according to the lockkeeper's later testimony, apparently stayed in the Nieuport area for the next couple of days.

The lockkeeper also stated that he believed that the officers belonged to the British Staff. Unfortunately we were not able to determine which staff he would have referred to. Quite likely they were an advance party of Major General Rawlinson's headquarters. His troops were disembarking in Ostend and Zeebrugge at the time and reconnaissance teams must have been swarming out from these towns to check the lay of the land.

Pretty soon the lockkeeper and his domain would be at the centre of the struggle for the survival of the Belgian kingdom.

Chapter III

Towards the West

Friday morning, 9 October, the king and his staff officers left on horseback for Eecloo, a small town 17km as the crow flies west of Selzaete. The queen took the same route but by motorcar. Along the way she distributed thousands of cigarettes to soldiers who cheered her on when they recognized her. The troops and refugees, crowding the roads with a most diverse collection of carts, made progress difficult. But still they were able to set a good pace.

The fate of the Second Army Division, left at Antwerp to cover the retreat, was still unknown and a major concern to all at High Command. Shortly before arriving in Eecloo though, while waiting at a closed railway crossing, the staff officers gave a sigh of relief: on a train rumbling by they noticed soldiers with batches of the 7th de Ligne Regiment, a unit part of the Second Army Division.

Queen Elisabeth arrived by 09:30 in Eecloo and was immediately directed to the Boelare House, residence of Lionel Pussemier, a Member of the Provincial Legislative Assembly. In those days all dignitaries visiting the region were attended to there. Today the house is known as the Loontjes Residence.

At 10:45 the king and his entourage arrived through Church Street. The remaining citizens were watching silently from the pavement. As he was rather small of stature one of them, Livinus Verstraete, had managed to get a spot on the upper step to the dean's house. Here Church Street narrowed, with the result that the compact group of military riders was forced into single file or defile. From his perch Livinus saw the monarch

The Loontjes residence in Eecloo where the royal couple stayed overnight on 9 October 1914. The house in Selsaete where they stayed the previous night has since been demolished. *Author's photo archive.*

27

The front of the dean's house in the narrow Church Street in Eecloo.
Author's photo archive.

approaching. The king looked grim and sat somewhat bent in the saddle. As he was about to pass the dean's house Livinus broke the eerie silence in the alley and shouted as loud as he could – and in French so the king would certainly understand him – '*Vive le roi!*'.

Immediately the king lifted his head, looked at Livinus and saluted him. This sudden outburst of loyalty by the common man and the subsequent royal reaction broke all barriers. The dumbstruck bystanders in the narrow street took up Livinus' words, which quickly turned into a jubilant cheer that rolled on with the riders to the Market Square.

Burgomaster Emiel Dauwe welcomed the monarch arriving on the steps to the Town Hall.

Immediately afterwards the king descended upon the Justice of the Peace Building in Station Street where General Headquarters had been set up. The news that the royal couple had arrived in town had spread like wildfire. The whole population was now out and about and cheered the royals wherever they went.

Since the Second Army Division had apparently escaped from Antwerp, one of the first tasks at General Headquarters was to find out if the British Naval Division too had been embarked outside the besieged city. The other pressing matter was to try to locate the exact whereabouts of all the different units of the Second Division. They were probably strung out over rail and road westbound along the Dutch border. After that it was time to return to the coordination of the ongoing movement of the entire army.

It was obvious to High Command that all the fighting power of the Field Army had been used up. The men were not only physically but also psychologically exhausted. Moreover, with the fall of Antwerp and the improvised retreat, large parts of the now redundant Garrison Army had intermingled with units of the Field Army in the march to the coast. As such the main objective for the staff officers was to find a way to extract this miserable collection from the battlefield, at least for a few days in order to give the men some rest and to carry out an urgently needed reorganization.

After lunch with the queen at the Boelare, the king, at 14:00, rejoined General Headquarters. Here the deliberation was now focused on the plans for reassembling the Army. Evidently there was one major growing concern: *where* would the restructuring take place?

Meanwhile Queen Elisabeth visited Our-Lady-ten-Doorn Institute where the Red

The Justice of the Peace Building in Eecloo where Belgian Headquarters was installed on 9 October.
Author's photo archive.

Cross had set up a hospital for wounded soldiers. The queen arrived at 16:50 accompanied by Mr Pussemier, Commander Daveux and her lady-in-waiting. A local journalist described the scene:

> The queen was wearing a very simple, navy blue skirt, a linen collar, a hat, white toque, white shoes and gloves. She had left her white cape in the car.

In these tragic circumstances the queen must have appeared to all as a magic figure. But she did not come to shine. Elisabeth was young, modern and walked expertly from patient to patient [1]. She managed to boost the morale at every step.

> With an exquisite kindness, a superior modesty and a perfect tact she walks from bed to bed, shakes the hand of a wounded soldier, asks the sisters about his condition. What does he suffer from? Where has he been wounded? How long ago did it happen – at which battle? At what dressing stations has he been treated already? Is he now well taken care of? She makes the remark to the nurses that this one has a fever, that one looks distraught.

Up until now nobody in town had ever met such a caring and well-versed high society lady!

Meanwhile the debate within High Command was at fever pitch. The National Refuge had been lost because the Franco-British Guarantor Powers had not been able to reach the Antwerp Fortified Place in time . . . or perhaps they had never been eager to engage in such an operation to begin with . . . ?

Now that High Command had to look for a new, temporary camp, the alternatives on Belgian soil were getting scarce. It was not only imperative to find a well-defined, battle-sheltered region on national territory. The king and his staff wanted to make sure that this time the Anglo-French forces would be, and would stay, in the vicinity to provide the indispensable protection.

After reorganization, and with the support of these forces, the king anticipated the French Generalissimo to assign the Belgian Field Army a sector in the – by then expected – advancing front line. As such the Belgians would be able to enter in line with the Entente Powers when they proceeded back east through Belgium. If a further deteriorating tactical situation would prohibit the establishment of a safe

Queen Elisabeth, during the war, visiting a school in Vinckem, behind the lines. She was a ravishing personality who embodied the 'mother at the front' for thousands of lonely soldiers. Always there, behind or in the trenches, to give you heart . . . *Someone to watch over me . . .*
Nieuport 1914-1918, R. Thys, 1922.

haven within national territory it was agreed to evacuate the army from Belgian soil.

Since the end of The Great War, now already eighty-eight years ago, quite a few historians – and as a result the Belgian population in general – have assumed that King Albert eventually would retreat with his army into France. If the army could not make a stand behind the Yser River it would cross the southern border. Personally, we regard this as a rather simple reasoning based on two axioms: first that from the outset King Albert wanted the army to make a stand at the Yser River and secondly that France was considered as being the 'strategic hinterland' of Belgium. Although our initial research was focused on the more technical aspects of the floods it became clear over the years – to our amazement – that nobody had ever taken the time to investigate historically both prejudices.

However, in the next pages we will see that, from Eecloo on, King Albert masterly organized and manoeuvred his army divisions – the cavalry divisions were a separate case – so as to be able to embark them for England at short notice. All this happened not only after consultation with his personal advisers but also under the noses of his Minister of War and his High Command, both of whom were known for their Francophile sympathies. Up to 14 October all infantry units would be kept in positions ready for an embarkation in Ostend or even Nieuport, rather than for a withdrawal into France. But let us return to our story.

There were not many choices left for a national safe haven. One possibility was the Bruges-Zeebrugge region. This area was protected in the north by the coastline and in the east by the Dutch border. Zeebrugge, with its new mole, could be the main supply port for the camp and the Ostend-Bruges and Bruges-Sluis Canals could act as perimeter. But, as rumours had it that German troops were already in the vicinity of Ypres, the risk of being cut off from the Anglo-French armies was quite substantial.

Another consideration might have been that the splendid medieval city of Bruges would have been in the front line. The Belgians were by now well aware of the devastating power of the German artillery.

Conversely, and with reason, they were wary of the British too. Winston Churchill was convinced that the BEF had to hang on to the Belgian coastline at all cost. Still, on 22 November he wrote to his friend Field Marshal French:

> If you push your left flank along the sand dunes of the shore to Ostend and Zeebrugge, *we would give you 100 or 200 heavy guns from the sea in absolute devastating support . . . .*

Just imagine what would have happened if a massive artillery duel had been fought out between the Royal Navy off the coast and the German mighty guns inland, over the Belgian heads and with Bruges in the centre!

Another region that could be considered lay south-west of it: the area between Ostend and Nieuport. It did possess the advantage that the army supply base had already been moved here from Antwerp. But the only protective obstacle was the Bruges Canal [2] and the rather narrow belt it provided along the coastline was too small to accommodate the full army complement and still give sufficient shelter from enemy heavy artillery. Moreover, the British were now using Ostend as their main debarkation port in Belgium and any Belgian occupation of the area would only complicate British troop movements in and out of the harbour.

This left the extreme western corner of the country, enclosed by the winding Yser River and known as the Furnes-Ambacht [3] region, as the only available option. Comparable in size to the Antwerp National Refuge, this zone was well situated against the coastline, wedged between the Dunkirk Fortified Place across the border and the British bridgehead at Ostend. So High Command in Eecloo agreed that, for the time being, the latter region offered the best alternative as a temporary refuge for the army within Belgium.

In Eecloo itself pure chaos reigned. An amalgamation of units from the Garrison Army, dragging along outdated material, slowly struggled along the main street on its way to the coast. Even after dark the tired troops and their squeaking carts kept moving.

It must be said that at this point the British were apparently concerned with the personal safety of the Belgian monarch. One source indicates that the previous evening General Rawlinson had sent a cavalry brigade to Eecloo but another source says this order was later cancelled. Indeed the tactical situation changed from hour to hour.

At 19:00 the royal couple had dinner at the Justice of the Peace Court after which they strolled back to their lodgings, only a few hundred metres away. Captain Commandant Galet, also staying at Mr Pussemier's, again had a troublesome night. Colonel Wielemans, Deputy Chief of Staff, woke him up with a disturbing message: a German column, six hours long, had been reported moving from Ypres to Furnes. This distressing news was enough for Galet not to sleep a wink anymore. Luckily, in the morning, the information proved to be another rumour.

But again, this alarm had brought home a very important question: while Belgian High Command hoped to assemble the army on national soil in the aforementioned Furnes-Ambacht region, it was still unknown what the strategic intentions were of the *Entente*[4] forces. Without their presence to protect the Belgian Army, any rest or recovery in that area would be impossible. With this uncertainty in mind the king decided to call a conference with the Franco-British representatives to be held in Ostend the next day.

Back in Antwerp, the British marines, after having crossed the Scheldt south of Antwerp, continued their march to Beveren-Waes. But instead of proceeding to St Nicolas where they were supposed to be entrained, they were directed towards St Gilles-Waes, 6km north of St Nicolas. A report had come in that the Germans had reached Lokeren, a town on the railway to Ghent. It had therefore been hastily decided to entrain the men in St Gilles-Waes and transport them to Ostend by the secondary railway following the Dutch border.

The last columns of the Belgian Second Army Division, still on their march towards Selzaete, got no respite either. Halfway between Stekene and Moerbeke, almost 35km west of the besieged fortress, a patrol was sent south to investigate claims that the enemy was nearby. Soon after the patrol left, fierce rifle fire was heard from that direction. Scared, the weary men got up and hurried on. The patrol never returned. While straggling on they barely noticed that here and there in the adjoining fields some dazed soldier would suddenly sit up. They were the remains of the Fifth Army Division whose columns had passed there the previous day. After a twelve-hour sleep these souls were woken up by the noisy passage of their comrades.

Around 12:00 the Belgian troopers arrived in the village of Moerbeke, still 12km from Selzaete and the life saving bridge across the sea canal. Many of the men fell asleep on the cobblestones almost instantly. But, like frightened animals, they got back on their feet when cannon fire woke them up. The officers managed to calm them down and lead them north, into the brush adjoining the Dutch border. Here one small, cobblestone track made its winding way to Selzaete. Tired, hungry and wet they finally crossed the Selzaete Bridge in the early evening.

The stragglers of the 1st Naval Brigade in Antwerp were not so lucky. Since the pontoon bridges across the Scheldt had been blown up before their belated arrival they had to cross the river by requisitioned steamer. After this time consuming effort they arrived in Zwyndrecht, a village halfway between Antwerp and Beveren. Here they found out, after some time, that the rest of the division had gone to St Gilles-Waes. There was nothing for them to do but to press forward. Amidst a crowd of refugees they could do no more than put one foot in front of the other and struggle on. When they finally arrived in St Gilles-Waes in the afternoon, they were told that their compatriots had left some eight hours previously. In the small rural station there was still one transport to leave for the west but all were not entrained yet when news arrived that the Germans had pushed beyond Lokeren to Moerbeke and had attacked a train in that location. What nobody knew yet was that this train had carried the British 10th Marine Battalion and refugees. One hundred and fifty marines had managed to escape and later reached Selzaete. The remainder could not get clear of the mêlée and were captured by the Germans.

Utterly exhausted by the forced march, without guns, ammunition, food or water, the commander decided to take his men north, covering the few kilometres to the frontier and surrender their arms to the Dutch. This was done and at about 17:00 some 1,500 reached the border. Thirty or forty men, together with one officer, decided to try to escape capture and flee along the border, an endeavour in which they miraculously succeeded.

Strangely enough, the next day the railway was still open. In fact after the Germans had retreated, a Belgian officer moved the train that had been attacked and another train with 200 British marines passed later still.

Meanwhile the violent skirmishes with the enemy around Ghent began to increase. Before 12:00 news arrived at General Headquarters that the *Groupement Clooten*, including the *Brigade de Cavalerie Independante* was being attacked by German forces on the south-eastern approaches to Ghent.

It is rather important to describe in a few lines the composition of the Clooten group as we will later see it evolve into a unit with a potentially much more important role to play.

Under the command of the Military Governor of Ghent, General H. Clooten, this detachment was a strange amalgamation of regular and second-rate units. It comprised elements of the special corps of the Civic Guard – the *Chasseurs à pied de Gand*, the *Chasseurs à cheval de Liège*, and *l'Artillerie de Bruxelles*, a squadron of *gendarmerie*, four battalions of (untrained) volunteers and the 4th Brigade of the First Army Division, including three artillery battalions. Temporarily added since the previous evening were the French *fusiliers marins* and two companies of French territorials.

The *Brigade de Cavalerie Independente* on the other hand was formed on 4 October with the cavalry regiments of three army divisions. After these divisions had withdrawn to Antwerp their scouting capabilities had become, in essence, superfluous. With the expected imminent arrival of Anglo-French reinforcements this provisional brigade had therefore been formed to guard the communication lines with Antwerp, i.e. the area north of the Scheldt river.

Soon this *groupement* would become the Second Cavalry division. Hence, from a practical point of view the Field Army was now largely divided into an infantry and a cavalry component. This suited the king quite well for the upcoming operations.

In the evening the British General Capper, arriving with his Seventh Infantry Division from Ostend, assumed command of the defence around Ghent. As a result of these reinforcements the same night the attacks by the Germans, advancing from Alost, were temporarily checked.

At about the same time in Eecloo, the Army Orders for the next day, 10 October, were drawn up. Now that High Command *grosso modo* had decided on the Yser region to reconstitute its Field Army and give its soldiers a few days of rest, it was a matter of getting the men there without compromising a worst-case scenario, i.e. a possible retreat from national soil. The various army divisions got their entraining stations assigned and a massive rail-lift was organized from the Ghent-Terneuzen Canal to the area west of the line Ostend / Thourout.

The Fifth Army Division was to entrain in Selzaete and Assenede, a few miles northwest of Selzaete. The Third Division was to entrain in Tronchiennes, just west of Ghent and the Sixth in Hansbeke, 13km west of Ghent. The Fourth Army Division finally would embark in Aeltre, 7km further west still. The Second was to stay in Selzaete for another day and destroy the sea-canal bridge. It would be the last to depart. The Second had arrived in Selzaete late on 9 October and would only leave on 11 October by rail. Its initial destination seems to have been the area between Bruges and Ostend since the Army Orders of 10 October at 17:30 indicated that the horses and rolling stock had to move to this region.

It is interesting to note here that this would leave the Second Division – together with the Fourth in Ghistelles – close to Ostend in case of an evacuation order.

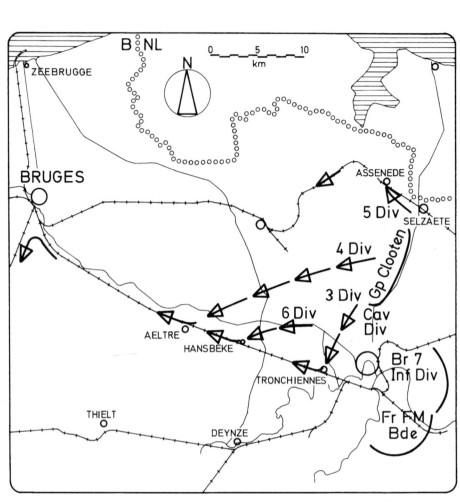

10 October

For the Third, Fourth and Sixth Army Divisions this meant the use of the railway line Ghent-Bruges-Thourout. For the Minister of War and his High Command this was a logical choice: from Thourout the railway continued towards Ypres, Poperinghe and Hazebrouck in France. King Albert too considered it a good decision: in Thourout a branch line split off towards Nieuport and its seaport facilities!

Although the majority of the army would be on trains for two days it was not considered a tactical risk. To mask the withdrawal the *Groupement Clooten* would take up positions along the canal and the Cavalry Division would cover the move south of Ghent.

It seems as if the decision to move General Headquarters to Ostend was taken at the last minute. The original and more logical destination would have been Bruges. The French Admiral Ronarc'h wrote on the evening of 8 October, in *Les Fusiliers-Marins au Combat*:

Le général [Pau] *ajoute que le G.Q.G. Belge est à Eecloo aujourd'hui, sera à Bruges demain, . . .*

On Saturday morning at 07:00, the king and his officers departed from Eecloo to Ostend via Bruges, again on horseback. The queen left the town by car two hours later. Along the road she again distributed thousands of cigarettes to the soldiers. By 10:40 the queen met the king at the 'Eecloo Gate' outside Bruges and together they rode through the medieval city where people, surprised by the sudden royal visit, still managed to cheer and applaud. Once past Bruges the small convoy could pick up some speed and at lunchtime they arrived at the royal residence in Ostend.

It is not clear though if the king went to the 'Royal Villa' on the sea promenade in Ostend itself or to the 'Royal Chalet', also with a seafront location, but isolated in the dunes 6km south-west of the city. On 15 December 1914 the Germans burned the latter down as it was seen as an excellent reference point for the British Fleet. Subsequently they constructed one of many heavy coastal battery emplacements in its place. Today the site is an important archaeological centre and open-air museum of coastal defence in both world wars.

The chalet with the adjoining windy dunes and sunken passages was more intimate and would have suited King Albert's nature better but for the planned formal meetings we assume that the more regal villa in the city was chosen.

Ostend was by now turning into a British town. The Naval Division, having narrowly escaped from Antwerp, was being embarked to return to England. But in case the Germans succeeded in breaking through near Ghent, the Admiralty planned the dispatch of three warships to Ostend to cover the withdrawal and an eventual evacuation of their base. Besides the over 5,000 men of the Naval Division, the British Navy was to embark some 12,500 Belgian recruits and volunteers for transport to Cherbourg. In addition to these troop movements, the orders provided for dealing with the removal of Belgian stores and up to 10,000 wounded then in the city.

All this work nevertheless was subject to the needs of Rawlinson's forces in case they required assistance. A special instruction indicated that enough vessels were to be kept in immediate readiness with steam up for the next forty-eight hours to re-embark all of the British forces should the emergency arise.

Meanwhile though a decision had been taken by the British government in London that would thwart the plans of the king of the Belgians.

With the full-scale retreat from Antwerp, the Expeditionary Force for the Relief of Antwerp had become in fact redundant. But since these troops were on the continent anyway they had been renamed Fourth Corps and made a part of the BEF under the overall command of Sir John French with headquarters in St Omer in northern France. This meant that Sir Henry Rawlinson now got his orders from Field Marshal French instead of the Cabinet in London. Since his supply lines still ran through the port in Ostend though, Rawlinson maintained his headquarters at the Terminus Hotel in this well known upscale seaside resort. Moreover he was still waiting for the arrival of the Eighth Infantry Division that had been promised to him.

This ambiguous situation on the ground is perhaps responsible for the fact that not only King Albert but also General Rawlinson and even General Pau, assumed that the Anglo-French presence in north-western Belgium would be further expanded. But Sir John French had other plans. Soon everyone would find out that the British Eighth

Division was to be diverted to France and hence the BEF, still in the process of de-training in the Hazebrouck area.

In the morning Rawlinson had a meeting with Pau in which both men discussed the withdrawal of the Belgian Army and the way in which to cover it. While General Joffre had advised Belgian High Command to have its army follow the Lys River from Ghent towards Courtrai and promised to cover this retreat with the *fusiliers marins* and the British Seventh Division, the Generalissimo became increasingly irritated by the apparent lack of action upon his directive. On 8 October, Joffre sent a cable to Pau inquiring about the whereabouts of the British Seventh Division. The end of it read:

> Let him [General Capper, the commander of the division] know how important
> it is for him to act with light units on the communications of the German Cavalry
> that is now in the Ypres-Menin area in a rather difficult position.

The area mentioned was 40km south of Ostend, far from Rawlinson's initial field of action and the movements of the Belgian Army. As long as the Belgians were not in a safe environment Rawlinson was apparently not willing to engage in any action that lay outside his orders from Kitchener. As such Pau had to inform Joffre in the late morning that he and Rawlinson had agreed on the protection of the Belgian Army and on the need to harass the enemy in the Ypres region, but:

> ... On this second point the execution has been suspended because of the oppo-
> sition by Lord Kitchener.

Joffre and French had always agreed on the fact that all British forces on the continent should act on a unified front, under a unified command. But Kitchener had sent Rawlinson and his force to Belgium for the purpose of assisting in the defence of Antwerp. Since the city had fallen, Rawlinson had been ordered to cover a quick Belgian withdrawal towards France. But the king of the Belgians, in taking his army along the long road beside the Dutch border and the Belgian coast, thus deprived Joffre of the use of a significant part of the British forces whom he, Joffre, anxiously wanted to deploy in the Lille area.

At 14:00 Rawlinson and Pau met the king in the Blue Room at the Royal Chalet. Also present were Baron Charles de Broqueville, the Deputy Chief of Staff, Colonel Wielemans, and the members of the Military House of the king, the Lieutenants General Jungbluth and Hanoteau and Captain Commandant Galet.

Before the meeting the king himself had written down the different questions he expected an answer to:

1. How many days will it take to rebuild our army and when will it be ready to take the field again?
2. What role can it be assigned?
3. What front will the army be able to take on in a defensive mission?
4. We ask that our army, as much as possible, can fight on our own soil.
5. What is the exact situation of the Allied forces so we can determine a safe region for the rebuilding of our army and allow our soldiers some respite?

The first question seems to be unrelated to the others that more clearly involved French and British cooperation. Strangely enough in his book, General E. Galet skips the answer to this question. Nonetheless, the shorter the time to reorganize, the closer the Belgian Army could stay behind the actual Anglo-French front line or, in other words, the greater the chance to stay on national soil.

The second and third questions considered a request to the Anglo-French Commanders to assign the Belgian Army a meaningful, but defensive, role in any future operations. To the astonishment of all General Pau replied that he had not been given any instructions on this matter. It confirmed the uneasy feeling of the king and his advisers that the Generalissimo saw this conflict as a pure Franco-German military feud: every available soldier, be it French, British or Belgian, was supposedly subordinate to the French cause.

After this surprising answer the king could only address the last and, in fact, the most urgent problem: the actual tactical situation and the related question of a safe haven. Fortunately here General Pau could be more specific.

The French were preparing the Dunkirk Fortified Place and wanted to keep the surrounding region free to manoeuvre. More south, at St Omer and Hazebrouck, the BEF was in the process of de-training and was being covered by the French 87th Territorial Division and French cavalry. To counter this assembly of forces the Germans were mounting an attack on this area from two sides: one from Courtrai in the north-east and one from Lens in the south-east.

The last question clearly indicates that King Albert was still in doubt whether or not the Furnes-Ambacht region would be the 'ultimate' safe haven for his army. As long as

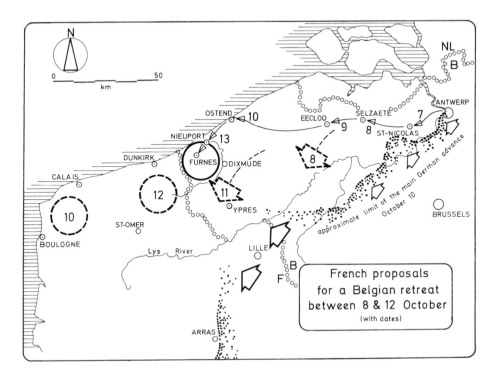

French proposals
for a Belgian retreat
between 8 & 12 October
(with dates)

he had no clear picture on the advance of the *Entente* forces into Belgium, there could be no talk of a safe haven on Belgian soil, hence his desire to stay close to the coast and its harbours.

General Pau proposed to transport the Belgian Army to the only rear area still free of any major military operations: Boulogne/Calais/St Omer. There the Belgians would be able to recover in safety. Simultaneously the Belgian base would be transferred from Ostend to the port of Boulogne.

All this clearly went against Joffre's plans. More than anything else this proposal appears to have been a private venture, hatched by a compassionate Pau and a sportsmanlike Rawlinson during their early morning meeting.

The king did not explicitly agree with the idea. After all Boulogne was already 70km from Belgian soil.

We suspect that, from the allied side, Pau had done most, or all, of the talking since Rawlinson did not speak any French. This would explain why the latter apparently mixed up the conclusions of the meeting and subsequently misinterpreted the reaction of the king. He wrote from Ostend:

> We [he and Pau] succeeded in persuading them to send the Belgian Army to France, *in inducing the Government to move to Dunkirk, and the king himself to go to Havre* . . . . [Our italics]

General Galet, after the war, used this quote in his book, but without the text in italics. Could this be a smoke screen by this royal *intimus* to cover the real intentions of his Master?

Nevertheless King Albert reiterated his desire for the Belgian Army to be assigned a sector on Belgian soil once the recovery stage was completed. All in all, the meeting did not last half an hour.

For the king and his entourage the results were disappointing. A retreat towards Boulogne would mean abandoning Belgian soil altogether. This was not a comforting thought and constitutionally a dangerous move. In the end it could even prove to be fatal for the survival of the country.

When the meeting had ended General Harry Jungbluth followed the government into exile to Le Havre. As Professor Emeritus Henri Haag wrote in 1990: '. . . a fictitious incarnation of the Sovereign . . .'.

On 9 April 1915 de Broqueville managed to have the royal mentor retire anew. Nevertheless, throughout the war Jungbluth and the king kept on meeting in secret, sometimes even from separate motorcars somewhere along the open road of unoccupied Flanders.

Why Jungbluth, in early October 1914, left for Le Havre has always remained a mystery. The future of the country was still very much in doubt, the front line was continuously moving in the wrong direction and the relationship with the friendly powers was rather formal, uncertain and littered with unfulfilled promises. The young monarch would certainly have felt more comfortable with the intellect and wisdom of his mentor on his side in the upcoming days. Definitely something more, unwritten, was at stake here.

If we indeed assume that King Albert's 'secret plan' had been all along to eventually evacuate his (infantry) troops to England instead of retreating into France the reasoning is as follows: His mentor in Le Havre could have taken command of both remaining cavalry divisions that would have covered the embarkation of the Belgian Army from Nieuport. Unavoidably these units would have had to retreat into France but would thus have been shielded from being absorbed into the French Army – a nightmare scenario for the king – because they would still have been under 'royal' command. Once in France they could have waited – as Jungbluth's 'private army' – and protected the Belgian government until the timely return of the monarch with a re-invigorated military force.

One of the king's personal interests had always been history and this proposal by Pau and Rawlinson brought to mind the precedent of President Benito Juárez of Mexico. This footnote in international history might seem quite unrelated to our story but for King Albert it was part of his family's recent past and to his government it was a rather unpleasant reminder of a royal adventure gone sour. To better understand the dilemma facing the Belgians in October 1914 it will help us to elaborate on this subject.

In 1861 a well-known lawyer of Indian descend, Benito Pablo Juárez had been constitutionally elected as President of Mexico. Two years into his term a French Expeditionary Force, in a wicked scheme put together by Napoleon III of France, occupied Mexico City and installed Ferdinand Maximilian Joseph, archduke of Austria, as Emperor of Mexico. Due to the campaigns by the French Legion Juárez and the forces loyal to him, had been forced into a series of retreats that had ended at Ciudad del Norte (nowadays Ciudad Juárez) on the Rio Bravo del Norte, opposite El Paso, Texas. In June of 1865 the French commander in Mexico, Marshal Bazaine, urged the 'Emperor' to resort to severe measures in order to silence the remaining opposition. To justify his proposal the Marshal appealed to an unconfirmed rumour, afterwards shown to be false, that Juárez had left Mexican territory and taken refuge in Texas.

Emperor Maximilian reluctantly agreed but, soon after the ensuing crack-down, across the border in the United States the American Civil War came to an end and the government in Washington became more and more nervous about the French military escapades south of the border. With President Juárez still on Mexican soil the Americans had a strong legal case against the puppet regime in Mexico City. Finally, two years later, in 1867 Napoleon III was forced to withdraw his troops. Soon afterwards the imperial reign in Mexico City collapsed, Maximilian was captured by Juárista troops and later executed.

At first sight this story has nothing to do with Belgium but it was King Albert's own, close family that had been involved in this ill-fated affair. Maximilian had married Princess Charlotte, daughter of Leopold I [5] and sister of Prince Philippe, Albert's father. As such of course, Empress Charlotte was King Albert's aunt. Shortly before Maximilian's capture by presidential troops in 1866, his imperial spouse had left Mexico and returned to Europe in an effort to raise financial and military support for her husband's enterprise. In fact Albert's father, in October of that year, had hastily rushed to Rome to escort his sister, then suffering from a severe nervous breakdown, to her Miramar Castle on the Adriatic. Later on, when her condition worsened, he had brought her to Brussels.

All this had happened almost fifty years before but Aunt Charlotte, although mentally very unstable, was still alive and being taken care of in a chateau near Brussels.

But here the story does not end. King Leopold I, in a paternal effort, had dispatched a corps of some 2,000 Belgian volunteers to Mexico to help his son-in-law establish the core of an Imperial Mexican Army. The campaign nevertheless was ill-fated: in September 1865 the Belgian Legion suffered a significant military blow at a place called Tacambaro which had caused great uneasiness among the political establishment in Belgium. The end came a year later when the force suffered an outright defeat at Ixmiquilpan, 120km north of Mexico City. Upon this news the embarrassed government in Brussels pulled the plug on this royal adventure and disbanded the corps at the end of 1866.

This unhappy enterprise nevertheless did set a precedent in international law from which King Albert could but draw two important lessons. First, as long as the legitimate head of state remained on national soil no foreign power would dare to establish a new regime in the country. Evidently, and with hindsight, it would prevent the German Emperor from setting up a pro-German regime in Belgium.

But King Albert, with his sharp view on history, was perhaps more worried about France's historical expansionist feelings towards its northern neighbour. When the French, as they predicted, made a swift offensive sweep through Flanders while the Belgian Army was being reconstituted in the quiet countryside off Boulogne, nothing could prevent Paris from abolishing the neutral status of Belgium by organizing a pro-French, perhaps even republican, government in Brussels!

Secondly there was the situation of the army itself. In Mexico the Belgian troops had been volunteers, mainly equipped and financed by the mother country. But, as they were fighting on foreign territory, they had been deprived of their Commander-in-Chief. A similar, or even worse, situation would arise if the Army withdrew into France. Without the financial and political support of a tangible fatherland, the troops would be totally dependent on French goodwill for food and equipment, while the king would no longer be able to head his troops. In the end his soldiers could be considered volunteers, or even mercenaries, fighting under the French *drapeau*. This was a nightmare the king wanted to avoid at all cost. Without his cautious and concerned leadership the men would be gobbled up by the huge French war machine and subjected to the ruthless offensive doctrines of the French military establishment.

On the opposite side of the front line, in occupied Brussels, there was German optimism that the Belgian authorities would soon leave the country, a move that would give the occupier a free hand in running Belgium. This is certainly evident from Hugh Gibson's journal[6]. Gibson had already made a few diplomatic – and adventurous – trips through the front lines to Antwerp and even London in order to stay in contact with this government in Washington without being hindered by blatant German censorship.

On the morning of Monday 12 October, Gibson met Freiherr von der Lancken, Head of the *Politische Abteilung* in Brussels. After the customary pleasantries, von der Lancken came to the point. According to him the German forces were rapidly advancing to the coast and it looked as if the Belgian government would soon leave the country. He asked Gibson:

And, my dear colleague, what will your status then be?

It was obvious that the Germans, once the Belgians were driven out of their country, would grab total power. Gibson was taken aback. But later that day, when the Spanish

Rodrigo de Saavedra y Vinent marquis de Villalobar, in 1914 the Spanish Ambassador to Belgium.
Ons Land, 1919.

Ambassador, Marquis de Villalobar, got the same question from von der Lancken, he replied:

> My situation will be just the same as yours. We will both be representatives of our country in a land that is not ours. We will still both respect each other and make the best of it in the given circumstances.

When a few days later the Germans had captured Ostend, Gibson intercepted through his many diplomatic channels in Brussels the rumour that the Belgian Government quite likely had left for the Channel Islands, in particular Guernsey. This was of course wrong, but if we accept that in every rumour there is a grain of truth it is interesting to look somewhat deeper into such a proposal. This destination would have been a handy diplomatic way out for the 'Belgian problem' within the *Entente Cordiale*.

The Channel Islands were of course British, but with a special status. Not only would the Belgian government be welcomed here but Guernsey and Jersey were large enough to even accommodate, on a temporary basis, the Belgian Army and its monarch.

After the conference with Rawlinson and Pau in Ostend had ended, two directives were drawn up. The first one concerned the transfer of the operational base from Ostend to Calais. This transfer would take place partly by sea, partly overland. As such the king did not yet approve of a definite move towards Boulogne. But with the choice of Calais he did acknowledge the desire of the French High Command to clear the area around Dunkirk.

The second memo advised the railways to transport the Second Army Division, to be embarked the next day in Selzaete, straight to Calais, at least according to General Galet. But, as we have seen earlier, at 17:30 the Army Orders for the next day stated that, while the troops were to entrain, the horses and rolling stock of the Second Army Division were to move to localities between Bruges and Ostend. These orders apparently did not indicate a final destination for the division. A railway report moreover indicated that on 11 October thirty-five trains were provided to move the Second Army Division to Bruges.

All other Army Divisions were to be assembled around their embarkation stations and prepare horses, artillery and other convoys for a march to the south-west.

General Pau, in the meantime, informed Joffre that the Belgians were in no mood to stick to the Lys river in order to join the Franco-British lines but that they rather would move along the coast towards northern France.

Rawlinson and Pau, during their meeting with the Belgians, had not only promised to protect their retreat, but had complied with the wish for a quick extraction from the battlefield. Both being closely involved in the northern theatre of operations they had seen firsthand the poor condition of the Belgian Army. While digging in around Ostend and awaiting further reinforcements, Rawlinson clearly expected the front line of his Fourth Corps to expand southwards and eventually link up with the bulk of the BEF detraining at Hazebrouck and directed towards Courtrai.

The same day, in the western corner of the Belgian countryside where two days earlier British officers had used the telephone equipment of the Nieuport lockmaster, the stage was being set for the epic story about to unfold.

Two high ranking British officers, presumably from Rawlinson's staff, called on the same lockmaster and asked for a private meeting. Once alone in the office they unfolded an ordnance map of the region and asked if it would be possible to inundate the area between the Bruges Canal and the dunes, in the direction of Ostend. The lockmaster's reply was negative. To clarify his answer he explained why such a manoeuvre was futile.

For one thing the only structures to drain the polder on the Nieuport side were the Nieuwbedelf Gates. These sluices had only three openings, each 2.50m wide and 3.45m high. This was really insufficient to flood such a large area in a short time. The only way to increase the flow would be to cut the western dyke of the Bruges Canal itself

Idyllic view of the head bay – from the Bruges Canal – of the Count Lock just before the war. The Café du Comte stood to the left of the towpath just out of sight.
City archive Nieuwpoort.

42

and open the lock doors to this canal at the tail bay in Nieuport, adjacent the Nieuwbedelf Gates. (see map on p. 105)

Secondly, even if this procedure was successful he maintained, the main part of the land, especially the dunes and major roads, would remain dry because their lay was above the high water mark. Moreover, with regard to the twelve hours plus tidal cycle and the inner and outer water levels, one could only enter water from two to three hours in Nieuport while in Ostend, or even Zeebrugge, one could drain the same area during a period of nine to ten hours. So in order to maintain the flood he argued, it was crucial to command the canal itself and the drainage structures in Ostend. Otherwise the invading water could be drained in the north.

Apparently not quite satisfied with this comprehensive answer, the officers subsequently wanted to know if eventually it would be possible to inundate the land east of the Bruges Canal. Here the lockmaster was more positive but added that it would be a slow process and that, again, they would need to control the canal and the drainage structures in Ostend.

Obviously the British officers were investigating the possibility of a flood around their main debarkation point, Ostend. A thin layer of water would turn the fields into mud flats, leaving only the main access roads to Ostend dry, thus facilitating the defence of the place.

It is understandable that after the lockmaster's explanation the British officers were still disbelieving: they were indeed in control of Ostend and its drainage structures and wanted to keep the access roads to the city open. The region west of the Bruges Canal could therefore, in their eyes, easily be flooded. But they kept their opinion to themselves.

One of the officers, fluent in French, translated the lockmaster's explanations for the other who carefully took note.

Quite possibly this perfectly bi-lingual officer was Colonel Tom Bridges. Having been Military Attaché in Brussels before the war, Sir John French had sent him to Antwerp on 4 October. Remember the famous midnight run with his open Rolls Royce? Since then Bridges had stayed around and was now British Liaison Officer at Belgian GHQ.

This was in fact not the first time in the war the British were interested in establishing a debarkation base at Ostend. It was not even the first time they projected a new bridgehead on the continent against the German invader.[7] As early as January 1913, with a continental war in the air, the ever-energetic Winston Churchill, then already First Lord of the Admiralty, had thrown one of his numerous 'fantastic' ideas onto the table of Rear Admiral Bayly. He wanted his staff to investigate the possibility of seizing a base somewhere along the eastern North Sea shoreline. Rear Admiral Bayly got a team working on the project and eventually these men came up with some eight specific landing points between the Frisian Islands and the Kattegat Channel in Denmark: the Dutch Frisian islands of Ameland and Borkum, the German islands of Heligoland and Sylt, the Danish town of Esbjerg and the Laeso Channel in the Kattegat. On the Scandinavian Peninsula they studied Kungsbacka Fjord in Sweden and Ekersund in Norway. The report eventually disappeared in an admiralty drawer until a year later the Great War erupted. So far for the plans.

On 21 August the small Belgian garrison of Ostend had been pulled out in order to join the concentration of the army at Antwerp. But in the evening of the same day the civilian authorities in the well-known *cité balneaire* got word that German cavalry was heading towards the town and might appear within a few days. As these troops, and perhaps more to follow, could jeopardize the supply lines of the Belgian Army, the British Admiralty was informed and here it was decided to make a demonstration off the Belgian port with a light cruiser and two divisions of destroyers.

Upon arrival in Ostend the next day, Admiral Christian commanding the flotilla found out that his naval guns would not be able to give off any effective fire on an enemy approaching the port. The sand dunes masked the northern coastal road leading into Ostend from his guns while the road from Bruges could only be held by ground troops occupying the canal bridge a few kilometres east of the town. The road from Thourout, coming from the south, was protected from naval gunfire by the city itself. Asking for further instructions by wireless he was ordered to withdraw the whole force.

Two days later however, Belgian *gendarmes* based in Ostend had to fend off an advance party of Uhlans coming from Thielt, losing five men in the skirmish. Subsequently, at 19:00 the Belgian Ambassador in London received a cable from the Mayor of Ostend asking for the urgent dispatch of British ships and a landing force.

The British Admiralty, eager to defend any Channel port threatened by the enemy, at first wanted to land a few hundred men from the ships to assist the *gendarmerie* in driving off any German cavalry but then the scope of the enterprise rapidly expanded.

The BEF, only recently engaged in the battle, had been on the retreat from Mons to Maubeuge and now to Le Cateau. The retreat would only end six days later and 130km further south, at the outskirts of Paris. Faced with such an overwhelming German wave, the BEF needed some immediate relief. The ever-imaginative Winston Churchill at the Admiralty was the only one in Great Britain who could offer a diversionary move. With his 1913 invasion idea still at the back of his mind he was eager to divert the German attention from his comrades in the embattled BEF.

For just such a venture the Royal Naval Division was being raised, but it was still in embryonic stage and quite unfit for service. The only troop available to him being the Marine Brigade a landing on German soil would be suicidal. In order not to aggravate the European conflagration it was also out of the question to land a diversionary force on the neutral Dutch coast. So the only possibilities left were the Belgian and French shorelines. It would be much more advantageous to land on friendly soil but nevertheless far enough north to draw prompt attention from the German Imperial Staff.

The result was that in the early morning of 27 August the Royal Marine Brigade – Devonport, Portsmouth and Chatham battalions – landed at Ostend. On account of its size and composition it was merely a show of force rather than a real fighting unit. But the brigade was to be considered an advance guard to seize a foothold for the arrival of further forces. It would signal German High Command that the British were determined to take them on, without having to rely on the protection of a 'safe' French debarkation port.

Perhaps not a coincidence, the commander of the force was one of the few officers that had worked on Winston's project for landing points on the German North Sea coast only a year earlier. Royal Marine Brigadier General Sir George Grey Aston had been professor of fortifications – in the late 1880s at the Royal Naval College – and by the outbreak of the war he was still working for the Special Services Branch of the Admiralty War Staff.

Once in Ostend he did not get any time to implement the rules that had been laid out in the scenarios they had developed for such a landing. As he later wrote:

> There was not even time to run round in a car and look at the lie of the ground. Early in the evening [of 27 August], I started in a borrowed car to visit the outposts and have a look at the country outside the town, in case we should have any fighting.

While the Royal Marines were in Ostend word came from the French that they were to embark 16,000 Belgians at Le Havre. These were the troops of the Fourth Army Division that had fought around Namur in southern Belgium and had withdrawn into France. The destination of this army division was for some time uncertain. At first Ostend was, for technical reasons, regarded as unfavourable. Then it was proposed to use Zeebrugge instead: the civil population there was small, the quay accommodation better and the naval artillery could provide better support by having monitors enter the canal leading to Bruges. Shortly afterwards the French even proposed to use Dunkirk to disembark the Belgians. In the end the Belgians were transported to Ostend where they arrived from 30 August on and immediately rejoined the Belgian Field Army.

The situation of the BEF though was getting more precarious each day and on 29 August Sir John French decided that his main supply base would have to be transferred from Boulogne and Le Havre on the Channel coast, to St Nazaire on the Bay of Biscay. This massive relocation brought about such an important shift in priorities at the Admiralty – St Nazaire was 300km farther away from the front line – that it was decided to bring the British ships from Ostend back to England and direct the Royal Marines to Dunkirk to await further orders.

To complete this interlude we want to add that in Dunkirk the marines joined the eclectic force of Commander C.R. Samson. This unit included some ten aeroplanes – the Eastchurch Squadron – sixty more or less armoured cars and a few hundred recently requisitioned double-decker buses. In London's society circles the force was belittlingly dubbed 'Churchill's Dunkirk Circus' but it cannot be denied that these daredevils in October 1914 made numerous hazardous but very valuable reconnaissance flights over, and road trips through, northern France and Belgium.

On 10 October, back at the Royal Chalet in Ostend, nothing seemed to warrant a Belgian withdrawal from national soil, for now at least. As the Germans had not shown up in front of the Ghent-Terneuzen Canal the king ordered the *Groupement Clooten* to stay put. As he feared that his own High Command might prematurely withdraw and disband this interim cavalry force, King Albert at first had confirmed that General Clooten would keep the forces assigned to him at least for the next day. In the mean time High Command itself was still interested in the French proposal: the cavalry division was warned to prepare:

> . . . in case you would be ordered to cover at a later date the movements of the army *on the left [west] bank of the Lys River* . . . [Our italics]

At 19:00 General Pau admitted defeat in his efforts to steer the Belgians along the Lys into France. In his cable to the Generalissimo he blamed his failure on the Belgian desire to avoid any contact with the enemy. He could only confirm what the king silently was working towards:

Tonight the Belgian Army will be in the region of Thourout-Dixmude-Ostende where it will rest. [sic]

NOTES
1. Elisabeth's father was a well-known German eye surgeon and she herself had been trained as a nurse. She spoke six languages and in her spare time played the violin.
2. This canal is locally better known as the *Plassendalevaart* after the hamlet situated at its entrance to the Ostend-Bruges Canal. Originally however the Ostend branch did not exist. We will refer to this canal as the 'Bruges Canal'. Plasschendaele is not to be confused with Passchendaele, the village between Roulers and Ypres, famous for the battle that took place there in October-November 1917.
3. *Ambacht* is an old Flemish word for a judicial subdivision in rural areas. In this instance the subdivision had its seat in the town of Furnes. Today the region is better known as the *Westhoek* [West Corner].
4. The *Entente Cordiale* was an agreement signed by the British Foreign Secretary, Lord Lansdowne, and the French Ambassador, Paul Cambon, in London on 8 April 1904 with the aim of settling long-standing disputes between both countries regarding their respective colonial possessions.
5. Leopold von Saksen-Coburg-Saalfeld (1790-1865). At twenty-five Lt. Gen. in the Russian Army. In 1817 widower of the British Princess Charlotte. First king of the Belgians since 21 July 1831. Remarried in 1832 to Louise Marie d' Orléans, daughter of King Louis Philippe of France.
6. Gibson was the secretary to Brand Whitlock, at the time American Ambassador in Brussels.
7. Exactly 100 years earlier British troops had already landed in Ostend and Nieuport to replace Prussian troops that had 'liberated' the then so-called 'Belgic Provinces' of the Netherlands from French rule after the abdication of Napoleon Bonaparte in April 1814.

Chapter IV

To Leave or Not to Leave

Early on the morning of 11 October, Baron de Broqueville sent a note to the French Ambassador asking permission for the Belgian government to enter France and install itself, if possible, at Le Havre. For the army he asked hospitality without any further specifications.

It is interesting to note that in the long declaration from Baron de Broqueville, dispatched by the French Ambassador in Belgium to his government, King Albert himself was not explicitly mentioned. But the reason given for the selection of Le Havre as a possible refuge read:

> With regard to our special friendly terms with England, the resources it provides us with ... especially in military matters, the government would like to establish itself in such a manner as to facilitate our connections with our English friends.

Is there a hint here that the king – and part of his Field Army – *in extremis*, might want to cross the Channel instead of following the ministers?

The French Mission at Belgian GHQ in the meantime had warned the Generalissimo that the Belgian Army would enter France and move to the Boulogne/Calais region. Twenty minutes after the arrival of this message, General Joffre had angrily answered that this proposal was unacceptable. Instead he reiterated his Lys River concept and advised General Pau to direct the Belgians towards the Ypres/Poperinghe area. But he left a door open:

> It is up to General Foch to prescribe other measures if the situation seems to be modified. Contact him immediately.

Indeed, Joffre had just appointed General Ferdinand Foch as his Deputy for the (French) 'Armies of the North'.

At 22:00 the Generalissimo forwarded a detailed order to Foch involving, among others, his immediate contacts with the various commanders of the armies in the north. Joffre's opinion concerning the French relationship with the British and Belgian commanders was expressed as follows:

> Manage to get along with the Marshal [Sir John French of the BEF] regarding General Rawlinson and with *General Pau* relative to the *Belgian divisions* ... [Our italics]

47

What had all of a sudden happened to the words 'King Albert' and 'the Belgian Army'?

In his orders to Foch, Joffre didn't seem to be quite sure about the Belgians complying with his directives. At the end of his message to Foch he added subtly:

I ask the Minister of War to settle as soon as possible the question of command of the Belgian Army.

It must have been quite irritating to the French Generalissimo that he was not able to give orders directly to the – in his eyes relatively small – Belgian Army as he did to the BEF. Anyway, regarding the latter that's what he thought he did!

The British troops were fighting for what he saw as the 'common cause' and as such acted within the French strategy. But what Joffre was unaware of was that Sir John French had strict orders from London not to engage in actions that would risk his Expeditionary Force.

Moreover the French people in general did not grasp the whole concept of Belgian neutrality and the resulting policy. Having observed strict neutrality and having been dragged into this conflict against its will and against international agreements, Belgium did not want to take sides and wanted to continue an independent course.

By lunch time there was still confusion about the final destination of the Belgian Army. Belgian High Command informed General Pau that the Army would be transferred to the Boulogne/Calais/St Omer region starting the next day.

As a result it notified the Cavalry Division at 13:00 to move from Ghent to Thielt, some 20km west, 'in order to be able to cover the march of the army to the southwest tomorrow'. More importantly GHQ also announced the formation of a Second Cavalry Division out of the *Groupement Clooten*.

This decision concentrated virtually all Belgian cavalry assets into two divisional units. It is another indication that Albert, King of the Belgians, was preparing for an eventual departure of his infantry for England. The Francophiles among the staff officers at High Command perhaps did not realize this but the royal advisers nevertheless managed to get it ordered. The stage was now set for the Belgian cavalry to eventually cover the embarkation – a vulnerable operation indeed – after which it would be able to retreat into France to join the government in exile. Moreover such a decision would save thousands of horses – still a valuable asset in those days – for which there would have been no room on board a flotilla.

Nevertheless High Command was overconfident in its appraisal of the situation. On the orders it read:

. . . the Second Cavalry Division will probably move to the Thielt region while you [the First Cavalry], no doubt, will move to Roulers.

Pro-French officers did not have to rejoice for long though: at 14:20 a new order for the cavalry divisions was issued by High Command. In it the move announced to Thielt and Roulers was cancelled and instead the cavalry was ordered to stay closer to Ghent guarding a canal running north from Deynze.

*   *   *

48

King Albert had a busy day at the Royal Chalet. Apart from the military matters that dominated his days since the beginning of the war there was now the impending departure of his government and the ultimate fate of his army. At 07:00 he asked for information on the naval transports. In Ostend alone some 10,000 wounded were without proper care or medical equipment. He and the queen wanted them evacuated towards safer ground as soon as possible.

Later in the day the king met twice with the Secretary General for Foreign Affairs, Léon Van der Elst and at 16:00 he met with Commander Bulthink, Head of the Nautical College and Professor at the Navigation Academy in Ostend. Baron de Broqueville rounded off the list of dignitaries with a visit.

A striking list of visitors indeed, and in a logical sequence. Mister Van der Elst was a long-time loyal civil servant, remarkably knowledgeable in foreign relations. Commander Bulthink of course was an expert in naval matters and an intimate friend of King Albert. Baron de Broqueville, as head of the cabinet, had to countersign any royal decision. Again, did they discuss a naval evacuation of the army to England?

General Foch, informed by Pau of the Belgian intentions, was furious. At 13:15, in a strongly worded telegram to Joffre, he explained that the Belgians were combat-wary, that they refused to follow Joffre's guidelines – in other words a retreat towards Ypres/Poperinghe – and were only interested in getting away from the enemy. Three quarters of an hour later Joffre ordered the French Mission at Belgian General Headquarters to halt all Belgian troop transports destined for France.

The latter order by Joffre was apparently not a reaction to Foch's telegram. It was somehow a simple practical decision: traffic on the rail network of the French *Compagnie du Nord* was already overstretched due to the arrival of the BEF from Soissons, large domestic French troop transports, the arrival of Belgian recruits and the fact that Dunkirk itself was being readied as an entrenched camp.

As a result the first train with Belgian soldiers, part of the Second Army Division arriving from Selzaete, was halted in Furnes on its way to Dunkirk. But the situation was now evolving fast. Half an hour later Foch, evidently in an effort to solve this major complication within Allied ranks, reported to Joffre the compromise he had suggested to Pau:

> If the Belgian Army cannot be assembled south of Ostend, with that city as a base, let it then assemble south of Dunkirk, with the latter city as a base; there it can rest and reform.

In the late afternoon reports arrived at Foch's headquarters that French troops had retaken Hazebrouck from German scouting parties and were advancing east on Lille, a city that was now besieged by the enemy. This positive news apparently convinced Joffre not only to support Foch's idea of a concentration of the Belgian forces south of Dunkirk or Ostend, where they would be close at hand, but it also strengthened him in his belief that this Belgian Army had to be under his overall command. At 19:00 he dispatched the following telegram to the French Minister of War:

> I again insist on the necessity to solve the question of command of the Belgian Army. At this moment it is essential for the development of the current manoeuvre that I can give direct instructions to this army.

Colonel Léon d'Orjo de Marchovelette, Belgian representative at Joffre's Headquarters, relayed an even bolder account to Belgian High Command:

> They wonder if, under the new conditions, that is the Belgian Army being reduced to a lesser strength and having to work with the Franco-British Armies, the king would not consider to delegate one of his generals to take command of the army . . .

Now, with an independent Belgium being reduced to a small strip of territory, King Albert more than ever rejected the idea of relinquishing his command. The only offer he could make to Joffre was that the French Generalissimo should communicate with him directly, in the way Joffre already did with British Field Marshal Sir John French.

Besides the fact that there did not (yet) exist a unified command – and as such the French and British could not really be considered 'allied' – the irony was that Joseph Joffre, at that moment still a general, in a hierarchical sense, could not exactly give orders to Sir John French, who himself was a field marshal!

It is interesting to note also that in 1918 General John Pershing, Head of the American Expeditionary Force, faced similar pressures from French High Command. He too would adamantly oppose any 'amalgamation' of his forces with the French Army.

All in all the tactical situation had not deteriorated throughout the day. In fact various reports indicated that the land west of Ghent and north of Ypres was still free of Germans. In the east the enemy was still a three-days' march away. The only threat might come from the Hazebrouck/Lille/Ypres area. But there only light German forces were operating which could be dealt with by guarding the bridges across the Yser river between the French border and the Ypres-Yser Canal. Consequently, there was no need for an urgent retreat and for the time being, the intended restructuring of the army in the Furnes-Ambacht region, as discussed in Eecloo, could go ahead.

At 17:40 orders were issued for the next day. The First, Second, Third and Fourth Army Divisions were to stay at their present encampments that were, in the same order, Westende, Furnes, Nieuport and Ghistelles (see map '12 and 13 October'). The Sixth Army Division was to move west from Dixmude and occupy the bridges across the Yser between the French border and the Loo Canal. The Fifth Army Division finally was to move from Thourout to Dixmude and guard the entrances to this last town.

Except for the First and Fourth, all army divisions would then be within the Yser perimeter, protected from sudden German intrusions from the south. The First Army Division, still in Westende, could be across the river within hours while the Fourth, 15km out at Ghistelles, was ready to deploy, if necessary, in an advanced position . . . or perhaps it could be in Ostend within hours to embark for Britain!

The decision to whether or not withdraw into France having been postponed momentarily suited King Albert and satisfied the Generalissimo.

At the same time the Second Cavalry Division was in formation in the area Deynze/Thielt: the *brigade de cavalerie indépendante* had been released by General Clooten and was being reinforced by the cavalry of the Fifth Army Division and other mounted troops. These were mainly two squadrons of Garrison Guides, three squadrons of mounted *gendarmerie*, two companies of cyclists, a group of horse artillery and divisional transports.

During the day some confusion arose concerning both cavalry divisions. First, at 13:00 High Command informed the First Cavalry to prepare for a move towards Thielt to be followed, probably the next day, by another transfer to Roulers. The Second Cavalry was to come after. But an hour and a half later the message was cancelled. The First was instead to guard the Lys north of Deynze while the Group Clooten was to stay in place west of the Ghent-Terneuzen Canal.

The next day, 12 October, the newly formed Second Cavalry left its southern encampments and travelled north to take up positions behind what was left of the *Groupement Clooten*. This apparent reversal in tactics demonstrates the desire of the king to guard the approaches to Ostend and Nieuport, rather than patrolling the right flank of the Field Army. Perhaps the king anticipated that Rawlinson's Third Cavalry Division had been assigned this task but on 12 October this division was already moving from Roulers to Ypres, thus exposing the Belgian right.

An hour after the army orders for the next day had been issued a written note arrived,

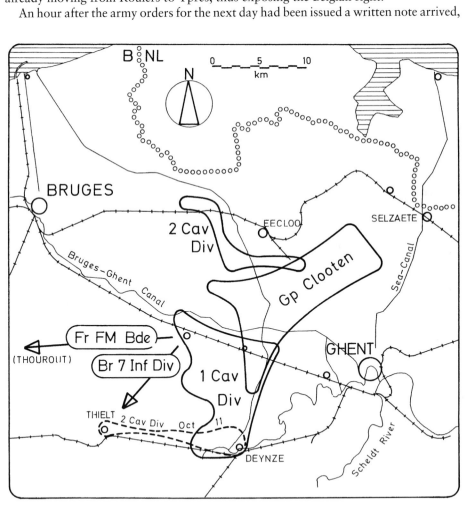

12 October

51

taken from a telephone conversation and emanating from Lieutenant Colonel Colin, Chief of Staff of General Pau, to the French Mission at Belgian General Headquarters. Colin (or Pau?) had agreed with Baron de Broqueville and Colonel Wielemans that the Belgian Army would concentrate in the Nieuport/Dixmude/Furnes area and would be ready for action within forty-eight hours.

While at lunchtime Pau had still agreed on a withdrawal towards Boulogne, he now expected the Belgian Army to be capable of action within two days! While Joffre, through this government, was trying to 'dethrone' the king from his supreme command, he relied on the acquiescent attitude of the Belgian Minister of War and his protégé, the Deputy Chief of Staff, to entice the Belgian Army into almost immediate – and certainly adventurous and perhaps even disastrous – action.

Meanwhile in Nieuport on the Belgian coast the traffic started to increase. Up until now the war seemed to have been a distant event experienced only by city people in Liège, Brussels and Antwerp. The only reminder that a war was on had been the occasional visit of British patrols, mainly motorized units from Commander Samson's base in Dunkirk, that would pass by at the locks, on the way to one of their outlying landing strips more east. The only stark reminder of the war was on 3 October when 2,000 Belgian recruits arrived.

Jules Vermeulen, Parish Priest in Nieuport from 1907 to 1920 described their arrival and subsequent stay as follows:

On Saturday October 3 all of a sudden 2,000 rookies arrived in Nieuport. That is how they called recruits in 1914. They arrived in their civvies and had left their barracks in Antwerp in great haste since these had been bombarded already. The men were starving and were exhausted. They hadn't gotten any food the whole day and had slept outside for two nights. As such the citizenry immediately welcomed them fraternally, yes enthusiastically. They filled them up with food and drink and in all schools and public buildings sleeping-places were organized. It was said that they would stay for some time and that they would learn the art of soldiery here. But after three days they suddenly had to leave without even lunch. They had to take the train and tramcar to travel France's way. After all, it was said, a German Army was on its way through Flanders to capture the young recruits.

With compassion the people of Nieuport saw the rookies off, not only because everyone had become sympathetic to them but also because this departure spelled doom for all of us.

Four days after the 'rookies' had left, Saturday 11 October, also in Nieuport things were getting even more serious. The city was informed by army authorities to prepare for the arrival and billeting of 10,000 soldiers – mainly the men of the Third Army Division. The Reverend Father Jules Vermeulen again strikingly described their arrival in the city:

Never have I seen a more sad spectacle. The army passed by in disarray, everything was grimy and slipshod, the superiors looked sorrowful and disgruntled. Soldiers and horses looked totally worn out and on all faces one could read despondency. Every citizen took it to heart to see our army in such a miserable state.

Everywhere soldiers were billeted – 2,000 on a hastily arranged carpet of straw in the church alone – and by the end of the week all pubs and stores were sold out. On 11 October one peculiar incident happened which we should mention.

In the morning a few Belgian soldiers wandered onto the locks, apparently showing up from nowhere and seemingly without any commanding officer. They got a hold of a couple of steel racks mounted on wooden beams that were meant to manipulate the lock doors. As they got ready to cut the timber to pieces lockmaster Dingens, alerted by one of his aides, arrived on the spot.

'What are you trying to accomplish?' he asked furiously.

'We want to cook our food.' the troopers replied.

'But these are my tools!' Dingens exclaimed.

The soldiers were imperturbable.

'You can replace them with ropes,' they said, 'it will work just as well. By the way, don't be too concerned, tomorrow the army will take over the place.'

A discussion followed in which the soldiers finally agreed to return the beams to the lockmaster. But, as they insisted on getting wood to cook their meal, they got a hold of the handles of the ice picks the locksmen used in winter to break up the ice along the gate- and lock doors. Fortunately, soon afterwards the troublemakers disappeared.

In the afternoon, the four British soldiers that had stayed at the lockmaster's dwelling for the past four days made preparations to leave. After courteously acknowledging the hospitality of lockmaster Dingens they finally left by motorcycle for Roulers. They were on their way to rejoin Rawlinson's forces that were now covering the Belgian right flank and were moving from Ghent southwest to Thourout and Roulers.

They had hardly left when a French speaking second lieutenant and a sergeant of the Belgian Engineers arrived on the scene. With an air of superiority they literally occupied the lockmaster's office and even prevented him from using his precious telegraph equipment. Dingens protested vigorously:

> It is my duty to do my work, and I will continue to do so until a higher ranking officer tells me, on his responsibility, to leave my post.

Being lockmaster in Nieuport was an enviable job [1]. You came to live in a large two-story house, built in between the dispersed locks and surrounded by an enjoyable garden. On duty you commanded a force of nine or ten lockkeepers and assistants who worked the locks and sluices upon your directives.

Thanks to your hydraulic knowledge, hundreds of farming families and thousands of artisans and small merchants living in the surrounding polders felt protected from the erratic seas. Through the Nieuport sluice complex 377 square kilometres of polder – or more than twice the area of Washington, DC – was drained. By manipulating the water levels in the different polders you, the lockmaster provided these people year round with the right amount of fresh water to grow excellent crops and thick, green pastures.

There had been earlier dark times, when no heavy wooden, double doors protected the low-lying land. A time when every major storm in the North Sea could wreak havoc deep inland and pull hundreds of helpless victims to their death.

As lockmaster you knew and met boat people from near and far and as such were the ambassador of your city. All this meant that you stood in high regard with the local

Lockmaster Dingens and his staff stand at the gantry of the Furnes Lock. In between the group we see a typical capstan to manoeuvre one of the flood doors.
Historical prints collection Callenaere-Dehouck.

people, from notaries and noblemen through merchants and fishermen to farmers and factory workers.

Lockmaster Gerard Dingens in October 1914 was no exception to this rule. On the contrary, being a determined self-educated person, he had become a respected public figure in Nieuport intellectual circles. Who was this man?

Gerard Dingens was born in 1849 in the Netherlands, in all likelihood in Sas-Van-Gent, just across the border from Selzaete. For unknown reasons and early on he emigrated to Belgium. At the age of twenty-eight he was already living in Nieuport as an employee of the Roads & Bridges department. The young man from Zeeland-Flanders apparently had a way with technical drawings since in 1876–77 he took part in the design and construction of the new lock-and-gate structures at the northern entrance to the city. At that time he also gained his Belgian citizenship. The young Dingens had a lightning career: six years later, at age thirty-four, he was appointed lockmaster-collector in his hometown. All this meant that by 1914 he had accumulated over forty years of impeccable service with the Waterways Department of the Ministry of Roads & Bridges.

As such it would not be surprising that Dingens was well acquainted with, and perhaps even friends with, several engineers and other high-ranking officials in the Waterways Department of the Coast. As we will see later on, these relationships would after the war be quite valuable.

The City of Nieuport was the man's whole life. Here he was a man of distinction: besides the fact that he was perfectly bilingual he was Secretary of the local Flemish Rhetorical Society and the Nieuport Savings-Bank. He was also a member of the Philharmonic Commission and Vice President of the Flemish-Liberal cultural movement *Willemsfonds*. On the job he directed his personnel with an iron fist and, proud of his locks as he was, he could talk in great detail about them to well-mannered outsiders. The British officers and later Captain Commandant Nuyten, were extremely well mannered, very polite and asked for his advice. They treated the lockmaster as one of their peers. But his strong personality and steadfast attitude were bound to collide with the invaders of his territory.

At first young, rude and practically illiterate soldiers invaded his domain and appropriated tools and equipment in the name of a so-called military authority. The proud lockmaster's office began to look like Grand Central Station: soldiers began to use it as a guardroom. They fumbled with his electric apparatuses and measuring tools and rummaged through his paperwork and books. All this fooling around made Dingens nervous and very uneasy about the future.

Understandably, given the circumstances, animosity was created immediately on both sides. Lockmaster Dingens evidently resented the French speaking, Belgian establishment, embodied by the engineer officer and his men invading his territory. The soldiers on the other hand, were afraid, in a general mood of 'spy-catching', that the lockkeeper, apparently a militant and intellectual Fleming, would wire strategic information to the other side.

On the morning of Monday 12 October, some 12km north-east in Ostend, the king had an early morning meeting with Baron de Broqueville in order to draw up a reply to the French president. It had been a quite chilly autumn night but the day brought an expectation of at least a few sunny breaks. Upon the request of the Belgians to take refuge in France, the French government had taken the necessary steps to grant official asylum status to the king and his government.

In his telegram to King Albert the French President, Raymond Poincaré, had written:

> I have been informed of the decision of the Royal Government [to move to France]. The Government of the Republic is deeply touched and will immediately take the necessary steps to secure the stay of His Majesty and his Ministers . . .

In his letter of thanks, drawn up in accordance with the Minister of War, the king acknowledged the hospitality granted by the President of the French Republic to . . . just his government!

> I am deeply touched at the hospitality that France is willing to cordially offer to the Belgian Government and the measures that . . .

By not mentioning his own person, the king officially indicated his resolve to stay with his troops, the bulk of which he clearly did not want to enter France. It represented his unflinching conviction that he was the Commander-in-Chief of the Belgian Army and the Symbol of the Nation.

In the middle of the afternoon the Belgian Colonel Léon d'Orjo de Marchovelette

The Yser Mouth with both palisades still intact before the war. On the opposite, left bank one can see the pilot house. Along both stockades and at the fisherman's wharf upstream, several troop transports could have docked simultaneously to embark the remainder of the Belgian Army.
Historical prints collection Callenaere-Dehouck.

arrived at the Chalet in Ostend for a meeting with General Jungbluth. Up until now nothing is known about the subjects discussed. But Léon d'Orjo, being posted at French High Command, was of course heavily exposed to the French 'offensive' mindset. Undoubtedly the king wanted him to understand exactly what his ultimate intentions were. Who better than Jungbluth to brief him? At about the same time, the king met Baron de Broqueville, also at the Chalet. General Headquarters meanwhile was again being packed up, this time to transfer to Nieuport-Bains.

If we think in terms of making a stand at the Yser River – a view which has been held by most historians for almost the last ninety years – Nieuport-Bains seems to be a most peculiar choice to establish Belgian General Headquarters. We only have to look at a map to conclude that, for the coordination of the defence of the Yser front, the obvious place for General Headquarters would be in the centrally located county town of the region, Furnes.

The choice of Nieuport-Bains is a lot more obvious though if we keep in mind that King Albert and his close advisers, for various reasons, had quietly favoured British support all along. Even the government had considered for a moment, before deciding on setting up at Le Havre, to transfer to England. This installation in Nieuport-Bains is just one of many indications that the king still kept the idea of a naval evacuation of his Field Army from Belgian soil to England at the back of his mind.

After Ostend, the small town of Nieuport-Bains was the best choice. It did possess a railway station and paved road within a minute's walk of a thousand metre long palisade in the Yser Channel. Here, and in the inner harbour, several sea-going vessels could dock simultaneously to embark troops. Moreover, the adjacent narrow-gauge railway line provided access to an extensive local inland network and would enable the transportation of the majority of the infantry by rail from its present, dispersed encampments (see map chapter XIII, p.188).

In the morning, news had arrived that the Anglo-French forces were on the verge of launching a major offensive. While French troops would march on Lille, the newly arrived BEF would move towards Courtrai on the Lys. Here they were supposed to join up with Rawlinson's Fourth Corps and the Belgian Army! To this effect Joffre expected the Belgians to move south to cross the Ypres-Poperinghe route and proceed to the Lys. The purpose of this project, in the French offensive spirit anyway, seemed to be the recapturing of Lille by French troops and an outflanking manoeuvre by the BEF, supported by the Belgians. That would mean another forced march with an army of which The Reverend Vermeulen just had written: 'Every citizen took it to heart to see our army in such a miserable state.'

Now that the Germans were on the move westwards again there was no question of transporting the exhausted and by now severely under-equipped Belgian divisions to Ypres or further east. From the localities they were now stationed, three divisions would have to march thirty-five or more kilometres, just to get to their starting point. Even supposing that the Belgian Army was able to make it to Ypres, there was no way that upon arrival, they could conduct any offensive action. While the stores of the Field Army were again being relocated, this time from Ostend to Dunkirk, no reliable supply line could be set up to support an operation of this magnitude. Moreover, by leaving the coast the Belgians would not only lose the protection of their left flank, a fundamental factor in their strategy since the retreat from Antwerp, but they also risked being deprived of their sole free link with England.

With this unrealistic plan Joffre discarded the notion that at the moment the Belgian

Navigating a narrow channel in foggy conditions can be hazardous. On Christmas Day 1923 the vessel *Jarrix* ended up on the breakwater lining the river mouth. Note that the palisade has not yet been fully repaired from the war's ravages.
Historical prints collection Callenaere-Dehouck.

Army was unfit to take to the field. His Deputy Foch, closer to the scene and with a more realistic view of the situation did solve the problem with the two *divisions territoriales*, the 87th and 89th, that had been protecting the detraining of the BEF between St Omer and Hazebrouck. He put both under the command of General Bidon, the Military Governor of Dunkirk, and ordered them to move east and organize a strong defensive position around Ypres.

Now that the threat of a German drive through western Belgium was becoming more real – enemy columns were reported to be moving from Ghent towards Bruges and Thielt – Foch cabled the following directive to Pau concerning the deployment of the Belgian Army:

> Under the protection of the Rawlinson Corps and the Belgian cavalry divisions, the five Belgian infantry divisions fit to take the field, will establish themselves on the line Roulers-Thourout-Ostend. They will be there tomorrow evening, 13.

This project was already a more sensible approach to the problem and a lot closer to the ideas of King Albert. Trying to outflank the enemy in the vicinity of Courtrai while he was closing in on the coast, along the Dutch border, was not so prudent a manoeuvre.

But in the end it was a matter of *déjà vu* all over again to the king. Maybe countries like France and Great Britain, with almost unlimited resources, could afford to organize an offensive involving such risks. His responsibilities towards his compatriots, exhausted, empty-handed and driven together onto the last square miles of national territory, dictated the utmost caution. A certain premonition, coupled with his personal knowledge of the Prussian military mind [2] warned him that a major confrontation was about to happen on the German right flank. Indeed, as long as the Channel ports were still free, the risk of the British Grand Fleet landing a second BEF in the German flank was too important to be neglected by German High Command.

The Belgian monarch realized that occupying the Belgian coast would be a priority for the enemy. There were enough indications in the field that the Germans were up to a major offensive in order to take what was left of Belgium and to conquer the Channel coast. The Second Cavalry Division, now west of the Ghent-Terneuzen Canal, reported German troops on the east bank of the canal from Selzaete to Ghent. So they too were skirting the Dutch border! More south, on the Dendre river, aerial patrols revealed that railway troops were repairing river crossings and installing debarkation ramps in the shunting-yards.

At 17:00 another meeting was held with the Anglo-French representatives. The king expressed his doubts concerning the planned attack towards Courtrai and proposed that his army should take up an entrenched position in the low-lying area behind the Yser River. For the Belgians, this front was easier to defend and not as advanced. With the Yser, its dykes and the multitude of ditches, the region was a bulwark, relatively simple to organize. Even in the event that the French and British did not reach Ypres, and as such not the Ypres-Yser Canal, it would only be a matter of occupying the left bank of the river from the confluence with the canal from Ypres, to Rousbrugge at the French border.

Finally a compromise was reached: it was agreed that the First and Fourth army divisions, supported by the *fusiliers marins*, would take up an advanced position some 12km east of the line Dixmude/Ostend. The Third and Fifth would start organizing the

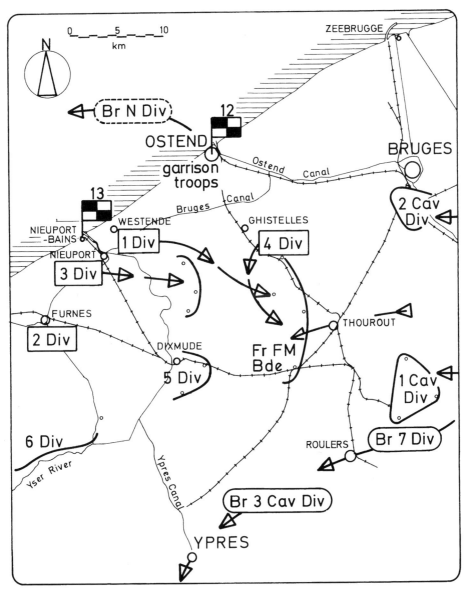

12 & 13 October

forward defence of the river while the Second would stay in Furnes and the Sixth guard the southern approaches along the Yser between Rousbrugge and Loo.

Not everyone agreed with the idea of exposing two divisions in front of the Yser position but in the end it was the Deputy Chief-of-Staff's point of view that won the day.

The two cavalry divisions, still west of the line Deynze/Ghent/Selzaete, were to stay in close contact with the enemy columns to test their forces and to determine their marching directions. Would they move north-west to Bruges and Ostend, or south-west to Thielt and Thourout?

Meanwhile, the French logistics had managed to organize the rear of the Belgian Army. The depots and recruits were to be directed by ship to Le Havre. As the Port of Boulogne was still heavily used by the British, the Belgian Army Base was to be established, for the time being, in the Calais/Dunkirk area. Measures were being taken to provide railway cars to transport stores and prepare for nourishment of the attending men and horses. In fact the French *Compagnie du Nord*, after previous refusals – notably 21 September, 5 and 10 October – to allow thousands of Belgian rolling-stock units onto its system now asked 300 to 400 cars from the Belgian Railway Company. As Belgian wagons and carriages were stuck for tens of miles on every available line near the border by now, they were provided immediately.

In the evening General Foch was quite optimistic about the mainly unopposed advances that the Franco-British troops had made during the day. As a result, he moved the detraining of the British First Corps up from the St Omer/Hazebrouck sector to the Hazebrouck/Bailleul area.

At Belgian General Headquarters attention was now being focused on the organization of the Furnes-Ambacht region as an entrenched camp. While on 9 October this region had already been mentioned as a possible temporary refuge for the army it was now obvious that the winding Yser River would have to be transformed into a defensive barrier.

The river and adjoining Ypres Canal were not unknown territory to the Belgian staff officers. As late as 1913, when war clouds were already darkening European skies, studies had been taken up on the principal lines of defence in the country. While the Meuse River had been scrutinized as the primary line against an aggressor from the east, a similar study had been made of the defence against an invader – France – from the south. Here the waterway from Nieuport to Ypres comprised the westernmost first line

The mail boat *Ville de Liège*, sister ship of the *Stad van Antwerpen*, was the first mail boat to return to Ostend harbour after having been in exile for four years.
Author's photo archive.

of defence. Facing the Dunkirk Fortified Place it was of particular importance to the Belgian defence and had been studied to some degree.

Now of course an unexpected situation had developed: instead of the Belgians facing west, the line would have to be occupied facing east! Nevertheless, as the general topography on both sides of the river was similar, the river offered good defensive properties along both banks. The flat terrain, criss-crossed by hundreds of ditches and canals and the scarcity of access points would hamper the approach of the enemy and made for a quite reliable position by a well-prepared, dug-in defender.

After the war quite a few authors directed a lot of criticism towards the army for not having studied the possibilities of inundating this region. Although some of this criticism can perhaps be attributed to a biased point of view by these authors, High Command, and the engineers in particular, should indeed not be blamed for this lack of understanding of the drainage system of this westernmost and low-lying part of the country. The knowledge of inundating a terrain for defensive purposes was well known – and still being taught – at the Royal Military Academy but mainly in conjunction with the defence of Antwerp, the National Refuge. The defence of the line of the Yser as mentioned earlier, was only meant as a temporary measure to delay an invader coming from the south. It was a first line of defence to gain time in order for the international guarantors to mobilize their forces and come to the rescue of the Belgian kingdom.

At seven in the morning of Tuesday 13 October the Belgian mail-boat *Pieter de Coninck* put to sea from Ostend. Concerned about the safety of the important passengers the British Admiralty provided escort with three river monitors that, as we will see later, would return in the ensuing days for shore bombardment. All the members of the cabinet – except the Minister of War – the Ministers of State and the Diplomatic Corps were aboard, heading for Le Havre. Half an hour later a second mail-boat, the *Stad van Antwerpen* put out for the same destination with civil servants of various ministerial departments. Under a low, overcast sky and with an icy drizzle it made for an emotional farewell to Belgian soil.

For those that were left behind a lot of work was ahead. Soon after, the Head of the Cabinet, Minister of War Baron de Broqueville departed by car from Ostend for Dunkirk, ready to organize the arrival of the military stores from Ostend. The Commander-in-Chief himself and his close advisors left on horseback for their new headquarters in Nieuport-Bains.

Shortly after the departure of both mail-boats an officer of the Military House of the King – unfortunately we do not know exactly who – made a seemingly mysterious, but nonetheless extremely interesting telephone call from Ostend to Deynze. As a result a unit of the *pionniers-pontonniers cyclistes* of the First Cavalry Division immediately disabled the switching and signalling apparatuses and destroyed other vital equipment at the Deynze railway station. Subsequently the small engineering unit withdrew across the Lys river and blew up the last remaining river crossing in that location, the railway bridge. What was the reason for this peculiar order, evidently emanating from the king himself?

It was expected that the enemy would occupy Deynze soon. If the railway in this locality was left intact, the Germans would be able to launch an armoured train on a 70km raid straight to Nieuport and alongside the Yser mouth. It might look like a suicide mission but it would have created tremendous havoc among the thousands of

The lightship *Dyck*, six nautical miles north-west of Dunkirk. At the outbreak of war all navigational aids like this one in the Channel had been removed, making a sea journey even more hazardous. One more reason why a British navy escort for the mail boats was appreciated.
Author's photo archive.

troops if they were ever assembled between Nieuport-Ville and Nieuport-Bains for an embarkation to England.

This fear for a surprise enemy raid behind the lines was certainly not unfounded. One story in the *Revue du Touring Club de France* recalls that in September 1914 a German open tourer and two trucks left Noyon (80km north-east of Paris), went round the front line and succeeded in reaching the Fôret de Lyons near Gournay-en-Bray, 40km from Rouen, by way of small unguarded roads. The raid was led by *Oberleutnant* von Gartner who, before the war, owned a hunting licence in this forest and who knew these woods like the back of his hand.

Unfortunately though, during a brief stop of the convoy a woman gathering brushwood spotted the Germans. She immediately informed the nearest *gendarmerie* where a 'posse' was organized with local farmers. With hunting rifles, pitchforks and clubs this diverse group attacked the Germans, in the course losing four men out of five. Nevertheless their brave sacrifice enabled the authorities to gain time: the German 'commandos' finally ran into a roadblock set up by Territorials. But the fact remained that the enemy party ultimately had managed to get 110km behind the French lines. And this was certainly not an isolated incident. On 4 October, at the outskirts of Lille, French Garrison *Chasseurs* exchanged fire and subsequently halted a German armoured train bound for Calais, 100 km to the west.

In the circumstances though the raid would have failed due to sheer coincidence: Colonel Brécard reported on 14 October to Joffre that twenty trains loaded with equipment from Antwerp were sitting on the railway line between Nieuport and Dixmude. As we will see though another strange rail incident would happen in Dixmude a few days later.

At General Headquarters the staff officers were more concerned with the direction the enemy columns took leaving Ghent. Were they heading north-west towards Bruges and Ostend, or south-west towards Courtrai and Lille? News had arrived that all Anglo-Belgian troops had left Ghent the previous evening and that important German columns were converging on the city. So a patrol was ordered to push to the western outskirts of Ghent and report on the enemy movements on the arterial roads.

During the day, as a formation of an estimated 10,000 Germans were marching from

Selzaete towards Eecloo, the Second Cavalry Division withdrew to Bruges while the First moved to the area north of Roulers.

Upon arrival in Nieuport-Bains Captain Commandant Galet crossed the Yser mouth and made a reconnaissance trip through the range of dunes west of the village of Lombartzyde (see map p.188). This statement was made by General Émile Galet in his book seventeen years after the war. One of his observations was that if they held the village of Lombartzyde, the Germans' artillery would be able to take the whole west bank of the Yser in enfilading fire. If the army was to make a stand at this river it was essential that the troops hold on to the village and the adjacent dunes. Nevertheless, in view of what has been argued earlier, we suspect that the investigation of the king's confidant on the east bank still had other, ulterior motives.

It looks rather strange that a member of the royal inner sanctum would occupy himself with such trivial tactical details, let alone remember them so many years later that he broached the subject in his book. There was indeed a more strategic reason for Galet's innocent excursion. We should not forget that he was one of the brains behind the royal strategy.

At that moment two infantry divisions were stationed east of the Yser. If these large units needed to be evacuated by sea to England they could lose valuable time crossing the river by the few small bridges over it. At the time though the mouth of the river was on either side flanked by a long palisade jutting into the sea. It would therefore be handy if troops stationed east of the river could also use the eastern jetty to embark. But unlike the western pier, which was near the railway and tram station, the location of the eastern stockade was isolated, adjacent to a large section of dunes and 2,000m from the nearest paved road.

Nieuport-Bains — La Digue Ii.

On 13 October General Headquarters was established in the Grand Hotel des Bains on the sea promenade in Nieuport-Bains, just steps away from the Yser mouth.
Historical prints collection Callenaere-Dehouck.

Ordnance maps from before the war indicate, nevertheless, that a single, narrow-gauge rail line branched off in Lombartzyde and ran up to the pedestrian entrance to the jetty. This line had obviously been built so visitors to the seaside resort of Nieuport-Bains, coming from Ostend and farther field, could avoid the long detour by the City of Nieuport itself and a probable wait at any of the three busy locks north of it.

In our opinion it is clear that the main reason for the Captain Commandant to cross the river mouth and make a walkabout in the deserted dunes was to check for himself the local topography, the physical situation of the railway line and the layout of jetty. Not only plans for a successful embarkation depended on his personal assessment; perhaps even the survival of the country as well!

Of course in 1931 there was no reason to mention this train of thought in his book: the allies had won the war so, for the sake of the nation, any alternative and desperate projects of 1914 could as well be buried.

After having left Ostend at 16:00 by motorcar Queen Elisabeth arrived an hour and a half later in Nieuport-Bains where she was to stay with her husband at the luxurious Crombez Mansion on the wind swept sea promenade.

The Crombez family was of wealthy Walloon stock. At the passing away of the childless Benjamin in 1902, his nephew, the young and dashing Henri, had inherited large land estates on this side of the Belgian coast.

At the end of the nineteenth century Crombez the Elder had initiated the development of Nieuport-Bains into an upmarket seaside resort. As such though he had come

King Albert and Queen Elisabeth stayed at the Henri Crombez Mansion on 13 and 14 October, a hundred yards from the Grand Hotel des Bains. To the left we see the glass roof of the adjacent covered garden.
Historical prints collection Callenaere-Dehouck.

64

into conflict with a formidable rival, King Leopold II [3] himself who at the time harboured similar plans for 'his' Ostend. But all this was history now.

Henri loved the good life and moved around in high circles with ease. In 1907 he had opened a large golf course with all amenities on the east bank of the Yser Channel to cater to the rich and famous. The narrow gauge railway had already been extended from Lombartzyde into the dunes and perhaps one day he also intended to develop Lombartzyde-Bains into a luxury resort. But Louis Blériot and his aviation exploits must have caught his attention and he soon got into the flying business. His pilot's licence, dated 18 October 1910, carried serial number 26. In 1914 he flew his own Deperdussin monoplane and with this machine volunteered for the *Compagnie des Aviateurs* when the war broke out. All volunteer aviators were organized into a new squadron, the 5th. Perhaps due to his connections in high places, Henri Crombez was appointed squadron leader. At some point he was even given the title 'the king's personal pilot'.

The Crombez Villa stood a good 100 metres west of the Grand Hotel des Bains where General Headquarters had been installed in the morning. Although this isolated, small sea resort, only 14km away from France looked dreary in the cold autumn wind, it was almost perfect for conducting the upcoming operations. Even here High Command still had excellent communication links with Britain. The army was not only still in possession of the undersea cable to England at La Panne but had also access to the wireless telegraph station near the harbour entrance lighthouse.

This wireless – or 'Marconi' – station had been the first in Belgium, being inaugurated in 1900 by the then Prince Albert accompanied by his wife, then Princess Elisabeth, and General Harry Jungbluth. The radio equipment had been installed in the small pilothouse on the sea promenade near the Yser Mouth. The aerial was erected on three wooden poles mounted on top of each other.

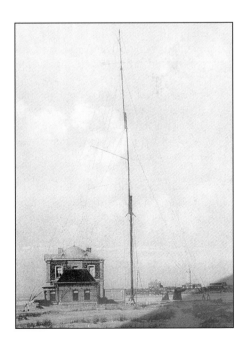

The wireless station near the harbour channel in Nieuport-Bains. Through this station Belgian Headquarters was still in permanent contact with London. In the background the lighthouse and villa at the golf course of Henri Combrez on the opposite bank of the Yser mouth (today the military domain of Lombartzyde).
Historical prints collection Callenaere-Dehouck.

Today an electronic beacon in the same spot as the wireless ninety years ago. *Author's photo archive.*

It must be said that the undersea cable at La Panne and the Marconi station in Nieuport-Bains were now of the utmost strategic importance to the Belgian Army.

As an example we mention here the incident that happened only a few weeks later on the other side of the globe. On tiny Direction Island, one of the Cocos Keeling Islands in the middle of the southern Indian Ocean, the British had installed a radio and telegraph station. Here the undersea cables of Australia, Africa and India all surfaced and interconnected. On 9 November the German light cruiser *Emden* landed a marine detachment with orders to destroy the radio equipment and cut the undersea cables. The marines did their work thoroughly – they even destroyed an innocent seismograph – but unfortunately for them the radio crew had managed to send a distress signal just prior to the enemy landing. For the *Emden* this meant the beginning of the end of an infamous, three-month marauding cruise on the high seas.

Back in Nieuport, in the cold, late afternoon an officer of the General Staff, Captain Commandant Nuyten, returning from an unspecified mission, had his car halted at the lock system and called on lockmaster Dingens. Nuyten later wrote:

> Returning in the evening from my mission, I halted my motorcar at the entrance to Nieuport-Ville, in order to inform myself with the lockkeeper, in charge of the locks at that location, on the possibility to inundate the land east of the Yser. The good man gave me a negative answer. I did not insist and continued to Nieuport–Bains to account for the use of my day to my superiors.

This was a quite peculiar post-war statement. Why did Nuyten not reveal the main goal of his mission on that day? Did he still have to conceal something important – just like his friend Galet? Why was a staff officer, with no engineering experience at all, interested in floods? From the limited context we can only suspect that Nuyten came from the direction of Ostend and from the lockkeeper's account we deduce that Belgian High Command, and/or the king, were still interested in – British – flood plans 'towards Ostend'.

Dingens, recalling the encounter in 1920, elaborated on the subject. At first the Captain Commandant had asked him where he could contact his superiors, the Superintendent and the Chief Engineer of the department of Roads & Bridges. Nuyten was highly surprised to hear that Dingens was unaware of the whereabouts of his supervisors.

From a post-war enquiry we know that the same day the Chief-Engineer and Head of the Roads & Bridges Service for the Coast, Mr Hainaut, had left Ostend in the morning for Le Havre, we assume even on the mail-boat *Stad Van Antwerpen* as mentioned earlier. We will later see under what circumstances Mr. Hainaut would return on 26 October.

'But then perhaps,' the Captain Commandant continued, 'You can give me some indication regarding the terrain, the canals and the bridges of the area. There has been talk about inundating to the east of the Yser River, towards Ostend: is that possible?'

This time the head-lockkeeper was a lot more compliant than with the francophone second lieutenant on Sunday, undoubtedly because Nuyten was an exception to the rule in the Belgian officer corps: he was Flemish, born and raised in the soon to become famous city of Ypres, just 30km to the south.

Prudently Armand Nuyten at age sixteen had enlisted as a volunteer in the Third de Ligne Regiment becoming a corporal after only three months. Within three years he was a sergeant and entered the Royal Military Academy. In 1895, promoted a second lieutenant, Nuyten returned to the infantry in the First de Ligne Regiment. By the time he turned thirty he was Staff Assistant at the Second Regiment Guides, while he was later posted to the Liège Fortified Place. In 1912, as Staff Captain Commandant, he was transferred to the Military Academy as a substitute Professor. Here, not two months prior to the outbreak of the war, he was appointed Professor at the Academy, responsible for the courses –Staff and Administration Services, Human Rights, Legislation and Military Law. With the mobilization of the army, in August 1914, he was attached to General Headquarters.

Now, two months later, the army had been cornered in between the French border and the coast with only two options left: make a stand or ultimately embark for England. In the ensuing days his knowledge of legislation and international law would enhance his role at General Headquarters. But for now his interests were more down to earth.

The area 'east of the Yser River' was in fact the same low lying region the British officers had referred to as 'east of the Bruges Canal' three days earlier. It is quite evident that Nuyten knew about the British investigations into the flooding of the Ostend surroundings. His information on this matter came through Colonel Tom Bridges, the British liaison officer at General Headquarters. Obviously Nuyten, knowing the land, had wondered why, according to his British counterparts, such a flooding seemed impossible. By asking the lockmaster he, Nuyten, wanted to verify this explanation for himself.

But again, the lockkeeper gave the same answer: it was possible, but it would take quite a long time and one had to be in control of the Bruges Canal and its branch towards Ostend.

For the time being though, Nuyten was more interested in information on the bridges crossing the Furnes and Loo canals. Unfortunately, in his post-war statement, Nuyten was not more specific about this last question. Or was he still bound by secrecy?

If the army would have to guard the line of the Yser, these bridges would have to be able to withstand the constant traffic of heavy equipment. At least these were the standard tactical difficulties a military engineer would be confronted with. But Nuyten, as we have seen earlier, was not an engineer and as a staff officer at General Headquarters

Colonel Tom Bridges was certainly a man of action. Here we see him on horseback on the towpath along the Furnes Canal, at the intersection with the road from Wulpen towards Oost-Dunkerke.
Thys Family Archive.

he was supposed to be dealing with problems from a strategic point of view. So one can wonder if he was not interested in these bridges because he worried what the enemy could use them for? The Furnes and Loo canals in a sense defined a bridgehead around the harbour at Nieuport. For instance, if the Belgians blew up these bridges at the right moment this would prevent the Germans from launching a surprise attack on the – by then embarking – Belgian forces.

Anyway, seemingly satisfied with this knowledge Nuyten took leave and continued to General Headquarters in Nieuport-Bains. We will return to this strange conversation in a while.

And here we have to organize a little scene. Upon arrival, presumably even over dinner, Nuyten met and talked with Colonel Bridges. Of course the question of the British defence of Ostend was mentioned. This was, after all, a crucial issue to the Fourth Corps ánd King Albert. One of the main Belgian worries for instance was the evacuation of the wounded from this city. On 11 October Queen Elisabeth wrote in her diary:

> . . . We have to absolutely evacuate the wounded from here. What a difficulty! . . .
> Here in Ostend we have over ten thousand wounded and no beds. We are short
> of everything: blankets, bread, milk.

As the situation stood on 13 October, Ostend was still General Rawlinson's embarkation port in case of an emergency. As three British corps – with the Indian Corps still at sea and on the way – were being deployed east of Hazebrouck there was a good chance of them forming a continuous front from Armentières, over Menin, Roulers and Thourout to Ostend. This last city would thereby be protected by floods along the Bruges Canal and supported by naval artillery. This way the Belgians would have the time to re-establish their forces in the Yser region, behind British lines. But things were now unfolding rapidly.

Later in the evening, Tom Bridges left Belgian Headquarters in Nieuport-Bains for Roulers – some 40km to the south-east – where Rawlinson now had his headquarters installed. Here Captain Commandant de Lannoy, his Belgian counterpart at Fourth Corps, had phoned Colonel Wielemans at 19:00 telling him that Sir John French had sent a message to Rawlinson ordering his Fourth Corps to march on Ypres the next day.

Over ninety years on, at the same spot where Colonel Bridges once stood. The house in the foreground is new but the dwellings further down the towpath, now a country road, still look very familiar. *Author's photo archive.*

Evidently Sir John French wanted to concentrate his BEF. He had never liked Kitchener's idea of a separate force operating independently in Belgium. Now that he had become the overall commander of British troops on the continent his main concern was not to take any risks, even if it had to be against the directives of General Ferdinand Foch.

Arriving by 23:00 at the Town hall in Roulers, Bridges met with Rawlinson and de Lannoy. While they were discussing next day's operations, the three of them agreed, in light of these new developments, that the best thing to do for the Belgians was to organize defensively behind the Yser River. Rawlinson's aim, as he had expressed to King Albert three days earlier, had to be abandoned. His forces would not be able to cover the whole northern front and protect the Belgian Army while it reassembled and re-equipped in a safe zone, behind the lines.

While they were still debating the opportunity of next day's move, Bridges apparently kept on pondering about those floods around Ostend and the rather negative reply he had received, first from the lockkeeper in Nieuport on 10 October and secondly, only a few hours earlier, from Captain Commandant Nuyten, but also emanating from the lockmaster in Nieuport. Suddenly Bridges turned to de Lannoy:

'What do they call *polders* in your language?' De Lannoy responded by saying that these were lands, below high water, from which dunes or dykes protected them.

'Well,' Bridges retorted readily, 'I asked around at Belgian Headquarters if there was no way of inundating the polders along the Yser with seawater and the answer was that it was impossible. However, Captain Commandant Nuyten will be instructed to study the question.'

But the tactical situation was by now rapidly changing. In fact the next day the German Third Reserve Corps occupied Ostend and the British Fourth Corps moved into Ypres. The need for a flood around Ostend had disappeared. But it shows the confusion the lockmaster had created among the British staff officers operating in Belgium.

In the afternoon, at General Headquarters in Nieuport-Bains, the atmosphere suddenly turned sour when a new French Mission arrived and *manu militari* took over the offices of the Belgian Operations Section. The French officers' attitude and intentions made it clear that the Generalissimo's directives were expected to be executed, not discussed. By the time Émile Galet arrived on the scene the arrogant

Frenchmen had made such an impression on the always-conciliatory Wielemans that he had already drawn up orders for the next day to move all army divisions into an offensive position close to Thourout. At the very moment when the whole army was being reorganized and needed to adapt to the battlefield such a major move would be pure suicide.

As we mentioned earlier – and on top of it all – they received, in the evening, the message from Captain Commandant de Lannoy in Roulers that Major General Rawlinson would be moving from Roulers to Ypres the next day. This came like a bolt from the blue to everyone. Field Marshal French was uncovering the whole northern front, on the one hand ignoring Foch's directives and on the other exposing all Belgian forces east of the line Ostend-Dixmude. The French officers for their part were simply outraged. 'That 's another dirty trick of them! They just do as they please and torpedo all schemes without warning!'

On the Belgian side it was utmost consternation. The king, who was not present at the time, had to be informed at once. Wielemans and Galet immediately left and headed for the Crombez Mansion, taking with them the operations map showing the advance of the enemy up to a line west of Eecloo.

By evacuating Roulers for Ypres, Rawlinson at once created a 20km gap between the Belgian troops and the BEF. Moreover, the army divisions just west of Thourout now stood in a position well forward vis à vis the Anglo-French forces. The king agreed that this was an untenable situation and that now, more than ever, all the units had to stay where they were and establish a strong line of defence.

NOTES
1. For a critical review of the role of lockmaster Dingens in October 1914 see Appendix I, The elusive keeper of the locks.
2. Not only was King Albert honourary commander of a German regiment and on several occasions had been present at German military manoeuvres, he had also studied Prussian tactics during his training at the Royal Military Academy in Brussels.
3. Leopold II (1835-1909), second king of the Belgians. Having no male descendants his nephew Albert, became third king on 23 December 1909.

Chapter V

Jacta Est Alea

With the Fourth Corps moving from Roulers to Ypres the decision on whether to evacuate the Belgian Field Army to England or whether to reorganize it on national soil had inadvertently been taken by Sir John French.

With no British troops north of Ypres, not only was any protection for the Belgians lost but also the support for an evacuation had vanished. It would only be a matter of time before the Germans would reach the coast where the Belgians had been left to fend for themselves. King Albert saw what was to happen: not only would the army have to be restructured in the Furnes-Ambacht region, at the same time it would also have to defend its new entrenched camp.

After two and a half months in the field, continuously confronted with an unstoppable superior war machine, the men were highly demoralized. Since the fall of Antwerp they had been marching for days with the enemy on their heels. Perhaps more importantly, the lack of a clear, made-in-Belgium strategic goal had been lost which weighed heavily on the morale of the rank and file.

Desertions during the retreat had been common. In 1986 Anthony Van Tilborg, who had made the march from Antwerp to the Yser as a recruit, told the author that quite a few of the young men in his column just had fallen out of the line and had disappeared in the countryside. As the army made its withdrawal through Flemish speaking territory there were proportionally more Flemish boys of military age being rounded up by the *gendarmerie* in the process. In turn these boys were more familiar with the land and could easily escape or make it across the border into neutral Holland.

To give them back a measure of self-confidence it was the king himself who issued a patriotic proclamation to his troops. In it he stressed the fact that from now on they would be fighting alongside the gallant French and British armies. They would only have to look forward and prepare with tenacity for the retaking of their beloved country.

Accordingly, Army Orders were issued with regard to the reorganization and reinforcement of the Field Army. Without any reserves that could be called upon, the only way to replenish the thinned ranks was to draw from the garrison units that had been able to escape from Antwerp. The infantry and artillery units would draw on the spot from their corresponding garrison units every able-bodied man. The divisional engineers would do the same.

At 23:00 another order was issued stating that the two army divisions west of Thourout should immediately organize a forward defence. The other four divisions

71

were to establish several bridgeheads east of the Yser and guard the corresponding passages over the river. Meanwhile the First Cavalry Division was spending the night west of Thielt while the Second billeted just south of Bruges.

The Head of the new French Mission that had arrived with so much ostentation was Colonel Brécard, and the same evening he paid a visit to King Albert. Unlike in the past, where the French had dealt with Belgian High Command, from now on they would have to communicate directly with the king. After the attempts of the Generalissimo to have King Albert relinquish his command of this army in favour of one of his generals, the king had notified the French Government through Baron de Broqueville:

> The Sovereign, in accordance with his government, intends to conserve the command of the Belgian Army, whatever its strength. But, he would be happy if the Generalissimo would act towards the Belgian Army as he acts towards the British Army and, accordingly, communicate directly with its Chief.

During the night High Command got a better picture of the advance of the enemy: a column of 2,000 men were marching west from Eecloo while 8,000 were on their way from Ghent to Bruges. A third column had reached Deynze.

At 10:00 on Wednesday 14 October, Colonel Brécard returned to General Headquarters with a message from General Foch. Having been briefed on the Belgian situation by Brécard, Foch agreed with a defensive posture by the Belgians along the line Roulers/Thourout/Ostend. But he asked them to stay in close contact with Ypres where the French were trying to establish a Franco-British centre of resistance. Foch did not exclude the possibility of the Belgians retreating but emphasized that they had to offer stubborn resistance. At any rate their ultimate line of defence had to be the Ypres Canal and its extension north.

Still these 'instructions' from Foch did not sit well with Galet. 'General Foch called us towards Ypres; we opted for Nieuport.'

Field Marshal French though had succumbed to the eternal French insistence on attacking: later on news arrived in Nieuport-Bains that the BEF was to embark on a general move east from Hazebrouck.

Sir John French, a cavalryman of the old guard, had seen at the Aisne River near Soissons what trench warfare looked like. So it was not difficult for the eloquent Foch to win French over to his offensive ideas. Besides, as we have already seen earlier, his friend Winston Churchill had convinced him that the Germans had to be kept clear of the Channel Coast at all cost. So Sir John French expected the Belgian Army to be able to march on his left between Roulers and Bruges. As a result, the staff officers at General Headquarters, with their French counterparts looking over their shoulders, had been drawing up plans for an offensive towards Thielt by three Belgian divisions.

When King Albert was informed about Sir John French's plan of attack the king was quite understandably pessimistic about the outcome of this new Anglo-French enterprise. But there was no alternative for him than to comply with the Field Marshal's wishes. After all there was always that slight chance of success and of course, in any advance through Belgium, Belgian troops had to be alongside.

As in the early afternoon word came from Rawlinson's Fourth Corps that it was to undertake a broad offensive towards the Lys river the next day, the Belgians reluctantly agreed to support the move by acting in the direction of Roulers.

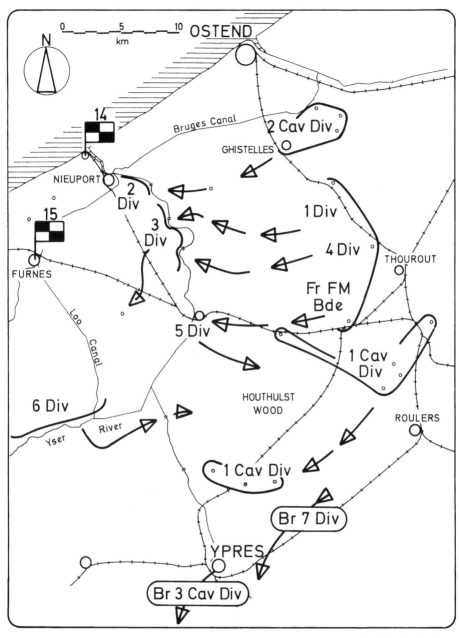

14 & 15 October

During the day the word had spread that the Germans had occupied Ostend. This of course also entailed the fall of the Port of Zeebrugge. From a naval point of view this was a more serious matter. The harbour with its new mole, large navigation lock and inland docks was perfectly adapted to act as an enemy submarine base. The British Admiralty had undertaken the work of evacuating the Belgian stores that had accumulated there in the previous weeks and subsequently wanted to destroy the mole and harbour works. But British Army Command for its part still hoped to return soon and objected to the destruction of the ports of Ostend and Zeebrugge.

This fateful decision of course would lead to the rapid use of both harbours by the German submarine force for daring attacks on allied shipping in the North Sea and the Channel. The British Fleet would eventually try to stop these deadly raids by the now famous and courageous but bloody blocking operation of both ports in the spring of 1918.

In the evening information arrived at Belgian High Command that four German columns, each 10,000 men strong, had arrived respectively in Bruges, south of Bruges, in Thielt and 15km north-east of Courtrai. This was a clear warning that the Germans were moving en masse towards the Channel coast.

Since their retreat from Ghent the French *fusiliers marins* had formed the open right flank of the advanced position taken by the First and Fourth army divisions west of Thourout. Upon receiving the news of the German advance, the marines' charismatic commander Vice Admiral Ronarc'h urgently asked to pull his brigade away from their exposed position south-west of Thourout and bring them more in line with the bulk of Belgian forces. The Belgian Deputy Chief of Staff finally had to concede that in the end a positioning of all troops along the Yser would be the more prudent move.

Army Orders for the next day were issued at 22:00. The First, Second and Fourth army divisions, together with the French Marine Fusiliers, were to move behind the Yser and prepare the defence of the accesses across the river from Nieuport to Dixmude. The Fifth and Sixth were to deploy east of the river, south of Dixmude. The First Cavalry Division would cover them to the east. The Second Cavalry was to patrol south of Ostend to monitor the German advance. The Third Army Division would be kept in reserve west of Dixmude. This was again a compromise: the defence of the river between Nieuport and Dixmude was taken in hand but to the south two divisions were kept in readiness to move east in case the British succeeded in their attempt to reach the Lys. The last sentence of the orders read: 'General Headquarters will be installed in Furnes tomorrow.'

Thus the dice was rolled. By abandoning the seaside settlement of Nieuport-Bains for the inland location at the county town of Furnes, the royal decision to stay on national soil was confirmed.

In the city of Nieuport the street scenes were by now beyond description. The main coastal road from Ostend to Dunkirk passed over the *route des Cinq-Ponts* – the Five Bridges Road [1] just outside town. A constant stream of horses, soldiers and refugees with children, bags and carts kept on flowing across the narrow bridges. Any manoeuvring of the drainage structures, let alone opening one of the bridges and thus blocking the main escape route was practically impossible. The situation for lockmaster Dingens and his aides was growing tenser by the hour. Orders and counter-orders created confusion, and certain scenes bordered upon the ridiculous. Flavoured with a strong anti-establishment undertone Gerard Dingens would recount the following incident after the war.

At a certain moment locksman Theo Provost, standing on one side of the Count Lock got the order from an officer to open the swing bridge across the lock. Simultaneously on the other side of the lock, a sergeant, who didn't know what was going on at the opposite side, howled at assistant Bogaerde: 'If you dare to open the bridge I will shoot you!'

Some time later the francophone officers simply requisitioned the handles for the bridges from the lockmaster. Apparently they had had enough of the lockmaster's perceived stubbornness. Unfortunately for all, the handles had disappeared. In all the confusion, but unaware to both parties, they had been taken away by other soldiers and moved to the Rattevalle Bridge, 3.5km upstream on the Bruges Canal. This was grist to each party's mill: Dingens being infuriated by this latest infringement upon his authority, the officers angered by what they saw as another trick of this alleged subversive Fleming.

For the officers in charge it was apparently time to take drastic action and the lockmaster was escorted to the general in charge, at that moment standing at the Nieuwbedelf Gates. The general, certainly quite uneasy about having to use the Flemish language and presumably aware of the vaudeville-like situation, choose to remain silent and act as the presiding judge. One of the escorting officers, a major, asked Dingens where the handles were.

'I don't know.' Dingens stressed again.

'You must know!' the major responded with a commanding voice.

'How am I supposed to know when your soldiers took them away without uttering a word?'

This was strong language from a humble civilian in front of all these 'stars and bars'! While the officers were still flabbergasted, Dingens turned his back on them and calmly returned to his office. If they thought they had a new recruit on the block they were wrong! But a young lieutenant, full of fire and eager to make a good impression upon his commanders

Much ado about a bridge handle. This picture was taken in 1991 at the swing bridge across the Furnes Canal in Furnes. The cylinder at the bottom fitted over a recessed key in the centre of gravity of the bridge. On top, through the pipe, a wooden pole would be pushed which, by turning, would lift the steel structure, thereafter it could turn on ball bearings. This swing bridge has since disappeared.
Author's photo archive.

rushed after the seasoned lockmaster, pulled him by the arm and with a loud, tremulous voice exclaimed: 'We will execute you!'

The lockkeeper, undisturbed by this absurd behaviour and senseless threat halted, took off his service hat and with a penetrating look at the young man calmly said:

'Execute . . . me? Why? . . . I'm sixty-five, am I still worth a bullet? You can put your five cents to better use but I do not fear the execution. Why would I have to die?'
The lieutenant was taken aback.

'Because of your churlish behaviour towards the general. You walked away without his permission.'

'Oh,' Dingens responded, 'is that a general? Well, tell him I'm only a trivial employee but I try to be just as honest as he is and if I'm rude by walking away without his permission he is even more impolite by not wanting to talk to me personally.'

And the lockkeeper walked on, leaving the bewildered lieutenant behind.

Nonetheless, Dingens started to phone around and after a while found out that the tools were in the shed of the bridge man at Rattevalle. The lieutenant wanted Dingens to have a man send for them. But along the Bruges Canal at least twenty-five requisitioned cars were sitting idle, their drivers having a nap, smoking a cigarette or just hanging

The swing bridge at Rattevalle [Rat Trap] on the Bruges Canal in 1993. After lifting the (iron) bridge structure by turning the key, the bridge guard manually rotated the bridge by pushing with his torso against the breastplate in the foreground while slowly walking over the ribbed arch in the background. Since at the Goose Foot in Nieuport two bridges rested on the median walls, a narrow, circular footbridge replaced this path over the spillway to the gate structure. The bridge above has meanwhile also disappeared.
Author's photo archive.

around. Perhaps this was a transport unit, unrelated to the guard detachment, simply awaiting new orders. But that didn't bother the lockmaster.

'Can't you send a motorcar?' Dingens tried.

'You send one of your men.' the lieutenant insisted.

'But a man cannot carry them, and there are six of those handles . . .'

'He can use a wheelbarrow.' the lieutenant insisted.

Dingens felt that the young lieutenant didn't understand what he was talking about. Presumably the officer imagined something like a wrench type of thing.

'Do you know how much one handle weighs? Four and a half kilograms . . . one man can not handle six of them at once.'

The lieutenant gave up and walked away.

Then a captain commandant came up to Dingens, curious to know more about the procedure.

'But lockkeeper, if you don't have handles, how do you then actually open a bridge?'

'Well, to swing the bridges we do not necessarily need a handle. Come, we'll show you how.' and Dingens winked at his assistants.

But the commandant didn't like the humiliation of an open air lesson in bridge technique and walked off. For now at least the nerve-racking incident was closed.

Later a chief sergeant of the Belgian *gendarmerie* showed up at the lockmaster's office with the message that the barges, still in the head bays of the three navigable waterways had to be locked through immediately and transferred by sea to Dunkirk, Calais or maybe even further. This new order made tensions rise again.

The tugboat *Amical* from Termonde, now an exhibit at the Maritime Museum in Antwerp, was built in 1914. If Henry Geeraert indeed was a tugboat captain in Nieuport as the story goes, then this vessel would be a good look alike for the ship he piloted in October 1914.
Author's photo archive.

Geeraert in his typical posture on what we believe is his barge, *Suzanne*. Unfortunately this picture could not be dated. *Historical prints collection Callenaere-Dehouck.*

Dingens replied that these barges were constructed to navigate on inland waters and that, if they had to be directed on Dunkirk, they could as well be locked and taken onto the Furnes Canal from where they could continue their journey to Dunkirk by way of the Furnes-Dunkirk Canal. Besides, women whose husbands had been drafted into the army manned some of the lighters. The chief sergeant, uneasy about this unexpected response, decided to consult with his superiors first.

When he returned to the lockmaster he could only confirm the initial order: the vessels had to be locked immediately. On this definite order Dingens phoned the marine superintendent Mr Aspertagh and asked for the services of a tugboat to transfer the barges into the tidal port. As soon as the tug pulled up in the tail bay Dingens had the seventeen barges locked through and his assistant Beke, was ordered to help the skipper in pulling the vessels to the harbour dock on the left bank, downstream of the Yser mouth.

What the lockmaster of course did not know at the time was that Army Command intended to load these barges up with stores and float them further west along the coast. A major evacuation line had been set up by sea and land from Ostend to the new Belgian supply bases in Calais and Dunkirk.

The enemy was moving up fast along the coast so in the end the barges were never requisitioned. In order to prevent the Germans from eventually using these craft to their advantage, one of the vessels was later sunk as a block ship in front of the dock entrance.

Once they were in the relative safety of the dock the skipper of the tugboat, Henry Geeraert, curious about all the military commotion in and around town, made his way back to the lock system to watch events from close up. The man could never have imagined then that this decision would change his life forever and in the end make him a national hero for generations to come. [2]

Henry Geeraert was born and raised in Nieuport. In July of 1863 he was born at 40 Long Street while his father was away 'on the great fishery to Iceland'. Mother Anna Veranneman was a housekeeper and lace-maker. Later father would turn to the less hazardous inland shipping where Henry would succeed him. At twenty-four Henry married Melanie Jonckheere and together they had eight children. Due to their travelling existence all children were born in various locations along France's waterways.

The only known picture of Henry Geeraert with his parents.
Nieuport 1914-1918, R. Thys, 1922.

Being married and raising children was certainly not Henry's favoured pursuit for at least from 1914 on his family was never mentioned again in any documents. After the war lockmaster Dingens would – for obvious reasons perhaps – not have a good word for Geeraert when he wrote: 'He is a great enemy of full glasses . . .' But then again this was probably not far from the truth.

With the aggravation caused by all this interference with his authority over the lock complex it went almost unnoticed to the lockmaster that the guard detachment of his beloved domain had been changed. A platoon of the Second Pontoneer Battalion, Second Army Division, led by Sergeant Jules Henry had taken over the surveillance of the locks and bridges. One of their orders was to prepare destruction of the southernmost bridge, the one across the Furnes Lock.

By the time their commanding officer arrived, on the evening of the next day, Sergeant Henry and his men had installed charges next to the heavy iron turntable underneath the swing bridge. This operation was later confirmed by the Army Order of 15 October at noon that instructed all divisions to prepare for the destruction of all bridges on the Yser and the Ypres Canal. This order for the first time actually confirmed Belgian Army intentions to defend its position behind this winding aquatic obstacle.

There is a slight geographical discrepancy though. Since Sergeant Henry did prepare the destruction of the bridge over the Furnes Lock and not the one on the Yser River/Ypres Lock [see detailed map at the beginning of Chapter VII] he left a narrow physical gap in the 43km long defence between Ypres and the sea. Theoretically the sergeant left the enemy an invasion route onto the left bank over an intact bridge on the Ypres Lock! But then again, the man only followed orders that we will see later, emanated in fact from French High Command. Was it perhaps to minimize destructions in view of a French offensive towards Ostend?

Shortly after midnight on 15 October, Baron de Broqueville in Dunkirk phoned the king's orderly officer in Nieuport-Bains telling him that in the morning Mr Augagneur, the French Minister of the Navy, would visit Furnes accompanied by Emile Vandervelde, Belgian Minister of State.

As daylight broke over another wet and cold autumn day King Albert departed from Nieuport-Bains at 09:00, this time for the County Town of Furnes. The queen also left the Crombez Mansion but an hour later. This time the small household staff had been able to arrange for the royal couple to stay at the Villa Maskens, which was some 10km

Front of the Maskens Villa in La Panne. Amenities were spartan: no running water, no central heating. In later years this historic building was levelled to make way for the lucrative beach tourism industry and its associated building boom.
Historical prints collection Callenaere-Dehouck.

further west. In her diary the queen wrote on 15 October: 'We are always the cuckoos that go in someone else's nest.'

Soon after her departure the queen's motorcar ran into a traffic jam near the locks in Nieuport. Refugees with handcarts and wheelbarrows, and hundreds of despondent soldiers once belonging to the Garrison Army crowded the roads. This miserable procession did not end on the road to La Panne. Every poor soul seemed heading for France.

The Maskens Retreat was a modest, brick residence at the seafront in the dunes near the resort village of La Panne, only a kilometre or so from the French border. For the royal couple it would be a relatively safe haven on home soil from the battle that was about to erupt.

The building was rather isolated and would be out of range of the German artillery if it would ever manage to get close to the Yser. In an emergency an aeroplane could even land on the wide open space of the beach to pick up the queen to take her to England. Fear for a large German landing here, behind the lines was not a concern for the moment: the wide belt of dunes, together with the few and far between, small, sandy accesses made for an unattractive landing beach.

At General Headquarters the staff officers had some encouraging news: the

A view of the royal bathroom in the Maskens Villa. Note the two bird cages on the windowsill and on the floor the ewer and the night bucket.
Historical prints collection Callenaere-Dehouck.

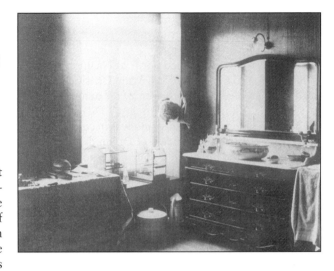

German columns did not seem to pursue any offensive actions against the Belgian units east of the river. General Foch in Doullens, the Somme Department, as always being self-confident, was even more outspoken. To the liaison officer arriving from Colonel Brécard in Furnes he said: 'At present the war is not complicated. The German infantry does not appear. It stays in its trenches because it is exhausted.'

Amidst all the messages arriving at Belgian General Headquarters one, at 10:00 was a proposal by General Rawlinson to inundate the polders along the right bank of the Yser. This was still a remnant of the nightly discussion between Belgian Captain Commandant de Lannoy and Colonel Bridges two days earlier in Roulers.

In fact the idea had not left de Lannoy and after some study he had come to the conclusion that the project, contrary to what the lockmaster in Nieuport had said, was indeed feasible. It seems he had made a similar proposal, just a month earlier to inundate the banks of the Dyle river, south-east of Malines. At that moment of course it still did concern the defence of Antwerp. But the Military Governor had rejected the idea on the grounds that the engineers had not studied the project in peacetime.

Now Rawlinson had sent this dispatch to Furnes. Reaction at General Headquarters was that 'the question would be taken into consideration' or . . . lets wait and see.

What still worried the French Generalissimo was the now widening gap between the British and Belgian Armies. The BEF was moving from Hazebrouck towards Bailleul and was expected to make contact with Rawlinson's Fourth Corps at Ypres soon. The Belgians on the other hand were stretching their exhausted forces to the limit by occupying a 43km front, from the sea to Ypres, with six divisions comprising barely 50,000 rifles.

His concerns were reflected in two messages he cabled to Foch, one in the evening of 14 October, the other the next morning. In both he urged Foch to prop up the Belgian right in order not to compromise the British left flank in Ypres. As a result Foch ordered the two territorial divisions that had covered the British detraining near Hazebrouck, the 87th and 89th, to the area north of Ypres, along the Ypres Canal. Joffre had also stressed not to weaken the Dunkirk garrison but have the place prepared as a bastion.

The preparations for the defence of the Yser were now well advanced. The Second Army Division, under General Dossin, was responsible for the sector from the Yser mouth to kilometre-stone (km) 4 along the river.[3] (see map p.97) Three advance posts were set up: one on the left at the village of Lombartzyde, one in the centre at Kets Bridge and one on the right across the Union Bridge in the village of Mannekensvere. A bridgehead was established north of Nieuport to cover the lock system.

From km 4 to km 10 the First Army Division guarded the riverbank. Here a bridge-head at the hamlet of Schoorbakke stayed in touch with a forward position at the village of Schoore. At km 10 the Fourth Army Division took over to km 16. With a bridge-head at Tervaete bridge the division was in contact with its advance posts at the villages of Keyem and Beerst. The town of Dixmude, just across from the Yser, was the main bridgehead on the right and under the responsibility of the French *fusiliers marins* of Rear Admiral Ronarc'h. In the area between Furnes and Nieuport two brigades of the Third Army Division plus the Second Cavalry Division were kept in reserve.

The king though, was not confident about the future. His troops had not been able to get enough rest, the ranks had been dangerously thinned and the integration and training of the garrison troops in the Field Army had barely begun. He warned Colonel Brécard that his men were demoralized and that, in the event that the enemy attacked in earnest, he did not expect a prolonged resistance. In two messages to Joffre that day Brécard informed him of the king's apprehension. But to reassure the Generalissimo he indicated in his second dispatch that General Foch would visit Furnes the next day.

In the afternoon the commanders of the Fifth and Sixth Army Divisions, still south-east of Dixmude near Houthulst Wood, informed High Command that their men were exhausted and would not be capable of any offensive action. Colonel Wielemans nevertheless upheld his orders. In the evening though, with the appearance of an enemy brigade to the north-east of their exposed position, the Deputy Chief realized the vulnerability of both army divisions and ordered them to fall back behind the Ypres Canal. Here they were to organize its defence from Boesinghe, where the French Territorials manned the trenches, to the Old Fort Knocke on the confluence of the canal with the Yser.

Since the French Minister of the Navy, Victor Augagneur, was in Furnes King Albert took the opportunity to see him. The king again stressed the exhaustion of his divisions and asked to convey to the French Government the message that his troops alone would not withstand the German pressure for long. Aware that the French did not have any sizable naval presence in the English Channel, the king did not ask the Minister for support from French naval vessels. Instead, he had sent Captain Commandant Galet to talk to Colonel Bridges. Galet was to inquire about naval artillery support from the British Fleet on the Belgian left along the coastline.

Now that the Germans had entered Ostend their advance against the Belgian line could be expected at any time soon. Only the British Fleet could strengthen the front with some heavy artillery in this corner. Bridges had transmitted the request from King Albert to Lord Kitchener who, in turn, passed it on to Winston Churchill at the Admiralty. This string of calls set in motion a long series of difficult and dangerous naval operations in support of the Belgian left flank. Churchill immediately ordered bombardment of the German held Belgian coastline to begin the next day.

The Admiralty was by now well prepared for a prompt and full response. Having anticipated the threat that enemy occupied Zeebrugge and Ostend could bring to the vital cross-Channel traffic a new command had been set up at the Admiralty on 12 October. Officially it was the 6th Destroyer Flotilla, but was generally better known as

The light cruiser HMS *Attentive* spent most of her war years on shore bombardment with
Dover Patrol. As such Captain Thys was quite familiar with the vessel's silhouette on the
horizon. So when he visited Dunkerque one day he took a picture of this unmarked war ship,
perhaps believing it was *Attentive*. But this was in fact a French Bouclier class destroyer, which
looks amazingly similar to the British Attentive class cruisers. On the quay to the right lay
several buoys, recovered from the Channel waters at the start of the war.
Thys family archive.

'the Dover Patrol' with Churchill's Naval Secretary, Rear Admiral Horace Hood in
command. His task force was comprised of no less than twenty-four Tribal-class
destroyers, the light cruisers *Attentive, Adventure, Foresight* and *Sapphire*, the 3rd and
4th Submarine Flotillas (thirteen B- and C-class submarines) and a number of auxiliary
patrol vessels and trawlers.

Since no coastal operations had been anticipated when the command was set up, few
vessels on the Navy List were adapted for the purpose and none were attached to Hood's
command. Fortunately the three shallow-water monitors that had escorted the Belgian
mail boats out of Ostend on the 13th were still at Dover so Hood immediately asked
for them.

These river patrol boats, *Javary, Madeira* and *Solimoes*, had had a short but already
peculiar history behind them. Originally the Brazilian Navy had ordered these three
vessels at the Vickers shipyard in Barrow-in-Furness. But when they were nearing
completion in August 1914 they were taken over by the British Navy. With the onset
of the war the Admiralty did not want to run the risk of seeing them one day reappear
as opponents. Although there seemed no immediate role for them in the fleet it was
obviously better to keep them in British hands. The Admiralty regarded them as being
monitors – floating artillery – but their light armament in fact did not reflect this classi-
fication: forward they had a twin 152-mm gun turret, aft a 120-mm howitzer on each

side and amidships two 3-pounder guns on the superstructure. One would rather call them oversized patrol boats, ideal for extended runs in the shallow Amazon basin.

The next day, the Generalissimo, unaware of the Belgian plea for British naval support, sent the following telegram to Lord Kitchener:

> Now that operations have extended towards the North Sea coast between Ostend and the advanced defence of Dunkirk it would be appropriate for the two allied navies to participate in this operation by protecting our left flank and, through the use of long range guns, act on the German right. The commander naval forces should act in cooperation with General Foch through intermediary of the Military Governor of Dunkirk.

It will be noticed that Joffre again 'forgot' to mention the Belgian Army and its Commander-in-Chief in the joint action on the left flank. But then again, perhaps he was more concerned about the defence of the Dunkirk Fortified Place rather than coming to the aid of the hard pressed Belgians in the open and muddy polders between Nieuport and Dixmude.

While the modest Belgian request had stated '. . . that a British warship was anxiously desired to flank the Belgian line . . .' Joffre's eloquent dispatch apparently carried more weight. Within two hours Admiral Hood had his orders.

In the evening, Second Lieutenant Lucien François arrived at the lock system in Nieuport to take command of the engineers' unit guarding the structures. Originally Second Lieutenant Coulon had been assigned but for unknown reasons it was François who took command of the detachment.

Lucien Alfred François François, barely twenty-one, was a native of Morlanwelz, a small community in the heart of Walloon coal mining country. At the start of the war he rejoined his engineer unit attached to the Antwerp Fortified Position and in October made the retreat from Antwerp to Nieuport. Here on 13 October, with the reorganization of the Field Army, he was posted to the Second Engineer Battalion, Second Army Division, under the command of Captain Commandant Borlon. His colleagues would characterize him as a *gentil gosse* — a nice kid.

At La Panne King Albert, returning from General Headquarters in Furnes, could only paint a gloomy picture of the situation for his wife. The queen later that evening wrote in her diary that they dined, as usual, with General Élie Hanoteau and Captain Commandant Émile Galet. If his two confidants could not bolster the royal morale that meant they too were pessimistic. Did they now regret the decision to forego an evacuation to Britain? Nevertheless Galet wrote in his field journal: 'While the situation is rather bad, for the first time I see it in a favourable light.'

Only the fact that all western troops were in line could appease their cautious military minds.

NOTES

1. The then official designation 'Five-Bridges Road' is certainly misleading. In 1914 it was the main road from Nieuport to Ostend. It left Nieuport to the east, made a semicircle across the six hydraulic structures and then turned straight north heading for Lombartzyde. In the mid-1800s though, the main road to Ostend left the town straight north, crossing the Yser Mouth via a wooden bridge (see map). The

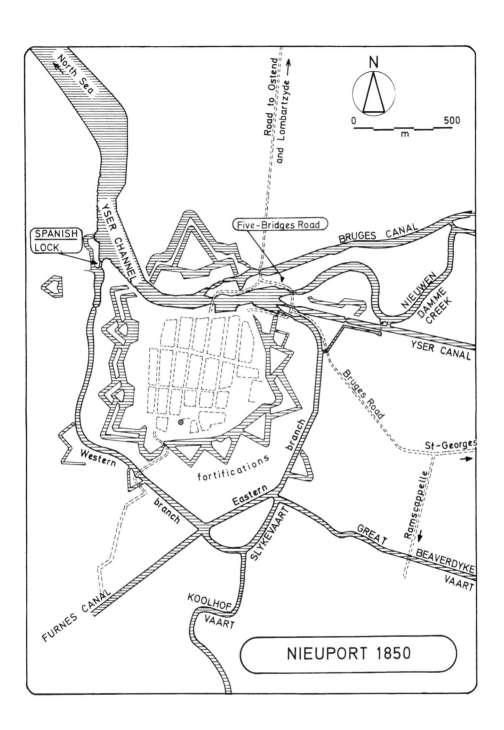

NIEUPORT 1850

Nieuwbedelf and North Vaart Gates, as well as the Count Lock did not exist then. Instead the fortifications surrounding the town had an East Gate leading to the Bruges Road. It was this road that passed five bridges: it crossed the fortress moat, the forerunners of the Furnes and Ypres Locks, the Spring Sluice and the Bruges Canal. As we will see later in detail by 1914 the only original – and peculiar – structure left on this road was the Spring Sluice. After the war the same road was moved 40m eastward to clear the lock chambers.

2. There are several, some times rather folksy stories about the way in which Henry Geeraert at first got involved with the military. The account that we put forward is the one that appears most often in the various archival records and the one that fits best in the detailed chain of events as we have been able to reconstruct them in the past fifteen years of our research. It is therefore, in our view, the most reasonable and plausible.

3. Distance measuring along the canalized Yser River is done by means of kilometre-stones, starting with km 0 [zero] at the Ypres Lock in Nieuport. The lock in turn is already 4km from the mouth of the river, measured along the Yser Channel.

Chapter VI

The Generals Come to Town

Being in line with the French and British armies did not automatically mean that the coming battles would be easier. It could be expected that German High Command would rather take on the Belgian twelve-month conscript than the French three-year soldier or the British six-year professional.

As one can expect the phrase 'fighting to the utmost' was unknown to the Belgian conscript. Military discipline was at an all time low within the rank and file, not because of contempt for its superiors but simply because of sheer ignorance. Nevertheless it was now a matter of pride, honour and national survival that the Belgian soldier should act as bravely as his French and British brothers-in-arms.

An energetic act was necessary to bolster morale and convince all ranks that a dynamic resistance and an ultimate sacrifice were required. From now on the Belgians would be equal to the French and the British: they had been entrusted, perhaps unwillingly but certainly too early, with the responsibility for the integrity of their own sector in the common front line.

To that end King Albert decided to personally make a tour of the divisional headquarters in the morning of 16 October and relay his message on the spot to his generals and their staff. The outline of his speech was straightforward:

> Our position in general is strong but more entrenching is required.
> We are tired, but so is the enemy.
> Wherever possible: let the troops rest now, before the battle.
> We must hold our positions, therefore:
> – The general whose troops retreat will be dismissed on the spot.
> – The officer whose troops leave their trenches will be dismissed.
> – Under no pretext, even if the line is broken, will there be a retreat.
> – The staff officers will be spread out along the respective front line sectors
>   and incorporated into the fighting units. They will stay in combat and
>   relieve the courageous leaders instead of complaining all the time.

General Joffre too was concerned about the fighting power of the weakened Belgian Army. As the Belgians stood with their backs against the French border and, as a result, on the perimeter of the Dunkirk Fortified Place, it fell upon them to protect this major common storage and debarkation base.

So that same morning the Generalissimo dispatched a couple of cables to Foch in order to underline his apprehension. He suggested that Foch should transport both territorial divisions from Ypres to the coast and he offered to send an active division to the north, available in Dunkirk on 21 October.

In reality though, in the ensuing days the 87th and 89th Territorials strengthened their positions along the Ypres Canal so the weakened Belgian 5th and 6th army divisions could be moved north behind the Yser. But we will track in detail the whereabouts of the active French division, the 42nd Infantry, that Joffre offered.

Foch himself also had his doubts about the combative spirit of the Belgian soldier. As *adjoint* to the Generalissimo, responsible for the northern theatre of operations, Foch could concentrate more on the issue. A few days earlier he had already mentioned to Joffre that he contemplated visiting Belgian High Command in Furnes. So on Friday 16 October he left his headquarters at Doullens, 65km south of St Omer, and paid his first brisk visit to the northern front, in order to assess the unstable situation. He took with him two bright young staff officers – Commandant Desticker, a native of the north himself and Lieutenant André Tardieu, a reserve officer and well known journalist with a thousand 'connections' both in civilian and military life. After the war the latter would become a prominent French politician.

In the morning Foch and his associates called on Sir John French in St Omer. For the time being the BEF was the only fist available to him with which he might stop the German progress. French and Foch had met before the war but did not know each other well. Sir John French feared that Ferdinand Foch might be another Joseph Joffre, seemingly unmanageable, rather aloof and at first sight slow of mind. But the clever Foch knew how to confront the white-haired Field Marshal.

A week or so earlier he had met Sir John for the first time since the war had started. In the best French style he had proved to be elegant, chatty and gentlemanly. Foch knew very well how to flatter the old Irish horseman. He had won him right over by telling him that he did not like General Henry Rawlinson operating in Belgium under direct orders from the British War Office. He had told him he would take steps to get all British troops on the continent under one command, understandably that of Sir John himself, of course!

The French used to nickname Rawlinson *le Nickelé* 'the Nickelled' for their inability to manipulate him. Foch's successful intervention with Joffre a few days earlier had eliminated Rawlinson from the upper chain of command and had left the more flexible Sir John French as the sole British commander he would have to deal with.

Both men discussed their planned offensive west of Lille. French too was convinced that the enemy had exhausted most of its reserves in the Battle of the Marne and that the most dangerous phase of the war was now over. During the conversation Foch, who had been briefed by Joffre, brought up the necessity of the cooperation of the Grand Fleet on the northern flank. After taking leave Foch drove the 40km north to Dunkirk, the first French fortified position along the Channel coast and now threatened by the German advance.

On several occasions in the past centuries this strategically located port had been disputed territory between the European powers. Noteworthy for instance is the date of 14 June 1658 during the Battle of the Dunes. In the morning the town was Spanish, at noon she was French, and in the evening she was in English hands. The English did not seem to be overly happy with their conquest since four years later they sold the

88

After the war, *Maréchal de France*, Ferdinand Foch.
Ons Land, magazine, 1919.

whole works again to France. The French name of Dunkerque in fact is derived from the Flemish Duinkerke, which means 'church in the dunes'!

Along the road, shrouded in fog, the three French officers had to halt every so often at road blocks set up by the French cavalry, say the password and present their identity papers, but finally they made it into the port city. Foch's main aim here was to inspect the state of the defences. This included overseeing the progress that had been made to prepare the flooding of the countryside around the city.

The canals and ditches in the polders around Dunkirk had already been filled to the brink by holding up the surface runoff. Once the order was given, it would only be a matter of a few hours to open the sea sluices and let the next tide roll in. Soon after, the waterways would overflow onto the land. (see map p.181)

As Baron de Broqueville was in Dunkirk, supervising the installation of the Belgian supply base, Foch took the opportunity to meet with him and throw out feelers about the mood at Belgian General Headquarters. The Belgian Minister of War vigorously defended the Belgian case. As a skilled politician he knew that the very existence of the kingdom was now at stake. Foch, every inch a soldier, grasped the psychological importance of the 'National Soil' issue for the Belgian fighting spirit. For him it was a matter of finally blocking the German steamroller with every infantryman available. So, although for different reasons, both men now saw an opportunity to counter the invader and they agreed to motor together to Furnes and meet King Albert and his staff.

The cobbled road from Dunkirk to Furnes, some 20km, would in normal circumstances not have taken long. But this time the small convoy of cars had to make its way against an endless stream of refugees pushing small handcarts that held their meagre belongings. The route, as it bordered the canal from Dunkirk to Furnes, had long straight sections, but the chauffeurs had to drive carefully, continuously manoeuvring to avoid the shuffling stream of miserable human beings.

Once in the small picturesque town of Furnes matters did not ease. The place was crowded with bands of Belgian soldiers, dressed more or less in their dark blue uniforms, a lot apparently without footwear as their feet were wrapped in rags.

Upon arrival Foch first went to see his liaison officer, Colonel Brécard to be briefed.

City Hall in Furnes today. The gas lantern in front of it has been replaced and relocated by a more modern fixture. Otherwise the outside – as well as the inside – of the building is identical to its appearance in 1914. The beautifully restored, ornate gilded façade looks perhaps even more vibrant than ever. *Author's Photo Archive.*

Then, accompanied by Brécard, the French General marched across the Grand Place making his way to the small renaissance town hall in the north-west corner. With a resolute pace the portly *bigourdan* [1] followed Baron de Broqueville, whirled passed the cast iron gas lantern in front of the building and, with a determined look, took the four steps underneath one of the finely decorated arches supporting the balcony.

Inside, in a room decorated with seventeenth century Flemish leather and a heavy oak ceiling, General Hanoteau, Colonel Wielemans and Captain Commandant Maglinse, welcomed the Generalissimo's deputy.

After the customary welcoming and greetings, the small group retreated behind closed doors. Here Foch began explaining the reason for his visit. This seemingly everlasting retreat had to be stopped now regardless of the cost. Instead the Belgians should switch to more aggressive action. To begin with they needed to dig themselves in.

Wielemans, although an admirer of this French rhetoric, was, by now, exhausted and pessimistic about the outcome of the coming hostilities. One of his arguments against Foch's point of view was the fact that groundwater in the region was practically at soil level, making it almost impossible for the men to dig trenches. General Hanoteau, for once in a more compromising mood and following King Albert's point of view – or was it orders – agreed with the notion to hold the Yser River but ruled out any forward adventures by his weakened fellow countrymen.

Foch kept trying to make his point – ranting and underlining his phrases with sudden, quick gestures. The Belgian staff officers endured the whole tirade. Through the heavy oak doors the other members of the staff and the remainder of the French delegation could hear Foch shouting: *'Attaque, attaque'*. After a while he calmed down, perhaps realizing that this kind of behaviour had no effect on the level-headed Belgians. He could not dictate terms as he had done with his confrères the generals Castelnau and Maud'huy on 5 October. Alone with Maud'huy in his office his staff officers had heard Foch screaming:

> I don't want to listen! You understand? I don't want to listen! I'm deaf! I know only three ways of fighting: attack, resist and run. I forbid you to do the last one. Choose between the first two!

Finally Foch ended his diatribe on a more sensible and practical note: he stressed that the town of Dixmude was firmly held by his *fusiliers marins* and that this presented a stronghold for the Belgians from which they had to build a defensive line further out along the river.

At the time Ferdinand Foch was mainly known abroad as a military writer, even somewhat disputed by his compatriots. The Belgians, having been subjected to overwhelming pressure by the German Imperial Army for more than two months, did not appreciate a lesson in basic tactics by a mere stranger. The French author Jean Ratinaud perhaps expressed the view of the Belgians best:

> General [sic] Galet, and his Master [King Albert], were of the opinion that they were facing a scatter-brain – *'un hurluberlu'*.

The north-west corner of the Furnes Market Square at the beginning of the war. In the corner on the left City Hall with its characteristic balcony. In front the Court House and behind it the Saint Walburga Church. Notice the gaping hole from a German shell in the church steeple. Although 9km behind the front line, the town was severely damaged from enemy fire during the war. After the war the square was restored to its original beauty and is now a major, year-round tourist attraction. *Thys Family Archive.*

After lunch, taken at the French Mission, Foch was informed that the king of the Belgians would receive him. The French officers returned to the town hall and made their way through the council chamber to the *salle des Echevins* [Alderman's room]. The king, in his dark blue uniform of lieutenant general, tall and slender, waited at the doorstep. As a welcoming gesture, and after shaking hands, the king amiably complimented the general on his military ideas, well known from his writings. With a short gesture of his right hand the general responded bluntly: 'The art of warfare? That doesn't exist!'

This rather tactless response chilled his audience. In fact it did not even reflect the doctrine he himself had promoted all these years! If this reaction startled everyone, it did not show on King Albert's face. One could well imagine seeing the king's eyes for a split second flashing over Foch's head to his senior advisors but then the monarch courteously invited the general in.

While the larger council chamber, lined with aged Malines leather and its rococo style fireplace, might have suited the flamboyant general, the Aldermen's Court corresponded undoubtedly better with the king's character. The room was smaller; the walls lined with seventeenth century Utrecht velvet, similar to the upholstery of the furniture. The fire had been stoked and was radiating a most welcome warmth on this cold and damp October day.

For General Foch it was the first time he had met with the Belgian monarch. The king, thirty-nine years old, could well have been his son. Nevertheless Foch felt rather embarrassed and did not know how to approach this affable young man; head of a neighbouring state and already famous worldwide for his honour and duty? He knew he had to control himself but at the same time he wanted to get his important message through.

At first the Frenchman was impressed. He defined the main lines of the *Entente* manoeuvre as it stood for the moment. Then again, he could only talk about offensive actions. The French-British endeavour would be directed towards Lille with the main northern drive by Ypres and Roulers towards Courtrai. The General wanted the Belgian Army to cooperate in this attack. He explained that he, himself, had pushed the enemy back at the Marne and, as the Belgians only faced newly formed German reserve units, there was no doubt in his mind that they would be able to throw these fresh, non-regular troops back.

But King Albert knew the situation in Flanders better than anyone. He explained to the General that, by being the Head of the Belgian Kingdom and bound by its constitution, he could only engage his meagre military resources after mature consideration, above all at this moment when the very existence of the nation was at stake. The king continued by explaining all the precautions that had been taken to defend the position along the Yser River. Nevertheless the nature of the terrain did not allow for a textbook organization. Besides, along the 40km long front line the troops were stretched out thinly with barely two brigades on stand-by. Physically and mentally the troops were not capable of any offensive action. The most that could be expected of them was a stubborn resistance, and even then only for a couple more days. The monarch told the French general also that, in his opinion, a major attack by the Germans on the Belgian sector could be expected soon. The only way to withstand such an assault would be the addition of major reinforcements within days. The king stressed that this would not only be beneficial to the Belgian cause but that it would serve that of the French and British also.

On this matter Foch could offer King Albert some solace: if the Belgians could resist another forty-eight hours on the Yser he promised help. At 8:00 a.m. Joffre had cabled Foch that he proposed sending an active division to the north and by lunchtime: 'The 42nd Division will detrain in Dunkirk starting the 19th . . .'

All in all Foch was quite disappointed about this first visit to Belgian High Command. His flamboyant theories on warfare collided with the common sense of a rather timid young man, not even a soldier by profession. His temper rose anew, his impressive theatrical personality once again took over and he attempted to inject a feeling of patriotism by stating:

> Nations that want to live need to defend themselves. The world would not understand that the Belgian Army would not be at our side at the very moment that we are to embark upon the conquest of Belgium. I myself, a Soldier of the Republic, I can assure Your Majesty that our cause is a just and exalted one and that Providence will grant us victory. [2]

After this emotional outburst Foch took his leave. It seems that the king shortly afterwards made the tactful remark to Colonel Brécard: 'I am happy to hear a French general talk like this.'

The general's quick-tempered, theatrical behaviour did not evoke the same emotions with the Belgian king as it did with Foch's own fellow officers. The monarch nevertheless was impressed with his sincere determination. It provided a much-needed boost to the royal morale.

In France itself the General Staff did not share King Albert's premonition of an imminent major German push along the Belgian coast. On the opposite side of the Flanders' front line though, the same day Duke Albrecht von Württemberg, Commander of the newly formed Fourth German Army, assigned the specific objectives to his different army corps.

It was a German custom that prominent members of the German Royal Houses led some of the different armies, in name at least. Although the orders came straight from German, or rather Prussian, High Command sometimes the leading royal would overrule these orders at his own army headquarters and have 'his' army act independently, much to the displeasure of the *Heeresleitung* and sometimes even to the detriment of the overall conduct of the war.

The goals of Duke Albrecht's Fourth German Army were to be reached within three days, by 19 October. The 3rd German Reserve Army Corps, still in the Bruges area, was to head towards Dunkirk while the 22nd Reserve Army Corps was to follow behind and reach the Yser between Nieuport and Dixmude. The 23rd, east of Thielt, was to arrive halfway between Dixmude and Roulers while the 26th and 27th were to converge 10km east of Ypres. German High Command saw this as the ultimate move to outflank the British army. Evidently speed was of the essence.

If Foch had been able to read the German Orders he would undoubtedly have sided with King Albert. The weary Belgians had still some very difficult days ahead.

It is interesting in this regard to note that Lieutenant André Tardieu depicted a remarkable scene related to these eternal 'outflanking manoeuvres' by both sides in the conflict. One late afternoon in October, Foch, dragging Tardieu by the arm towards the muddy fields, said:

Let's have a walk! In all this confusion we had better refresh our minds by a walk in the open air. Did you notice that since the beginning of the war, we, just like the Germans, are always late? Without these delays the war would have been over by now. Because of them, the war continues. They sent me here to manoeuvre, but late. I do what I can, but it is not brilliant. This endless alignment of opposing forces bores me.

In the evening, back in Doullens, Foch had time to sit down and write his daily report to the Generalissimo. First he described his meeting with Sir John French in St Omer and then his inspection of the defence of Dunkirk. On his visit to Furnes he could confirm the measures taken by the king in order to prepare a stubborn defence of the Yser line. He added: 'The King and the President of the Cabinet [Baron de Broqueville] . . . have understood that these days it is Belgium's existence that is at stake.'

Apparently Foch saw himself as having finally succeeded in convincing the Belgians that in order for their country to have any future they had to stick to their guns on their own soil.

Although he knew from Joffre that the 42nd Infantry Division would arrive in Dunkirk from 19 October onwards and could be used to reinforce the Belgian Army, his explanation on the matter was ambiguous: 'Albeit this is not indispensable, I would have reinforced the [Belgian] left with a quality unit, if I had it available. I only had a territorial division. It seemed to me, in everyone's interest, that it was better to put nothing.' Or was it perhaps a matter of '. . . let them suffer a bit longer'?

Then he continued with an overview of the French forces in the region: Ypres on the right, Dixmude in the centre and Dunkirk on the left. That Dunkirk, and not the Belgians, was indeed his main concern we learn from his postscript: 'Yet, if you do possess troops of real value to put on the Belgian left, they will do well from all points of view.'

From a second report to Joffre, the same evening, we can conclude that Foch leaned heavily on the patriotic sense of the Belgians to resist along the Yser River. As an alternative he could always count on the Dunkirk defence and have the Belgians eventually fall back on an inland position between Ypres and Dunkirk.

The 'Belgian left' was, of course, the coastal area with the main road from Ostend to Dunkirk. This narrow strip of sandy high ground along the shore was now indeed the most vulnerable sector of the Dunkirk defence and the obvious route for a large scale German assault on the French port city. Directing the Belgians away from here, towards Ypres, would allow Foch to have the defence of this dry land taken over by French troops.

At General Headquarters in Furnes, the staff officers could heave a sigh of relief. The German columns that had reached the line Ostend/Roulers on the 15th, had seemingly not moved on the 16th. Only a light unit had advanced on Dixmude but had been beaten back by the *fusiliers marins* and two Belgian units. A bizarre incident nonetheless happened just outside Dixmude. It ties in with the mysterious 'royal telephone call' of 13 October after which the installations of the Deynze railway station had been blown up by Belgian engineers.

The French Marine Fusiliers, patrolling the railway near Dixmude suddenly witnessed a locomotive pulling three cars coming from enemy lines. At great speed the

Rolling stock was not only used as a weapon but was also a target. Here we see a few destroyed cars on a Belgian track apparently far behind the front line. The load consisted apparently of steel pipes. Victim of an aerial bombardment? *Thys Family Archive.*

train rammed a lone locomotive abandoned in the station. As a result two of the carriages jumped the tracks and rolled over. After careful examination of the steaming wreckage the machine proved to be unmanned, but a note was found, apparently written by a soldier taken prisoner by the enemy. It read that 50,000 to 60,000 Germans were marching west.

The 16 October was also Second Lieutenant Lucien François' first day as commander of the engineer's detachment at the lock complex in Nieuport. Since their arrival on 14 October, the engineer troops had been billeted in the house of the lock-master. In the ensuing days, as the defence of the bridgehead north of Nieuport was taking definite shape, François received several orders related to the destruction of the various passages across the different waterways. Also any equipment in the surroundings that the enemy might seize to attempt a crossing, like barges or rafts, was to be destroyed.

At some point François had an argument with a Belgian artillery officer who was supposed to retreat across the bridges with his gun battery. The officer maintained that he would not let certain barges be sunk for he wanted to keep them in reserve in case he had to withdraw in another direction than the one that had been assigned to him. Did he perhaps expect to be evacuated by sea? François nevertheless had the vessels later destroyed by Corporal Ballon.
Furthermore he got listings of the various army units that had to return from the bridgehead before any demolition could take place.

The remaining citizens of Nieuport saw a bleak future in front of them. The Reverend Father Jules Vermeulen expressed their feelings as follows:

On Friday the sixteenth the Germans arrived in Westende and immediately started digging trenches between Westende and Lombartzyde. They had let the Germans pass, without a fight, in Ghent, Bruges and Ostend. We thought that they would let them through in Nieuport also without fighting. But no, the Army Brass decided to halt the Germans, at least for some time, at the Yser.

This was the death sentence for Nieuport. As in previous centuries the town would again be the sacrifice for the well-being of the country. The bridges were turned, trenches were dug in all the streets, and machine guns were installed on the quays and near the locks. Nieuport was put in a state of defence.

The next day a German high-level meeting took place in occupied Ghent, the ancient capital of the Counts of Flanders. Three high commanders and their respective chiefs-of-staff came to discuss the various options open to them in Flanders. General Erich von Falkenhayn, Chief of the *Oberste Heeresleitung*, presided over the gathering together with Duke Albrecht von Württemberg, Commander of the Fourth Army and Crown Prince Rupprecht von Bayern,[3] commanding the Sixth Army. Since the middle of September von Falkenhayn had taken over as Chief of the General Staff from Count von Moltke the younger.

The Sixth Army, between Arras and Ypres, was facing the British while the newly formed Fourth Army was to advance between Ypres and the Channel Coast. Depending on the actions of the BEF both German armies would react differently. If the British continued their flanking manoeuvre east, the Sixth Army would hold its position and the Fourth Army would run into the British flank from the north.

If, on the other hand, the BEF turned north to face the Fourth Army, the Sixth Army would go on the offensive and try to separate the British from the French. The last possibility, a British retreat, would be answered by the Sixth Army with a pursuit along the upper Lys River while the Fourth Army would push south into the British flank.

Evidently the Germans did not reckon with the presence of the Belgian Army. It had been withdrawing, albeit slowly and reluctantly, since the beginning of the war and it was expected to continue to do so.

Along the Yser front line on 17 October it was another day without widespread German action. Only sporadic bombardment of Dixmude in the south reminded everyone of the proximity of the enemy. In spite of the cold the soldiers were relieved that the rain of the previous days had stopped. Now at least their shivering bodies stayed dry. But there was mud everywhere the men turned. The heavy wet clay stuck to every object that came in contact with it. Digging or walking, it was all a gruellingly slow affair, so it was no surprise that in the relative quiet of the flat and naked countryside one could hear men, painfully bent over, swearing and gasping for air.

At 08:30 King Albert left La Panne for Furnes. Here the news coming in from the front line was more upbeat. Three French cavalry divisions had occupied the north and south side of Houthulst Wood supported by the Belgian First Cavalry Division. Meanwhile a British cavalry division was operating south-west of Roulers. But the enemy was definitely getting near. Information arrived at General Headquarters that the Fourth Ersatz Division was marching from Ostend towards Lombartzyde while the Fifth Reserve Division was on a parallel course but more to the east. The Sixth Reserve Division was concentrating 7km east of Dixmude. Further messages warned of major westbound troop movements inland.

During the day separate intelligence reports arrived in Furnes from the French and British armies that a new German Fourth Army was in formation in Flanders, to march between the North Sea coast and the Lys.

General Foch, finally realizing that a major battle was soon to erupt in the north, decided that the 42nd Infantry Division would be sent to reinforce the Belgian left flank.

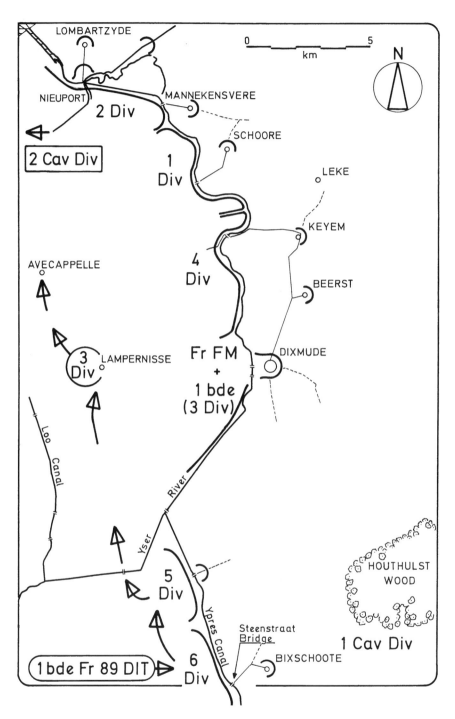

LOMBARTZYDE

0   5
km

N

MANNEKENSVERE

NIEUPORT

2 Div

2 Cav Div

SCHOORE

1
Div

LEKE

KEYEM

AVECAPPELLE

4
Div

BEERST

3
Div

LAMPERNISSE

Fr FM
+
1 bde
(3 Div)

DIXMUDE

Loo Canal

River

Yser

HOUTHULST
WOOD

5
Div

Ypres Canal

1 Cav Div

Steenstraat
Bridge

1 bde Fr 89 DIT

6
Div

BIXSCHOOTE

16 & 17 October

He also informed Belgian General Headquarters that he would strengthen his territorials behind the Ypres Canal. This news allowed the Belgians to withdraw their Fifth Army Division from the canal and bring it in reserve west of Dixmude. As a result the Belgian sector was shortened by some 7km and every kilometre less was a saving in precious manpower.

Now that the defence of the river and the bridgehead north of Nieuport in particular was taking shape, the military became ever more nervous about the presence of the locksmen in this strategic location. It was felt that these civilians apparently did not realize that soon their lives and that of their families would be in danger.

> Father Vermeulen:
> Saturday October 17 the cannons began to roar. Our guns were located partly along the river at St-Georges, partly by the Groenendyke and partly along the Yser channel between Nieuport and the sea. Added to our guns came the British war fleet that made our whole city tremble and shake.
> Until then the people of Nieuport had not worried that much. They hoped that Nieuport would be spared as an open city and that they would shoot at each other over the city and next to it.
> But in the afternoon the burgomaster got the following letter from the general of the Belgian Army, sector of Nieuport.

> My dear Burgomaster,
> I regret to inform you that the Germans will bombard your city and that perhaps our troops will do likewise to stop the enemy entering. As a result I urge you to immediately leave or, if this is not possible, to take refuge in a cellar as soon as the first shells starts to fall.
> Yours sincerely etc.
> (Signed: Daufresne)

With the thunder of the German guns drawing nearer, the restrictions on Dingens and his men became tighter. Officers, sometimes even soldiers, kept on telling them: 'Why are you still here? Leave! It is getting dangerous! We took over the locks, there is nothing more you can do.' But the lockmaster would not give up that easily. These were 'his' locks. 'Don't try to save your furniture,' they would say to him, 'but save your life! Come back in eight days when the battle will be over.'

At the end of 1914 this was, of course, still the prevailing idea of the military on both sides of the conflict and even the population in general. This was a war in motion. The enemy would eventually be stopped somewhere and then be thrown back quickly. This general state of mind explains a lot of situations and the decisions that were taken at the time.

In the city itself the army engineers were taking precautionary measures. The large brick towers were excellent reference points for the German artillery and could not be left standing. The fourteenth century tower of the Grain Hall was the first on the list to go. But the engineers underestimated the strength of the old brickwork. After a first set of charges had been detonated and the smoke had cleared there appeared to be a series of large holes in the tower but the structure was still proudly standing. At noon,

The Gothic Grain Hall in Nieuport at the end of 1914. Like the other Belgian front-line cities of Ypres and Dixmude, Nieuport too was totally flattened by the end of the war. Today the buildings around the Market Square have been rebuilt and reflect their pre-war splendour.
Thys Family Archive.

after a second set of charges had been installed and detonated the tower gave way and toppled with a thundering noise onto the Market Square.

In the afternoon work on the 300 year old church tower started. All the citizens who had not yet fled crowded together to view the spectacle. But again the engineers did not live up to their name. It took them several attempts before finally, around 18:00 the church tower and its beautiful carillon came down with a horrifying crash. A lot of the worried spectators, mainly the elder ones could not but brush away a tear. The Grim Reaper was floating over the doomed city.

At noon on 17th a message arrived from Sir John French indicating that 6,000 of the enemy were advancing on Nieuport from Ostend. The Field Marshal also anxiously inquired about the arrival of the monitors.

There was genuine British apprehension that the Germans would move troops by sea to La Panne in order to bypass the front line on the Yser. As we have seen the Belgians, who knew the local topography better, did not worry about such a possibility.

In the afternoon the first cruisers and destroyers of the Dover flotilla arrived off the coast of Nieuport. By 15:00 the three monitors too were able to set sail.

The brand new, ex-Brazilian monitors had been re-named *Humber*, *Mersey* and *Severn*. Although their shallow draught and low freeboard excluded them from

HMS *Humber* (ex-*Javary*)

navigating in rough seas this characteristic proved to be their main advantage for this type of operation. With their draught of 1.5m they could easily come to within a few hundred metres of the low-water line along the shallow Belgian shoreline and shell with deadly accuracy German positions 4 and 5km inland. This flotilla posed a formidable threat to the Germans. Their efficient and constant bombardment, especially in front of the Second Army Division, would soon force the Germans to shift their main attacks more inland. All in all it was a welcome support to the Belgians, dangerously short of capable heavy artillery.

So at 17:00 the British naval squadron under Rear Admiral Hood arrived off La Panne. But according to an eyewitness, three days earlier on 12 October, three British warships had bombarded the coast north of Ostend from 11:30 until 15:00.

It was not so much an impressive as a heart-warming sight: eight torpedo boats, followed by two cruisers and two monitors. The dispatch had been fraught with delays. The three monitors, with a division of destroyers to protect them, had been supposed to sail the previous evening from Dover to Dunkirk. But that night the weather had been so bad that the monitors could not put to sea.

In the evening, in a small dwelling in Long Street in Nieuport three officers gathered and discussed the defence of the lower part of the Yser River.

Here the canalized river ran west for 3km in a straight line, after a winding course coming from the south. Due to this rather sharp change in direction the defenders of the lower river section would be taken by enfilading fire from the enemy approaching from the east along the Bruges Road. Major Holman of the First Regiment *Chasseurs à Cheval*, explained this inherent weakness of his position to two officers of the Second Engineer Battalion, Second Army Division: Major Georges Le Clément de Saint-Marcq and Captain Robert Thys.

The British Dover Patrol in action off the coast of La Panne. Left a monitor, to the right a destroyer. In the foreground a fishing vessel on the beach.
Nieuport 1914-1918," R. Thys, 1922.

Immediately after firing a salvo the monitor changes course seaward to avoid counter-battery fire. Belgian soldiers, relaxing on the beach, watch the proceedings.
Nieuport 1914-1918, R. Thys, 1922.

In order to solve this problem Captain Thys, after studying the ordnance map suggested inundating the right bank of the river. By doing so the Bruges Road would be flooded around the village of Mannekensvere, thus barring an enemy approach from the east.

Unbeknownst to him this was the original idea discussed by the British officers – and later Captain Commandant Prudent Nuyten – with lockmaster Gerard Dingens almost a week earlier. Nevertheless the objective of Thys was totally different.

While the British initially wanted to isolate Ostend from the mainland by flooding the land south of the Bruges Canal, Thys proposed to set a flood east of the Yser river, this time between the Belgian and the German armies. Coincidentally both projects involved the same area since 'south of the Bruges Canal' also meant 'east of the Yser River' (see map p.179). Flooding this road would prevent the Germans from moving field guns past the village of Saint-Pierre-Cappelle and it would protect Major Holman's entrenched position along the river from accurate shellfire.

Since both engineers agreed that this plan looked quite feasible Major Le Clement put in a request with their commanding officer, Lieutenant General Dossin, head of the Second Army Division. According to one source, someone other than Captain Thys subsequently still sought the advice of the lockmaster. But Dingens again refused to cooperate. Obviously Dingens, for the second time, did not want to get involved in an action that would ruin the livelihood of the population in the polder. As Robert Thys later described it: '. . . for fear of the responsiblities'.

That the land in this region could be inundated was common knowledge amongst the local population, especially the schoolteachers who kept that knowledge alive and passed it on to their pupils. The following incident confirms that the military too did not ignore that valuable source of information.

On 15 October, Lieutenant General Dossin had established his divisional headquarters in Wulpen, a village halfway between Nieuport and Furnes. Two of his artillery officers were billeted with Germain Van Marcke, the local schoolmaster. One morning the good man was having breakfast with the two officers and he put the question to them why the army did not inundate the land. After all Nieuport had done so in 1793 against the invading French Army. The officers were quite interested in the teacher's story and as a result General Dossin invited Van Marcke over to his headquarters the next day. There the schoolmaster gave some information about flooding the region.

101

Nieuport-Ville. — L'Ecluse sur l'Yser.

The tail end (sea side) of the Ypres Lock. In the front left the lock doors, on the right the iron gantry with (on top) the manoeuvering platform with ten gearboxes to lift the doors. The layout of the Furnes Lock was identical, save for having only four openings instead of five and the lock being on the opposite side of the gates. After the war the gantry structures were not rebuilt and the lift mechanisms were installed at ground level. In the background on the right the so-called 'Greek Temple'.
Historical prints collection Callenaere-Dehouck.

However, a few days later when another staff officer asked him to accompany him to Nieuport, Van Marcke declined and referred the man to the locks men, since he himself was unfamiliar with lock operations.

Germain Van Marcke himself wrote down the account of this particular incident nine years later. Hesitant though, he put the date of the discussion as 16 October. For various reasons this is quite likely to be a bit too early. We suspect that the events as described happened a week later as we will see in Chapter IX. The gunnery officers in question were Colonel Le Roy and Captain Commandant Leopold Geerinckx.

At General Headquarters in Furnes a note was handed to the French Mission outlining the following request:

The enemy seems to have concentrated his forces in front of Nieuport-Dixmude. If these forces attack this front it would be quite advantageous if the French Cavalry Corps [positioned in the Houthulst Wood area to the south] would make a flanking manoeuvre or even take them in the back. If this happens at least the Belgian Cavalry Division will support this action.

NOTES

1. Ferdinand Foch was born in Tarbes in 1851, the county town of the ancient French county of Bigorre at the foot of the Pyrenees.
2. We found one other English translation in Émile Cammaerts, *Albert of Belgium, Defender of Right* (1935), but in our opinion this one does not exactly reflect the mood of the times: 'The nations which wish to continue their existence as such must defend themselves. At the moment when we set out to reconquer Belgium, it would seem extraordinary if the Belgian Army were not at our side. I, a soldier of the Republic, assure Your Majesty that our cause is a just and righteous one, and that Providence will give us Victory.' We let the reader judge.
3. Crown Prince Rupprecht was also Queen Elisabeth's uncle.

Chapter VII

The Battle for the Right Bank

The area known as 'the coastal plain of Flanders' is a fertile, narrow stretch of land that runs from Calais in France, north-east through Belgium, to the mouth of the Westerscheldt in the Netherlands. This flat land is protected from flooding at high tide by a ridge of sand dunes, varying in width from 1,000 metres in the south-west to a mere 100 metres in the north-east.

Although the plain is below high water level it is, unlike most polders in Holland for example, above low water. As such there is no need for mechanical devices like windmills or pumping stations to evacuate the surface water. Instead it runs off from the inland canals by gravity as long as the tidal cycle is below the polder water level [1]. Final drainage of the land is achieved through a few breaks in the line of dunes. The three

The Furnes Lock, seen from the Furnes Canal (downstream view), soon after inauguration in 1876. To the left, the gantry with four gates, to the right, the doors to the lock entrance. People lifting or lowering the gate doors could be seen from afar. That was one of the reasons why the gantries on both locks were not rebuilt after the war. The Five-Bridges Road was also moved upstream – closer to the camera – so the new bridges would clear the lock chambers. The lock houses were never rebuilt.
City archive Nieuwpoort.

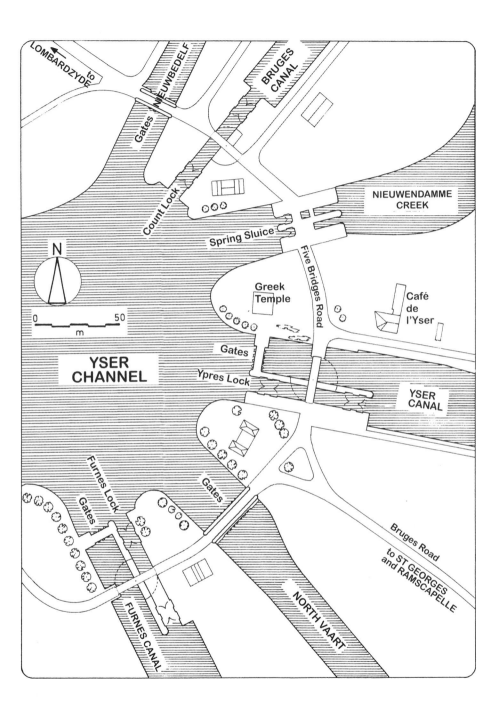

main outlets in Belgium are at Zeebrugge in the east, Ostend in the centre and Nieuport in the west.

Of these three the drainage facility in Nieuport is unique in the sense that there is also a river, the Yser, which empties into the North Sea through the Ypres lock-and-gate structure.

Besides the canalized river, two other navigation canals end up in the bay at Nieuport. First there is the Bruges Canal, connecting Nieuport with Ostend and Bruges. It ends in the Yser Channel through the Count Lock. This is the canal the two British officers talked about with lockmaster Dingens during their meeting on 10 October.

The second canal is the Furnes Canal, ending in the Furnes lock-and-gate structure, which comes from Furnes in the south-west.

No surface water from the adjacent polders is drained into these three canals since the canal water level is higher than the water level in the surrounding waterways.

To complete our round up of hydraulic structures in the Nieuport tail bay we have to mention the three drainage sluices that are wedged in between the three navigation locks.

First there are the Nieuwbedelf Gates in the north that drain the polders west of the Bruges Canal. This is the structure the British were first interested in when they talked to the lockmaster on 10 October. Secondly, south of the Count Lock lays the Spring Sluice. This sluice drains the region between the Bruges Canal and more or less the Yser River itself. Finally we encounter the North Vaart [2] Gates situated between the Yser and the Furnes Canal. When we near the end of the story these gates will become the focus of our attention.

All together these six structures form a complex, build in a fan-shaped design around the bay at the end of the tidal Yser Channel. Due to this shape the people of Nieuport call the complex 'The Goose Foot' (Ganzepoot), or in French, 'patte d'oie'.

To avoid swamping the reader with technical jargon, it will be easier to treat the main hydrology of this region in two separate chapters. Here we will give a quick overview of the northern drainage basin and later on in the book we will cover the southern area. The watershed between the two basins, also important to our story, is not exactly the straight stretch of the canalized Yser River but is in fact the more or less parallel winding road/dyke from Nieuport to St Georges and the Union Bridge: in other words, the Bruges Road. But first a bit of history.

In the early seventeenth century neither locks nor sluices existed at The Goose Foot location. The lower part of the Yser – between the Union Bridge and Nieuport – had a meandering riverbed following more or less the course of what is now called the Nieuwendamme Creek. The river, coming from Dixmude turned north near the Union Bridge towards the Old Fort Nieuwendamme. Here the riverbed turned south-west again to reach the spot where later the Spring Sluice would be built (see map p.108).

But over the years the still tidal Yser was silting up and hampering navigation on the lower river section. To solve this problem the city of Nieuport, in 1643, straightened out the river by digging a three-kilometre long bypass, almost due east – west. With the construction of the first hydraulic structure, a navigation lock called Ypres Lock at the tail end, the lower section of the river was now canalized while an excess of surface water automatically drained through the still open, old bed of the winding river. To provide for drainage of the strip of polder south of the new section that had now been

The North Vaart Gates, a few years after inauguration in 1875.
Kunstmatige Inundaties in Maritiem Vlaanderen 1316-1945, J.Leper, 1957.

cut off from its natural drainage basin, a culvert was built underneath the new canal some 400m upstream of the lock.

The beginning of the nineteenth century saw the appearance of larger barges with deeper draughts that in turn required deeper waterways. Now it became a priority to find a way to deepen the river channel downstream from Ypres Lock. As mechanical dredging was almost non-existent in those days a more familiar technique, known as sluicing, was used.

Sluicing works on the same principle as a toilet. When flushing a toilet the water in the tank rushes into and scours the bowl. Sluicing does the same, but on a larger scale: water is held up in a reservoir at high tide and released sometime before low water. At that moment the outgoing water creates a strong seaward flow, flushing out the accumulated silt in the river channel. For this purpose a peculiar type of sluice was built in 1820 at the mouth of the Old Yser, now called Nieuwendamme Creek, just north of the Ypres Lock. This so-called Spring Sluice did in fact serve two purposes: a civilian one and a military one.

In those days Nieuport was still a fortified place with heavy brick walls and earthen ramparts combined in an intricate design. To augment the defence, the low laying surrounding lands could be inundated to prevent siege artillery from approaching and sappers from building a siege trench network. As such the Spring Sluice was designed not only to maintain depth in the Yser Channel but also to inundate the Nieuwendamme Polder with seawater in case of a military crisis. In fact the sluice had been designed first and foremost as a flood sluice.

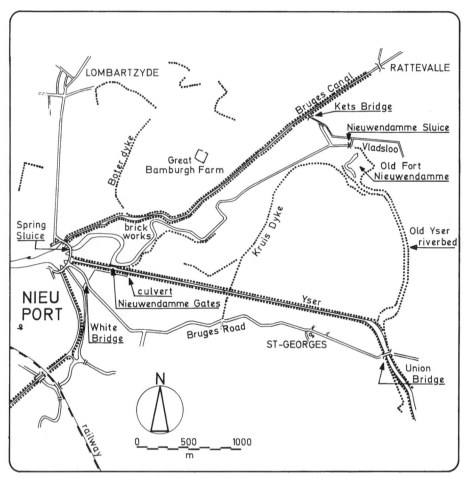

Nieuwendamme Creek

In 1794 the French, who had come from Ostend, had besieged the city. They had placed three cannons on the north side of the Yser Channel opposite the Old Spanish Lock situated north-west of the city, in order to destroy the lock doors and thus create an uncontrolled flood to the west and south of the city.

Twenty-six years later, when the Spring Sluice was being built, the city's magistrates took this possibility into account. This time their new sluice was built in a 'bombproof' way. Not only were the vital lift mechanisms faulted but also the structure was built with two long and narrow parallel channels. Since the structure was now part of the defensive belt of the city, an enemy could only fire at the doors from the east. With the doors and stop planks located far to the west in the channels they made for a very small and well-protected target. Only by positioning a few guns at a well determined, high spot 1,000 metres from the sluice was there a slim chance for the aggressor to hit the doors. And even then it had to be a bull's eye with a bomb in a low, straight trajectory

108

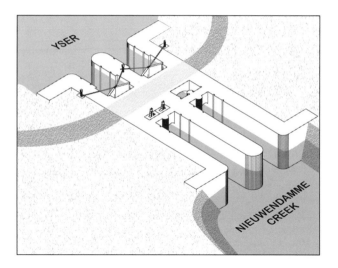

A schematic aerial view of the Spring Sluice as it existed in 1914. Only from a distance of 1,000 metres could a besieger target the lift doors, set far back in the narrow sluice channels. Scoring a direct hit was still another matter at the beginning of the nineteenth century.

since the slightest deviation would make the projectile ricochet from the heavy, rounded masonry on the upstream side.

Unfortunately by the end of the Great War this original sluice was totally destroyed. Although rebuilt and again operational in 1921 the structural changes have been so profound that its functioning in 1914 is unrecognizable today, yet for some unknown reason the outer recesses of the downstream flood doors were restored although no doors nor median wall to support two additional doors were ever installed! Nonetheless the bluestone used in the restoration is of a unique and detailed design worth admiring. But we should return to the tactical discussion of the three officers in the Long Street.

It looked quite simple to execute the proposal by Captain Thys. At ebb tide the doors of the Spring Sluice were to be opened to let seawater rush inland. At high tide the gates would then be closed and retain the water. The procedure was to be repeated at every tidal cycle to boost and enlarge the flooding. However, if Thys had been able to take a closer look he would have noticed that the floodwater would not have gone very far.

Indeed, between the Old Fort Nieuwendamme and Kets Bridge a structure called Nieuwendamme Sluice regulated the drainage of the whole region further east of the river, up to Dixmude. Until the construction of the Spring Sluice in 1822 this structure had been the first line of defence against the ravages of the sea.

Any attempt to flood this large polder depended on the control over this sluice. But within hours of the discussion in Long Street this sluice would be a mile in front of the Belgian lines.

On the morning of 18 October King Albert was on his way to inspect the bridgehead at Dixmude, occupied by the French *fusiliers marins*. In order to be able to hold on to the whole of the Yser the Belgians needed firm control over the Nieuport bridgehead on their left and Dixmude on their right. But as the guns of the British Fleet were now covering Nieuport, the king's foremost concern for the moment was the defence of Dixmude.

Meanwhile the Germans were attacking the main guards left in the villages of Leke,

The Nieuwendamme Sluice near the Napoleonic fort with the same name, provided drainage of the polder on the right (north) bank of the Yser River, as far south as the town of Dixmude. Further upstream the waterway is called Vladsloo Vaart, downstream it becomes the Nieuwendamme Creek. As this hydraulic structure was situated a mile in front of the Allied front line the Germans were more or less in control of the drainage of their side of the front.
Kunstmatige Inundaties in Maritiem Vlaanderen 1316-1945, J.Leper, 1957.

St Pierre Cappelle and Westende. After several hours of heavy fighting the troops defending these locations had to fall back on their respective advance posts. Subsequently the German 6th Reserve Division captured Leke and Keyem, the 3rd Reserve *Jäger* Battalion took St Pierre Cappelle while the 4th *Ersatz* Division captured Westende.

The Belgian advance posts, battalion-strength units dug in at Schoore, Mannekensvere and Lombartzyde were, in turn, bombarded but managed to hold on for the remainder of the day.

At 3:00 Admiral Hood, who had arrived on the Continent around midnight, was able to announce that the monitors would be in position at daylight. Their main goal would be to check with their fire the enemy advancing on Nieuport and prevent any landing of German troops between Nieuport and La Panne. From 9:30 they started bombarding German gun emplacements around Westende, and later on shifted their attention to two enemy positions, one in the hamlet of Lovie and the other near Blokhuis Farm, north of Rattevalle on the Bruges Canal. But owing to the height of the dunes, the effect of the fire was difficult to ascertain from the crow's-nest and the forward fire control from the shore was not yet established.

For the queen the whole naval spectacle was breathtaking:

> The bombardment becomes so powerful that we leave the house and walk up the dune to watch the ships. We can see the flash each time a gun is fired.

The Nieuwendamme Sluice in 1992. The piers were still the same but, removing the massive median wall and replacing it with a third lift gate, had enlarged the opening. *Author's photo archive.*

Between 14:00 and 15:30 it becomes almost unbearable, windows vibrate, we feel the shaking."

As a result of the heavy shelling the German 3rd Reserve Corps decided to hold back its 4th Ersatz Division in front of Nieuport and have its main body pass inland behind the 5th Reserve Division.

To the south the German attacks were fierce and the weary Belgians lost Mannekensvere, Keyem and Schoore. Once driven in the open fields local commanders desperately organized some counter-attacks and by sunset Keyem, part of Mannekensvere and Schoore were back in Belgian hands.

The Franco-Belgian cavalry divisions, roaming the countryside east of the Houthulst Wood, could still reach as far as Roulers but the offensive by the British towards Courtrai and the Lys River was not advancing as planned.

During the day several intelligence reports arrived at Belgian General Headquarters concerning the strength of the German Fourth Army. Among them was the message that the city of Courtrai had been advised by the German occupier to arrange billeting for 30,000 men. The enemy was preparing for a decisive battle.

Foch, informed that the fighting on the Nieuport-Dixmude front had erupted, sent the Belgian liaison officer attached to his headquarters to Furnes in order to ask the king to hold the line on the Yser at all cost. He also announced that the 42nd Division under General Paul François Grossetti would be able to intervene from 22 or 23 October. But if the Belgians thought that the 42nd would come to reinforce their ranks they were wrong; the French had not yet given up their offensive ambitions along the Belgian coast.

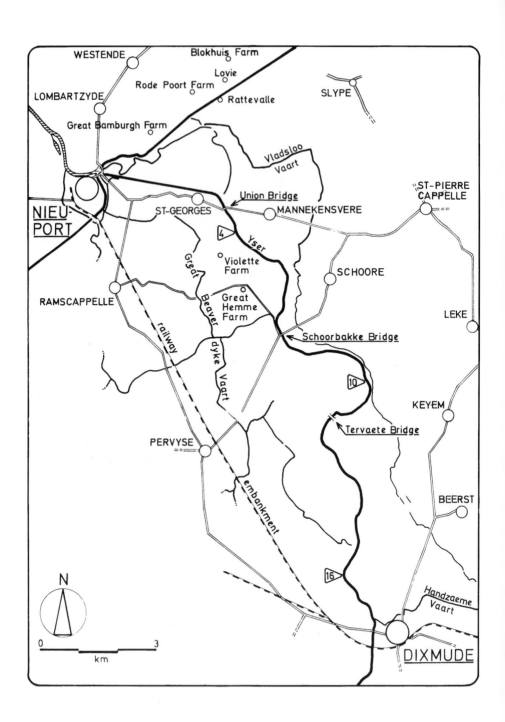

By noon General Bidon, commanding the French Territorials behind the Ypres Canal, visited Furnes. He too was planning an offensive action, departing on the left from Dixmude, with the *fusiliers marins*, supported by a regiment of *goumiers* [3] and his own Territorials on the right. The move would be coordinated with the Cavalry Divisions already operating east of Dixmude. This action was to be a part of the overall plan outlined by Foch in his report to Joffre:

> When the 42nd has arrived it will support the Belgian left; the marines will be in the centre; the Ypres Group will be on the right. *Perhaps we can now think of acting*. . . . The morale of the Belgian Army has completely recovered. I hope to use it.

While the previous attempts by Joffre to gain control over Belgian High Command had failed, Foch was now simply trying to 'frame' the Belgians. By interspersing them with French troops, under a vigorous French commander – that would soon prove to be General d'Urbal –, the Belgians would be forced to cooperate with a French offensive.

By the time evening arrived no enemy had yet been spotted in front of Dixmude. As the Germans seemed to be concentrating their assault in the northern sector, Belgian High Command turned back to its idea of the previous evening. At 18:00 a dispatch was sent to General Bidon asking if it would be possible to direct the French Cavalry Corps, assisted by the Belgian Cavalry in the direction of Thourout, turning north before reaching the town and attacking the enemy from the rear. To protect this move on the left flank, the Belgians asked Bidon to move his Marine Fusiliers from Dixmude north-east and his Territorials to the north of Houthulst Wood.

Belgian High Command saw this merely as a 'hit-and-run' action: only the combined cavalry force would attack the German rear.

While usually on Sundays Nieuport was a quiet, mostly devout fishing port, 18 October 1914 was totally different: the first German shells whistled overhead and exploded in and around town. Most civilians had fled, the streets were deserted. Only soldiers and officers in their different dark coloured uniforms could be seen galloping, riding or marching through town. Around The Goose Foot the situation grew tenser by the hour.

In the midst of all this commotion lockmaster Dingens could not refrain from voicing his opinion on the ongoing military operations around his domain. As he saw the carnage approaching he tried to persuade the military, even if it were only the men around him, that their actions were futile. In a discussion with a few soldiers of the guard detachment he tried to convince them that the Belgian Army was not strong enough to withstand the German war machine – that the government would be better advised to offer the Germans free passage without putting up any resistance. Sergeant Henry, upon hearing these defeatist views could not but admonish the lockmaster strongly and forbade him to use similar language in the presence of the soldiers in the future.

In the morning, 3km south of the locks in the village of Ramscappelle, farmer Pieter Ghewy had attended mass. Pieter owned the Blue House Farm a kilometre north-east of the village. For three days already a battery of Belgian field guns was stationed in his yard but Pieter quickly noticed that the Belgian cannons were no match for the German artillery firing from Mannekensvere across the river. Pieter later wrote down his tale:

Sunday October 18 after mass I noticed that the Belgian staff was installed at the village school. Determined I walked in and asked if I could talk to the commanding general. The guard did not let me pass but a young officer noticed me and I asked him if I could meet his superior while I showed him my passport. He told me that not everyone could just walk into the general's office but he asked me to give him the message which he would deliver. I insisted though and finally I was allowed to enter.

I presented myself as the owner of the Blue House Farm and told the general that from the attic of my house, 30min walking from the river, I could see the enemy positions across the river. If these positions were not inundated immediately the Belgian Army would have to retreat soon.

Amazed the general looked up at me and asked if such a decision was actually to be taken by a simple farmer. But I insisted and was allowed to continue my story. . . . I begged him to open the locks in Nieuport at high tide and flood the whole countryside up to Ostend, Ghistelles and even further so the Germans would drown before they would trample us all.

I told him also that the farm of my grandparents in Oost-Dunkerke had been inundated twice, in 1813 and 1814 to cover the retreat of the French Army. That my grandparents had had to move their cattle into the dunes and that the land had been barren for a few years after the flooding in 1814 with seawater.

The general informed me that they had been thinking about it but that exactly *the fear for ruining the farmland had made them waver.* . . . [Our italics]

This was a remarkable story from a farmer in the polder indeed. It was another testimony that everyone knew about the military floods – and its consequences – in the past. But not only does it prove that the army did consider this option, it also highlights the fact that High Command feared for the negative environmental impact and its effect upon the livelihood of the local population.

Monday morning, 19 October, King Albert left La Panne at 8:30 for Furnes. The fog, lingering in the air, produced an icy feeling. But the weather did not prevent the Germans from launching new attacks on the villages of Lombartzyde and Keyem. To reinforce the latter the king ordered a brigade of the Third Army Division to Nieuport, but Keyem fell for the second time. The loss of Keyem was an important tactical defeat. From this locality the enemy had access to the Tervaete Bridge across the river. From here they would be able to aim flanking fire on the men defending the Yser between kilometres 8 and 12 in the so-called 'Tervaete Loop' of the river.

In order to retake Keyem and simultaneously relieve the pressure on Lombartzyde the king decided at 9:00 to launch a counter-stroke from Dixmude to the north. To secure the right flank of this attack the king wanted the cooperation of the French Cavalry Corps towards Thourout. At 10:30 the king put his request to Colonel Brécard. But neither the request from the previous evening to General Bidon nor the appeal to Colonel Brécard seem to have had any positive reaction from General Foch. His priority at that moment still seems to have been to cover the left flank of the already stuttering British offensive towards Courtrai in the east.

Without waiting for a French reply the king ordered the Marine Fusiliers, supported by Belgian artillery, to march from Dixmude towards the village of Beerst, 3km to the north. The Fifth Army Division followed but with the objective of reaching Vladsloo, a village 3km east of Beerst. In the absence of French support the First Cavalry Division was to cover the right flank.

At first the results were favourable: both villages were retaken. But by four in the afternoon an aerial reconnaissance announced the march of several German columns [4] from the east and north towards the Dixmude area. Simultaneously Belgian and French cavalry were under attack some 10km east of Dixmude. To make matters even worse news arrived that the French Cavalry Corps had been forced to evacuate Roulers.

Incoming intelligence reports now even indicated that at least four German infantry divisions were marching towards Dixmude. These alarming messages prompted King Albert to recall his small attack force back across the Yser.

Unlike the Belgians, General Foch was not concerned about the strength of the enemy. In the morning he still cabled the Generalissimo:

> The total enemy forces in this region are estimated at about 10,000 men, very tired and belonging to the most diverse units.

In the evening, sending in his daily report, Foch reiterated his proposal to mount an offensive with the available French troops, including the Belgian Army, from the coast to Ypres. He explained that he hoped to launch his attack on 22 October after the arrival of the 42nd Division. He expected the Belgians to hold the Yser line until that date and if they did not he would start from the line Furnes-Ypres.

While shells were now exploding constantly in the Nieuport bridgehead, the British squadron off the coast was again pounding German artillery positions. The sand dunes prevented any point-blank fire but forward observers within the Belgian lines on shore now designated various targets. The bulk of the bombardment was directed against a series of German batteries located between Westende-Bains and Slype. The firing was so fierce that by 14:00 the ships' ammunition was getting low. Admiral Hood therefore asked to be reinforced with some older gunboats. Such vessels were not suitable anymore for fleet operations but they would still pack a good punch when used in shore bombardment. At the Admiralty the suggestion was immediately adopted and some otherwise obsolete vessels were readied for sailing.

Undeterred by the British shelling on the one hand and the rain showers falling relentlessly out of the heavy overcast sky on the other, the German infantry advanced steadily along the Bruges Canal. The Belgian forward defenders on the south side of the canal were thinly spread with the result that Kets Bridge, the Old Fort Nieuwendamme and the intermediate Nieuwendamme Sluice were soon lost to the enemy.

With it any hope of large scale flooding of the right bank of the river, as suggested by Captain Thys, had now evaporated.

On the opposite, north side of the Bruges Canal, 1,000m downstream, the Belgians withdrew towards the Great Bamburgh Farm. This amalgamation of sturdy old buildings with their vaulted cellars and moat provided a stronghold for the Belgians, but the Germans, advancing along the towpath of the canal, threatened to cut it off from the Nieuport bridgehead. When darkness fell nonetheless the defenders, cooped up in the farm, gave a sigh of relieve: they had kept the enemy at bay – but for how long?

* * *

Back in La Panne, King Albert was pessimistic about the situation. It was now certain that the Germans were concentrating on an all-out assault on the Yser line. Without immediate French reinforcements his troops would not be able to hang on to the river-bank. General Foch kept on talking about launching an offensive east of the river by 22 October but meanwhile he had not even provided cavalry support for the Belgian flanking attack. So when Foch bombastically predicted that he would be in Ghent by 26 October the whole affair indeed seemed unrealistic. Didn't French High Command realize what was really going on in Flanders? And was it worthwhile to go on sacrificing hundreds, even thousands of young Belgian lives?

The king was so convinced about the desperate situation of his army that, before the royal couple went to bed, he made certain that all their belongings were organized in such a way that they would be able to leave the villa at the slightest notice.

Early the next morning, 20 October, the Germans opened a heavy bombardment on the Great Bamburgh Farm, followed by an infantry attack supported by several machine guns. Soon the Belgian defenders, in pouring rain, were forced to withdraw towards the Boter Dyke, only 600m from the lock system. Immediately the Germans occupied and fortified the farm buildings. Unfortunately from here they could now strike St Georges, Lombartzyde and Nieuport with direct fire.

Since Admiral Hood was afraid of a nightly submarine attack, the Dover Patrol flotilla in the evening retreated to Dunkirk. But at 6:30 the next morning eleven British vessels returned from Dunkirk, this time followed, at noon, by three French men-of-war, including the brand new destroyers *L'Aventurier* and *L'Intrépide*. They were heavily engaged with the German artillery positioned between Middelkerke and Nieuport.

As the enemy attack reached its crisis point and the battery at Westende was still firing, Admiral Hood rushed inshore at full speed with all the destroyers, firing rapidly in the hope of creating a diversion. Naval gunners were well accustomed to firing accurately while at speed but Hood counted on the inexperience of the enemy land artillery in coping with fast moving targets. The effect was reported to be good and he kept it up till finally the enemy guns hidden in the dunes got the range. As a result the destroyer *Amazon* was so badly holed that she was put out of action. Later on targets indicated were a number of heavy batteries in the area of Westende/Middelkerke/Slype: in the late afternoon also the Blokhuis Farm and troop concentrations at Westende-Bains were included.

British naval support did not end with shore bombardment. During the day the Belgians had asked the Admiral for a machine-gun detachment to work with them ashore against the Bamburgh Farm. Lieutenant Wise of the *Severn* and twenty-eight men from the naval squadron landed in Nieuport-Bains and proceeded along the Yser Mouth towards the Nieuport bridgehead by mule and cart.

While the men were heading across the open fields towards the fortified farm the Germans had their rifles trained on them. Chilled Belgian troops in the neighbouring trenches shouted a despairing warning but their Flemish and French words were not understood. At fifty metres from their target the Germans opened fire. The young officer was killed almost instantly together with sixteen of his inexperienced men. In shock and in panic the survivors retreated to friendly lines. After Belgian stretcher-bearers had dressed their wounds temporarily the unlucky party returned empty-handed to the relative safety of their ships.

To lighten the load on the men defending the bridgehead a battalion of the Third Army Division was dispatched to retake the farm. The men, in reserve in Triangle Wood west of Nieuport, crossed the town on the double: Church Street, Market Square, Long Street, Ypres Street. When they arrived in front of the open land surrounding the locks German observers in a kite-balloon above Mannekensvere spotted the reinforcements. A barrage of fire was laid on the Five-Bridges Road and soon the dead blocked the pavement while the wounded, groaning and crying, tried to crawl for shelter. In the end, after a murderous approach, only eight soldiers and one lieutenant reached the foot of the farm buildings. It had been a useless exercise in bravery. Utterly depressed the men retreated and, surprisingly, made it safely back to the Belgian lines.

Almost at the same time and only a stone's throw away, the village of Lombartzyde was also lost to the enemy. A counter-attack by hastily organized reinforcements proved fruitless. In such a precarious tactical situation General Dossin was forced to order the troops in the bridgehead to fall back on a new defensive line, only a few hundred metres in front of the locks at The Goose Foot. Meanwhile he ordered his engineers to investigate the possibility of establishing footbridges across the Yser mouth, sheltered from enemy view, in case the safe passage on the open Five-Bridges Road became utterly impossible. To this end Major Le Clément and Captain Thys arrived at the locks in the afternoon to investigate the situation at first hand.

With the Belgian bridgehead so small the Germans now held it by continuous heavy shelling. Any movement around the sluices was promptly answered by machine-gun fire. This situation was becoming too much for the lock personnel and their families still living in the battered houses nearby. Lockmaster Dingens finally gave in to the unbearable pressure and in the afternoon told his loyal staff that they should leave the locks, their homes and gardens and flee. That morning Dingens had phoned his colleague in Furnes, Lockmaster-Collector Victor-Cyrille Kemp, to tell him that he was forced to leave and that he, Kemp, could expect similar treatment from the military soon.

In spite of the heavy bombardment, one of the aides, Theo Provost, still managed to reach his house, located between the Ypres Lock and the Spring Sluice. While shrapnel

The flood doors of the Spanish Lock before the First World War. In the background the Yser Channel.
Kunstmatige Inundaties in Maritiem Vlaanderen 1316-1945, J.Leper, 1957.

The West Vaart with, in the background, the Spanish Lock. Before the opening of the Furnes Lock on the north-east side of Nieuport in 1876, barges on their way from Dunkirk to Bruges passed here. By 1914 the vaart was only used for draining the polders west of the city. Through a culvert under the 'new' Furnes Canal the vaart was still connected to the polder south of Nieuport. *Nieuport 1914-1918, R. Thys, 1922.*

had already torn pieces of the front and a machine gun rattled from a position east of Lombartzyde, Theo ran down the brick stairs and into the vaulted cellar to get his wife and children. Sheltered with them were the elderly couple Quyo, the Nieuwendamme Sluice keeper and the family of Constant Dugardein; in all thirteen terrified people. When he reappeared the brave locks man was carrying his crying children in his arms. Theo quickly made his way along the hedges, across the narrow lock doors and into the relative safety of the nearby first row of houses. But halfway in their flight his wife stumbled, fell and fainted. Undaunted Theo ran back, somehow got his wife back on her feet and supporting her they both made it unscathed across the lock doors.

On the west side of Nieuport, in the open fields a few hundred metres from the railway station lay the lone and abandoned Spanish Lock. This structure had been built in 1820 to replace the original 'Old' Spanish Lock that had been threatened with destruction by French troops in 1794. In spite of the thunder of the guns and the presence of the soldiers a lone lockkeeper daily showed up and went about doing his job until one day an inquisitive officer asked: 'What do you do here every day, locks man?' Since the Spanish Lock was not maintained for navigational purposes it seemed illogical that a lockkeeper showed up each day at such a deserted structure. The locks man told the officer that, although the doors were closed and locked the gate paddles in the doors, which are underwater shutters, had to be lowered or raised according to the drainage requirements in the adjacent canal and the polder west of the city. The man was ordered not to come back. Nobody could have guessed then that soon, during a few nerve-racking nights, this disused lock would become the gateway to the survival of the nation.

Despite the investigation by Le Clément and Thys to facilitate the retreat from the bridgehead, Le Clément sent the following written order to Lieutenant François:

> In anticipation of an important offensive movement in the near future the lieu-
> tenant-general [Dossin] commanding the division repeats his order to preserve

118

all the bridges until the very last minute and not to blow them up until no other course of action is available. October 20, 1914.

With the enemy advancing along the south side of the Bruges Canal into the Nieuwendamme Polder, the right flank of the Nieuport bridgehead and the Five-Bridges Road were now under deadly fire. This situation made the bridgehead tactically untenable.

As a result the engineers of the Second Army Division revived Captain Thys's idea to inundate the creek. If they could only flood the polder up to the Old Fort Nieuwendamme and the abandoned former river bed, then the right flank of the bridgehead and the locks would be protected. It would have the added advantage that the defence along the Bruges Road could be relaxed in favour of the forward defence – to the east – of the hamlet of St Georges and the Union Bridge. To this end Major Le Clément put in a new request to General Dossin the same day, this time for a smaller, tactical flood rather than the large project that had been proposed three days earlier.

Early in the afternoon heavy German shelling broke out on all the advance posts and the Dixmude bridgehead. The bombardment was so severe that Belgian High Command decided at 16:00 to recall all its troops still on the right bank towards the river crossings except for the strongpoint of Dixmude and the Nieuport bridgehead.

At the junction of the First and Fourth Army Divisions, at km 10 in the exposed Tervaete Loop of the river, the enemy shelling was so severe that both divisional commanders agreed to pull back from the river levee and reorganize the defence along the chord of the loop. Shells of 210-mm created a bloodbath among the exhausted and badly equipped Belgian defenders.

The geography of the loop was indeed a weak point in the overall defence along the river. Perhaps this was an inevitable move, but at this point in the fighting it was still a very risky decision. Releasing one foot of dyke meant that the enemy would jump at the chance to cross the Yser. When High Command heard about the local decision it swiftly repeated its order to hold on to the entire riverbank at any cost. Was this the weak spot in the defence the enemy was looking for?

By the time the king returned to La Panne the British warships had halted their fire. They had expended all their ammunition and Admiral Hood had to send his destroyers to Dover to replenish,

The French General Grossetti, commander of the 42nd Infantry Division. The reinforcement by his division in the 'Tervaete Loop' struggle prevented a German breakthrough near Pervyse.
Onze Helden, R. Lyr, 1922.

and his monitors to Dunkirk to await the arrival of their ammunition stocks. He himself kept up the patrol in the damaged destroyer *Amazon*.

Undeterred by the darkness, the Germans continued their bombardment along the whole Yser front, but less violently than during the daytime. King Albert now saw the situation in a more positive light. The troops had held magnificently under the enemy fire. Galet, this time also more optimistic, wrote: 'Tomorrow we will still hold, the day after the French will get into the action.'

In order to launch his long announced offensive along the coast, General Ferdinand Foch needed to organize the various French contingents engaged in Belgium under a single command. These units were of a very different nature and value but would soon be reinforced by excellent elements. For the moment the new command would be called *détachement d'armée de Belgique* (DAB) and would be headed by General d'Urbal.

The Marine Fusiliers Brigade under Rear Admiral Ronarc'h was undoubtedly the best unit in this new detachment. They had already been under British General Rawlinson's command in Ghent and had later been transferred to Belgian Command while withdrawing to Dixmude.

Courageous Frenchmen, with their characteristic blue berets topped by a red pompom, they had proved to be an invaluable reinforcement of the Belgian Army. Their heroic resistance on the Yser front would be remembered by the French *Marine nationale* in 1946 by renaming the former British escort carrier HMS *Biter* as *Dixmude*.

The Second Cavalry Corps operating east of Houthulst Wood, and the 87th and 89th Territorials along the Ypres Canal made up the remainder of the French DAB. However,

Another view of the Furnes lock-and-gate structure, this time shortly before the war.
City archive Nieuwpoort

120

on the same day, from 11:00 onwards, the 42nd Infantry Division under General Grossetti, started to detrain in Furnes. But let us return to the flooding of Flanders' Fields.

Apparently on the same day two French officers had spoken to the mayor in Furnes concerning possible floods but he had given them an evasive response. When the good man later informed Belgian General Headquarters of the incident the burgomaster got a rather cool reception. Obviously these French officers were preparing the floods around the Dunkirk Fortified Place, a project that would interfere with the drainage on Belgian territory. But, for the moment, this problem was not yet of concern to the Belgian engineers.

At the French Mission the reports to the Generalissimo concerning the Belgian front sounded reassuring in spite of the heavy fighting. By noon a cable went out about the German attack on the Nieuport bridgehead and Dixmude. But it ended: 'Everything goes well.'

Close to midnight Colonel Brécard's men did send an overview on the day's events. In it they complimented the Belgian troops on their behaviour and closed with a phrase, well reflecting the spirit of the time: 'A good day, stimulating for morale.'

At the British Mission the report was equally flattering. Colonel Bridges wrote: 'The Belgians fought very well today; they made a number of counter-attacks and lost 2,000 men.'

NOTES

1. We would like to indicate to the reader that our concise overview of the water managment of the region reflects the situation as it was at the beginning of the twentieth century. Major reconstruction afterwards – some of it even immediately after the Great War – has sometimes changed the hydrology. Our exposé will also enable the dedicated reader to distinguish between old and new.
2. *vaart, \'vart*: a Flemish word, originally used for a serpentine, tidal channel in mud flats. After the flats had been reclaimed from the North Sea, the channel, by then a shallow canal, was maintained for drainage and local navigation. We will use this word for the larger waterways in the polder to distinguish them from the navigation canals mentioned earlier. Locally the canals are also called *vaarts*.
3. North-African (Algerian) cavalry. *Gaum* is the Arab word for tribe or troop.
4. This was the German 22nd Reserve Corps (43th and 44th Reserve Div), arriving somewhat later than the 3rd Reserve Corps to the north.

Chapter VIII

Flooding the Creek

On the north bank of the Yser River, strategically located in front of the Ypres Lock and along the Five-Bridges Road stood the Café de l'Yser. It was one of several haunts for boatmen waiting for their barges to be locked through and for townsfolk who gathered and spread the latest gossip from Nieuport, Ostend or Dunkirk. Another tavern stood between the Count Lock and the Spring Sluice. Then there was the watering hole 'A la nouvelle écluse, chez Lobbestal' [In the New Lock, owned by Lobbestal] in front of the Furnes Lock and walking from the Furnes Lock towards the town one encountered six more pubs.

Certainly in those days impoverished Flanders was littered with drinking-houses. It is said that in the mid-nineteenth century in Belgium, for breweries alone, the count was 2,900.

Since the war had started, most of the talk had been of the approaching danger and, throughout the preceding months, as more and more people left Nieuport for what they hoped would be safer grounds, patronage had dropped accordingly. Now, in mid-October, only a handful of curious or perhaps reckless customers had stayed. They were the ones who wanted to know firsthand what was really going on.

One of them was a bargeman in his early fifties named Henry Geeraert. His weather-beaten face, accentuated by a strong nose and heavy moustache, was always topped by his worn out skippers kepi. Although a jolly good fellow, his talk gave the impression

The Café de l'Yser early in the war. Since it had a strategic location and was used throughout the war as a reinforced observation post, by 1918 the Germans had bombarded the place into a pile of rubble.
Hotel Restaurant l'Yser.

Picture of Henry Geeraert used as the basis for the design of the 1,000 francs bank note. *Nieuport 1914-1918*, R. Thys, 1922.

that it was he who would halt the Teutonic masses here, right in front of the Café de l'Yser. Since September he had seen British and French servicemen coming and going but more and more Belgian uniforms had been coming into the region. It was a pitiful clutter at first, people demoralized by the perpetual retreat and desperately trying to hang on to the basic needs of life. The gradual disintegration of command had turned them into a bunch of poor peasants and tired labourers, disguised in some sort of uniform. Henry felt sorry for these disheartened young lads carried off from their homes and kicked around the land by a merciless Prussian tidal wave. His good nature and his father-like approach quickly made him popular with the young pack. But the war went on and so did most of the soldiers.

On 14 October Henry had been ordered by the marine superintendent to take some barges in tow with his small tugboat and pull them to the safety of the downstream harbour dock. But his curiosity had driven him back to the locks to follow events from close by.

A sapper platoon was on guard at the locks and he had seen a sergeant putting explosives under the swing bridge across the Furnes Lock. To re-establish some order the soldiers had expelled everyone non essential to the workings of the drainage structures. In all the confusion Henry Geeraert, eager to hang around, had managed to recover the cap of an assistant lockkeeper and now, wearing this official head gear, he could circulate on the Five Bridges Road undisturbed.

Unlike lockmaster Dingens, he had an uncomplicated philosophy; he did not care what language someone spoke or what kind of clothes a man wore. He seemed to be able to get along with everyone. And that an officer was a college man who knew a lot more than he did, he would gladly admit. It was no wonder army personnel didn't bother him on his harmless strolls across the bridges and soon the sappers were on friendly terms with him.

Although the German guns had started shelling Nieuport and the lockmaster had taken off for safer quarters, Geeraert was undeterred and stayed with his newfound friends. They provided the action and excitement he had been looking for all his life.

During the night of Tuesday and early Wednesday morning the German artillery kept the pressure up. At 01:00 it launched a bombardment along the whole Yser front followed, one hour later, by an infantry attack on Dixmude from all three exposed sides, by the 44th Reserve Division on the north-east and the 43rd on the south-east side of

Joseph-Jacques-Césaire Joffre, *Maréchal de France*. From 1914 until 1916 he was the Generalissimo of the French Army. *Ons Land, 1919*.

the town. The French Marine Fusiliers and the Belgians were well entrenched and managed to repulse the assault but the Germans came back at 12:00 and again at 15:00. Each time they were driven back.

The defenders of the Nieuport bridgehead were more fortunate: there the German activity was weaker and the Second Army Division, with reinforcements from the Third, was able to enlarge the perimeter somewhat.

While the monitors were awaiting their ammunition in Dunkirk, the scout cruiser *Foresight* arrived off the coast with the destroyers *Lizard*, *Lapwing*, *Crusader* and *Cossack*, accompanied by the torpedo gunboat *Hazard*. Admiral Hood transferred his flag to the cruiser and ordered his crippled *Amazon* home for repairs. By 07:00 his flotilla opened fire on Lombartzyde. An hour later, upon Belgian request, he extended his fire inland along the German trenches as far as the Great Bamburgh Farm where apparently bridging material was being collected. Later came a signal to turn attention to an area south of Westende where one of the naval balloons had located a heavy battery. But, even at a distance of 3,600m, the German fire upon the aerial observer was so accurate that he had to descend within five minutes. The balloon was hence transported to Coxyde-Bains and sent up there, at 8km from the enemy. There it was out of range and from this point it was able to direct the ships' fire on a battery at Rode Poort Farm, which was soon in flames and the guns silenced.

In the evening Admiral Hood reported that the squadron had fired for eleven consecutive hours, his cruiser alone expending 1,100 shells.

The sector St-Georges/Schoorbakke along the river suffered a heavy-calibre artillery attack but the infantry assault was headed off by Belgian 75-mm field guns. The lack of heavy guns was a major impediment for the Belgian Army throughout the battle. The Belgians had only fourteen 150-mm howitzers while the Germans were pounding the defenders with 210, 150 and 100-mm artillery. This was the second day in which the Germans were testing the Belgian defence to find the weak spot that would allow them to establish a bridgehead on the left bank of the river.

At 13:00 the French Military Attaché with the BEF, Colonel Huguet, wired to the Generalissimo:

British High Command informs you that the Russian Attaché in Belgium has learned, from a bona fide source, that the Germans have decided to take Calais at any price.

124

Behind the Belgian lines, despite the grave situation, the mood improved when the first units of the French 42nd Division promised by Foch arrived in Coxyde. Consequently, as the French Generalissimo himself paid his first visit to King Albert at 16:00, both men had no further propositions concerning the role of the Belgian Army: Joffre didn't insist on taking the offensive; the king did not ask for any more reinforcements. Afterwards both Commanders-in-Chief reviewed, from the steps of the Furnes Town Hall, a battalion of French *Chasseurs*. At last the Belgians did not feel alone anymore in this clash of arms.

At General Headquarters the composition of the opposing German forces was by now well known: the new German Fourth Army, between the coast and Courtrai, was fielding eleven full-strength divisions. Of these, five or six divisions were suspected of being deployed in front of the Belgian Army between the coast and Dixmude. The German order-of-battle was as follows: The 4th Ersatz Division in front of Nieuport and the 5th and 6th Reserve Division between Nieuport and Keyem. The 43rd and 44th Reserve Division north of Dixmude and the 45th and 46th Reserve Division in front and south of the town. Somewhat in the rear, towards Houthulst Wood, the 52nd and 53rd Reserve Division.

With Belgian manpower reduced to the equivalent of perhaps four under-equipped and battle-weary divisions, the arrival of the French 42nd Division was a blessing and would turn the scale closer to a tactical balance.

King Albert and his advisors had always assumed that the French division would strengthen the defensive position of the Yser. Thanks to the support of British naval artillery along the coast, the Nieuport bridgehead was relatively safe from being breached. Past the village of St Georges, nevertheless, the situation was totally different: here the river followed a sinuous course exposing the troops to dangerous flanking fire in several locations. But the Belgians hoped that with the French 42nd Division any German attempt at crossing the river here would be countered. In good spirits the king returned to La Panne around 19:00: his troops had withstood all German attacks and would soon be reinforced by first-class French troops.

Half an hour after the king's departure General Paul-François Grossetti, commander of the 42nd Infantry Division turned up unannounced at Belgian General Headquarters in Furnes. To everyone's dismay the Frenchman informed the Belgian staff that he was under immediate French command and that his mission was to mount a coastal offensive from Nieuport towards Ostend. For the Belgians it was déjà vu once more!

The king, who had just arrived at La Panne was quickly informed about this sudden and unexpected reversal of fortunes. He therefore had Colonel Wielemans draw up the following message for General Foch at 21:30:

> The situation as explained in the 21 October dispatch is very grave; all our reserves are engaged in the line. Tonight or tomorrow the line of the Yser can be forced, or at Dixmude, or towards St Georges and Schoorbakke. It is very urgent that our line shall be supported at the right and that reinforcements should be ready to re-establish the situation where necessary. Our troops have been exposed to an uninterrupted bombardment and violent attacks for four days on a 28km front while we only possess approximately 50,000 riflemen (including the *fusiliers marins*).

The establishment of the French division north of the line Furnes-Nieuport is of no help to us and as such we cannot guarantee that we can hold on to the Yser.

Earlier on another French General, Victor d'Urbal, had arrived at his newly formed headquarters in Rousbrugge, the first Belgian village on the Yser across from the French border. From here he would lead the DAB in its offensive against the Boche. He was the kind of man Foch could appreciate because he was a vigorous cavalry officer imbued with the offensive spirit he himself had been advocating for years. At 01:00 d'Urbal had already issued the following order to his troops:

> To Admiral Ronarc'h: contain the enemy offensive in front of Dixmude and hold on to its exits to facilitate our offensive on Thourout, while the Belgian Army holds on to the Yser between Nieuport and Dixmude. To General Grossetti: attack on Slype in order to take the exits of the Yser towards Ghistelles.

Reinforcing the Belgians on the Yser line was obviously not part of his overall assignment either!

On Wednesday morning, 21 October, orders finally arrived at the engineers' unit from the commander, Major General Daufresne (6th Brigade/2nd Army Division), to inundate the so-called Nieuwendamme Polder [see map p.108]. Accordingly Major Le Clément sent the following order to Second Lieutenant François:

> By order of the General commanding the Sixth Brigade you will immediately set a flood between the Bruges Canal and the canalized Yser, up to the Old Yser branch. On this matter you will contact the lockkeeper and agree with him; it will probably be enough to manoeuvre the gates at the fourth bridge, on the

View of the Spring Sluice from the tidal bay. In the background we notice the Café Ecluse du Comte on the Bruges Canal. Note the heavy, rounded median wall of the sluice, which would act as a deflector for a nineteenth century shell.
Nieuport 1914-1918, R. Thys, 1922.

waterway called Nieuwendamme Creek. You might have to open a gate or cut the dyke called Kruis Dyke.

In any case you will make sure that the floodwater does not extend east of the Old Yser branch; as soon as possible you will report back to us while indicating the approximate hour the terrain will be submerged.
9:15, October 21, 1914.
P.S. Very important: Do not take any executive measure until the confirmation that I will send you eventually after I have met the General of the Sixth Brigade.

From the tone of this statement, written a day after the lock personnel had left, it would seem that the lockmaster's claim six years later that he and his staff were 'evicted' from the locks by the military is rather exaggerated, if not untrue.

The order to restrict the flood to an area west of the Old Yser branch supports the notion that Belgian High Command still shied away from a large scale flooding of the right bank. We suspect that, at this time, the main reason was the French obsession for an offensive. A flood was, after all, a purely defensive measure. It created an obstacle for both warring parties!

Nonetheless François was faced with a problem: the lockmaster and his personnel not only had left the previous day but had forgotten to hand over any of the special tools needed to operate the structures. We suspect that Dingens, as well organized as he was and to avoid any misuse, had locked away all the gear before his departure. It should not be forgotten that the man was responsible, not only for the proper workings of the lock complex but also for the safety and well being of hundreds of inhabitants of the polders.

François contacted his superior officer asking for detailed instructions on how to execute the manoeuvre. As a result Le Clément replied:

1) Please try to find the tools to open and close the gates.
2) In the absence of any equipment please look into the possibility of fabricating it urgently.
3) In any case we must be able to open and close the gates at will.
4) You will keep the gates open as long as the water level in the channel is higher than in the Nieuwendamme Creek. You will close the gates between this creek and the channel (fourth bridge) when at receding tide the water level in the channel will be lower than in the creek.
5) You will make sure that the water from the creek can overflow on the adjacent land. If necessary you will make cuts in the north and south banks of the above-mentioned creek (50 cm wide with the spade).
6) If at all impossible to manoeuvre the doors, you will initiate an intermittent flood by keeping all the gates open permanently (if need be by breaking the doors) and by making the necessary cuts in the dykes of the Nieuwendamme Creek. October 21, 1914.

At 11:10 Major Le Clément and Captain Thys arrived at the guard detachment in order to show Second Lieutenant François exactly what to do to inundate the creek. The three of them then went to the Spring Sluice to inspect for any shell damage and to check the mechanical equipment.

The Spring Sluice was of an unusual design which certainly made the young lieutenant unsure of how to manoeuvre the swing doors, lift gates and stop planks, all at the same time, in order to achieve a flood of the polder.

The tide had been rising since early morning and in a little over two hours (13:20) it would be at its highest. The pressure on the closed flood doors was already too strong to allow any manoeuvring at this point so it was decided that François would return in the late evening with some men from his guard unit, open and lock the flood doors in their recesses and lift the doors.

Le Clément also repeated his order to François that he could only blow up the bridge across the Furnes Lock at the very last moment, which was when the Germans would have arrived at the second bridge, the one spanning the North Vaart Gates. At that moment all other structures, including the Spring Sluice, would have already been lost to the enemy.

The corporal of the detachment, Benoit Ballon heard from François that headquarters was planning to open the Spring Sluice and inundate the Nieuwendamme Creek. François apparently told him also that, being unfamiliar with the local situation and with the lockkeeper apparently gone, the engineer's staff hoped to find someone who could give them more information on the drainage system of the region.

Upon hearing this Ballon soon got a hold of his new friend Henry Geeraert and inquired if he would be able to provide his superiors with details concerning the local waterways.

This was just what Henry wanted: that big institution called the Belgian Army asking for his advice! Promptly Corporal Ballon brought Henry in contact with François and their commanding officer, Captain Commandant Borlon. Henry was delighted.

As the Five-Bridges Road was under constant artillery fire the small party retreated

to company headquarters in a small house not far from the locks. With the ordnance map on a shaky table, Borlon brought Geeraert up-to-date on the intentions of the division and revised with him all the details his engineers had worked out. Attentively Henry followed Borlon's explanations. When Captain Commandant Borlon had finished Henry slowly felt pride bubbling up; after all, the army did seem to need him!

Did they know that some 600m east of the Ypres Lock a culvert under the river connected the creek with the polder south of the Yser? Borlon was surprised. This meant that, by inundating the creek, they

Henry Geeraert, wearing clogs, somewhere in the ruins of Nieuport.
Historical prints collection Callenaere-Dehouck.

A typical capstan as used in
the Nieuport area in 1914.

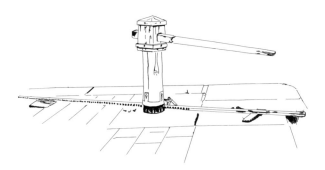

would just flood their own lines if they didn't block that escape route! Geeraert never-theless reassured him: if they closed the small culvert with two sliding gates at White Bridge on the Bruges Road, some 200m from the Ypres Lock, they would prevent the flood water from invading the main polder south of the river. The small strip of land between the Bruges Road and the canalized river would not be greatly affected. Here the land was higher than north of the river, rising towards the Bruges Road, the natural watershed. The culvert itself could also be blocked, but for that they needed to drop stop planks in place. This would not only take a lot of precious time but it would also be extremely dangerous. In view of the tactical situation, the men working on the crest of the Yser levee would be exposed to direct enemy fire.

Geeraert said that he knew how to operate the sluices and he reassured the officers that he would be able to find the tools to open the floodgates and the windlasses to lift the gate paddles. Obviously Henry was well aware of the wheeling and dealing of the lock people. When the officers proposed that the bargee should accompany them that night Geeraert agreed immediately and with a grin on his face.

In the discussions leading up to the issuing of the flood order it seems not only Major Holman wanted to get some protection for his troops. Major General Daufresne himself had hinted that this flood could be extended to include Mannekensvere and even go as far south as the exposed left flank of the Dixmude defence. But that was of course Captain Thys' original proposal of 17 October. Daufresne had suggested cutting the levees of the old Yser branch and use the Vladsloo Vaart as a carrier for the floodwater further south. This way the land could be inundated as far as the Handzaeme Vaart on the outskirts of Dixmude.

But the proposal never got to High Command for two reasons: first, the engineers argued that it would take too much water and time, in fact the same argument Dingens had used towards the British officers ten days earlier, and secondly it would hamper a possible eastward offensive: in other words the 'French Connection'.

Later in the day, presumably because of the proximity of the enemy, the order to cut some dykes in the creek to facilitate the flooding was withdrawn. Instead the artillery was put in charge of this operation.

After the war this new directive did create some confusion among authors. At some point it was argued that, in order to speed up the flooding, the Belgian artillery had breached the southern dyke of the Bruges Canal, a few hundred metres from the lock system. Engineer Captain Robert Thys nevertheless vehemently contradicted this statement and wrote in 1920 that the artillery '. . . has never intervened in the manoeuvering for the flood'.

There is no evidence to suggest that the dyke of the Bruges Canal – or any other 'wet' levee for that matter – was ever breached by the artillery. But given the tactical situation at the time and the topography it was indeed feasible for the artillery to 'soften up' one or two spots in the much closer dry *Kruis* Dyke (see map previous chapter) which acted as a subdivision of the polder.

In the evening Second Lieutenant François, Sergeant Henry and Corporal Ballon, accompanied by Henry Geeraert and fifteen soldiers of the guard detachment made their way in the dark to the Spring Sluice. The first manoeuvre to accomplish was to open the mitred flood doors. For that they needed the steel racks and wooden poles to turn the capstans. As he had said, Geeraert soon found all the tools needed. Under his guidance and that of the soldiers Cop and Van Belle, they opened the flood doors and locked them in their open position. Incidentally Frans Cop and Kamiel Van Belle were also bargemen.

Locking the doors once open was accomplished by flipping a heavy, cast iron gate hook into an eye at the outer end of the door. This hook was attached to an upright ring anchored in the blue stone top adjacent the gate recess. This detailed explanation might seem trivial to the reader but later on in the story we will run into a similar situation, but this time with quite different consequences.

In December 1914 the men of the inundation company received a Christmas parcel. That was an excellent moment to capture a few of them on film. From left to right: Henry Geeraert (now in army outfit), soldier Cop, Miss Fyfe (who presented the gifts), Captain Robert Thys and the soldiers Van Belle, Lequarré and Fulgoni.
Nieuport 1914-1918, R. Thys, 1922.

The decades old mystery of untimely closing lock doors solved! Here we see the cast-iron hook on the lock platform of the small East Vaart Lock. Just left of it the worn out groove and hole where once a previous ring and hook assembly stood.
Author's photo archive.

At 23:00 the men were able to raise both gate paddles in the southern sluice channel. Ebb tide had been around 20:00 so once the doors started to move the seawater immediately began creeping inland. Since the water level in the creek was at +2.40m and the expected high water would be over two metres higher, the seawater would soon be rushing in like a torrent. Being too dangerous a place to stay the team did not wait to watch the results and returned to their quarters.

When a cold, autumn night fell over the polder no German infantryman had as yet been able to crawl up the right bank levee and see the Yser river. But that would soon change.

Chapter IX

The Tervaete Debacle

The sector line between the Second and First Army divisions was at km 4, just south of the Union Bridge. Southward from there the First Army was in charge of the defence of the river, up to km 10. Access from the east bank was across the Schoorbakke Bridge where the division still held a small bridgehead.

Past the Schoorbakke Bridge, the river started a wide, outward loop forming a vulnerable salient for the Belgians. At the top of the bend stood the km 10 marker, from where the Fourth Army Division took over the defence. It was then in charge up to km 16, 1,500m north-west of the town of Dixmude. In its sector, at the base of the so-called Tervaete Loop, lay the Tervaete Bridge as the point of passage for the division. Dixmude itself was occupied by the French *fusiliers marins* and a Belgian detachment.

During the night the Germans had tried to cross the Yser at a few points but each time the Belgians had been able to throw them back. Unfortunately, in the early morning of Thursday 22 October, still under cover of darkness, two battalions of the 26th Reserve Infantry Regiment/6th Reserve Division managed to sneak into the thinly occupied outposts of the First Army Division on the east bank. Not a shot was fired, no unnecessary noise made, only bayonets and knives were used. Some of the Germans managed to cross the river on a makeshift footbridge used at km 10 by the Fourth Army Division. Around 06:00 enemy patrols were already infiltrating the west bank defences.

By daybreak several enemy companies of both battalions had already crossed the river on hastily laid additional footbridges. Once the defenders noticed the scope of the incursion, fierce machine-gun and rifle fire erupted on both sides. Only crawling through the heavy mud or bending over and sloshing through the water-filled ditches could now prolong one's life.

When, some time later, the news finally reached Furnes, the seriousness of the situation did not sink in at High Command. The message was not deemed alarming. It was considered something that could be handled by a local counter-attack.

The failure at General Headquarters to treat the initial reports of this intrusion more seriously can perhaps be explained by the lack of reliable communications. By then virtually all dispatches had to be sent by a messenger on foot to the nearest field telephone or carried further on horseback or by bicycle. This haphazard system certainly made for an unreliable transmission of messages. We should also not forget that the action took place in an isolated, exposed and waterlogged area of the front some 14km from Furnes.

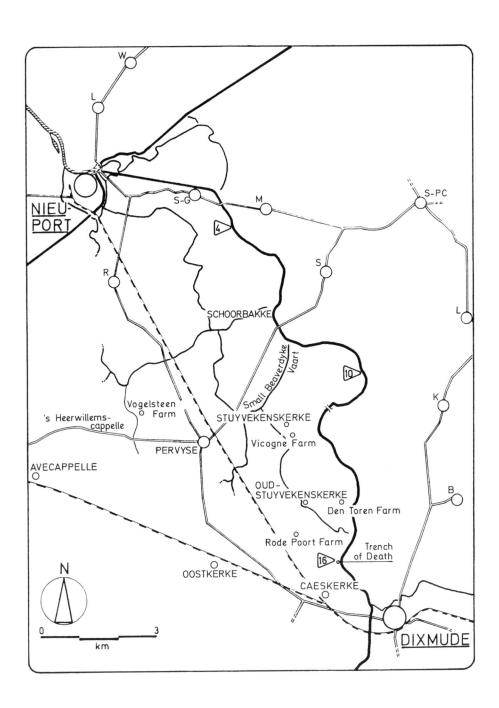

At the same time just to the north at the Schoorbakke Bridge, the 4th de Ligne Regiment, still defending the small bridgehead, could ward off a strong assault by the Germans. In Nieuport and in Dixmude meanwhile unremitting enemy shelling kept up the pressure.

'Collateral damage' was perhaps not exactly the phrase used by the British at the time but the queen wrote that evening in her diary: 'The British shell Nieuport by mistake.'

In the narrow Nieuport bridgehead the 1st Regiment *Chasseurs à pied* and the 9th de Ligne Regiment of the Third Army Division took advantage of a realignment by the German troops to attack and advance their positions towards Lombartzyde and the Bamburgh Farm but in the end they were unable to reoccupy either one of these positions.

Meanwhile the British squadron off the coast was fearful of a submarine attack. One of the monitors had been attacked on the day of its arrival, but no submarine had been spotted since. The previous day a report had said that a German submarine was in Ostend but later the message proved to be false. The next day however German submarines attacked two of Admiral Hood's ships. Due to the tactical inexperience with this new weapon on both sides the attempts failed and the subs eventually escaped. As a result of these encounters French warships had laid a protective minefield east of Ostend during the night. So in the morning the British monitors were back, escorted by the gunboat *Bustard* and together they kept up a curtain of fire on the German rearward batteries.

Around 11:00 General d'Urbal arrived at General Headquarters in Furnes. His message was not comforting for the Belgian staff. He declared anew his intention to launch an offensive from Nieuport, Dixmude and Ypres the next day. Overconfident, the tall, corpulent Frenchman predicted that this move would clear the Belgian front. As a result of this call-to-arms the battle weary Belgians had no choice but to again reverse their cautious defensive strategy and prepare for some kind of offensive. With the approval of the king, Colonel Wielemans drew up orders for the next day to recapture Lombartzyde and to hold on to the bridges at Schoorbakke, Tervaete and Dixmude at all costs.

In the Tervaete Loop, despite incessant Belgian artillery support, the situation had been deteriorating steadily. German guns had been brought in close to the eastern river embankment and they now pounded away mercilessly at the crumbling Belgian defence. A hastily arranged but fierce local response failed to throw the Germans back across the river.

By the time a major counter-attack was organized in the afternoon, the enemy strength west of the river had grown to two battalions with a dozen machine guns. Belgian Grenadiers and Carabineers attacked heroically but the flat, treeless landscape did not offer a lot of protection against the murderous bursts of bullets now coming from every direction. The countless waterlogged ditches prevented rapid advance. In the end a handful of brave Grenadiers under the command of Major d'Oultremont managed to reach the river embankment. But it was all in vain. The enemy kept pouring in more infantry and machine guns and the main Belgian assault wave got stuck a few hundred metres from the river. By nightfall, in order to establish a defensive line, the few Belgians left forward had to retreat for the night. High Command had to concede that the vulnerable Tervaete Loop had been lost in its entirety to the enemy.

At 17:00, while the Belgian defence was crumbling in the centre, the generals d'Urbal and Grossetti met King Albert in Furnes. They once more explained their planned offensive. d'Urbal even expressed the wish that the majority of the Belgian Army should follow his move east by crossing the river. The king was not impressed. He in turn aired his misgivings about the feasibility of the project and repeated that his troops were unable to take to the field again. Rather, he wanted to see the existing, shaky defence strengthened.

The king's remarks did not throw d'Urbal off balance: he distrusted the combativeness of the enemy and, as a well indoctrinated French officer, engaged in promoting the virtues of the offensive. This behaviour had the opposite effect on the king: he made the wry comment that if that were so, why were the Franco-British forces not yet at the Rhine instead of the enemy occupying Belgium and a large part of France?

In the evening Admiral Hood docked in Dunkirk to meet Colonel Bridges and the French Admiral Favereau, recently appointed commander of the French forces in the Channel. The British squadron was now being considerably strengthened: the old Apollo class cruisers *Brilliant* and *Sirius* and the sloops *Rinaldo* and *Wildfire* were arriving in Dunkirk. Since the British Fleet was now providing escort services world wide for various large army convoys from all over the Empire and bound for Europe, it was stretched to the limit. So any reinforcement that the Dover Patrol could get was greatly appreciated. Winter was approaching and Hood had to point out that a sudden northerly gale would probably force an end to the involvement of the monitors and the gunboats.

But the French offensive now in the works justified taking a risk. The cooperation of the British squadron was essential to the planned drive along the coast. By recovering Ostend the French would not only reopen the port to British reinforcements but they would also deprive the Germans of naval support on their right flank.

While Hood and Bridges were conferring with Favereau the order from General d'Urbal for his offensive towards the north-east arrived at Belgian General Headquarters. It stipulated three main drives: the first from Ypres towards Roulers with three French divisions in accordance with the British left attacking towards Courtrai; the second thrust would depart from Dixmude to Thourout with the *fusiliers marins* and the Belgian right; the third pointed from Nieuport to Ghistelles with the French 42nd and the Belgian left. The king's advisors were stunned. Where Joffre and Foch had not succeeded in laying their hands on the Belgian Army, now it was d'Urbal's turn to give it a try.

Reality forced Wielemans to send Colonel Brécard to d'Urbal informing him that the Belgians would not be able to comply. Instead he asked the general to direct his 42nd Division towards the centre of the Belgian front rather than to Nieuport. But Brécard returned empty handed. Reluctantly General Headquarters issued a new Army Order at 02:15 on the morning of 23 October, asking the troops in the Nieuport bridgehead to:

> . . . cover the exit for the French 42nd Division; for the Marine Fusiliers and Belgian detachment in Dixmude to prepare for an offensive, . . . but that they would have to wait for orders through the intermediary of the commander of the Fifth Division; that the other troops keep their current mission until the situation in the Tervaete Loop has cleared.

Again a seaside view of the Spring Sluice but this time from a lower angle (see picture p.126). On the left a set of flap doors installed during the war by the inundation company to replace the regular doors and stop planks that were systematically destroyed by the enemy artillery. *Nieuport 1914-1918, R. Thys, 1922.*

In fact this order was a mere delaying tactic. Belgian GHQ was sitting on the fence, waiting for the inevitable to happen.

After the icy morning fog had dissipated, Major Le Clément and Captain Thys returned to the Spring Sluice. To their satisfaction they discovered that a large part of the Nieuwendamme Polder was flooded. Via the culvert under the Yser the water was even up to the village of St Georges and the Bruges Road. To make sure that the flood was maintained François was ordered to open the lift doors at each rising tide to raise the water level even more. This was done until 26 October when his guard detachment left the locks.

As pointed out earlier the Germans were theoretically able to drain the water via Ostend. This initial flooding should have been an omen for them of what was possible in this low lying part of the country. But fortunately the German Army Staff never realized what could happen. The reader will find more about the reasons why they ignored this sign at the end of the book.

The next day, Friday 23 October marked the sixth day of relentless combat for the Belgian troops. During the night the small bridgehead at Schoorbakke had become untenable because of the enemy machine guns that were now taking the men under flanking fire. Before daybreak the defending battalion of the 4th de Ligne Regiment evacuated the bridgehead and blew up the Schoorbakke Bridge. But by now the Germans were already building footbridges in several locations. Soon afterwards the 3rd de Ligne had to stop an enemy attempt to break out from the Schoorbakke hamlet, a few houses leading to the river levee by the bridge with the same name.

With regard to the French offensive the results were not encouraging and seemed to

The French Rear Admiral Ronarc'h, commander of the Marine Fusiliers Brigade. After their heroic defense of Dixmude the brigade would often lend a helping hand to the Belgian inundation company at the Goose Foot in Nieuport.
Onze Helden, R. Lyr, 1922.

be more consistent with what the Belgians had anticipated. In Ypres, where the French Ninth Corps was supposed to attack, the British were still awaiting the latter's arrival, while in Dixmude a more realistic Admiral Ronarc'h was of the opinion that:

> . . . An offensive undertaken with exhausted troops will lack vigour . . . and that . . . the offensive will be halted at a hundred metres from its starting line . . . because of the proximity of the German trenches.

The enemy was certainly not cooperative: the whole morning the town of Dixmude and the river embankment north and south of it were bombarded with shrapnel and high-explosive shells. Around 12:00 an infantry attack followed after which, between 16:00 and 17:00, the shelling resumed.

From 22:00 the 84th Brigade and one battalion of the 83rd, both from the French 42nd Division crossed the lock system in Nieuport and the Yser Mouth by means of makeshift footbridges. While they were advancing through the dunes towards Lombartzyde and Westende the German artillery opened up heavy shelling and the infantry made a violent attack on the Belgians in the front line. The latter, driving them back with the help of the British naval artillery in turn managed to capture two machine guns and a lot of prisoners. But the French were not able to get far beyond the Belgian lines. The heavy packed *poilus* had trouble advancing in the loose sand of the dunes. Although they made some progress towards Westende they came to a halt in front of Bamburgh Farm.

General d'Urbal was completely frustrated with the Belgian unwillingness to take the offensive. He made this clear in his report to Foch at 9:25:

> Following its operational order the Belgian Army attacks little or not at all. It is necessary that it attacks, if only because it was to put on airs.
>
> Yesterday I attacked on my front and thanks to this, not only did I keep the position on the Yser intact, but I also gained terrain.
>
> It will be the same for the Belgian Army if it attacks. If it stays passive on the Yser it will end up being pierced at one point or another.

For days the British naval squadron had been in a serious dilemma. The planned French advance on Ostend required any help the ships could give but they could never do their utmost if they were in ever-present danger of submarine attack. As long as Ostend was open to German vessels the sea would not be safe for an hour. As such the Admiralty wanted to bombard the harbour and disable its facilities. On the other hand, if the advance was to achieve its ultimate objective, Ostend had to be left intact as a port of re-entry for the army. Finally, at 12:00 on 23 October Admiral Hood was authorized by Belgian High Command to shell the port.

Back in Britain steps were being taken to minimize the risk run by the squadron. Trawlers with anti-submarine sweeps were sent across and another division of destroyers was dispatched. Barges with nets were being equipped for the protection of the larger ships when in action. At midnight the Admiral did receive specific orders from London on how to destroy the Ostend docks and railway station. Meanwhile block ships for closing the port were being prepared and Hood was to report on the feasibility of running them in under protection of his vessels and sinking them in the entrance to the harbour.

This scheme was actually not implemented until 1918. Then, on 23 April, the afore-mentioned *Brilliant* and *Sirius*, now transformed into block ships, headed for Ostend but due to German trickery with the buoys both vessels ran aground east of the harbour entrance. Another attempt on 10 May, with the cruiser *Vindictive*, was nevertheless more successful.

On both sides of the front the guns thundered violently the whole day. There was no better panoramic view of these dramatic events along the Yser river than from atop the church tower in Furnes. Since it was a clear sky it came as no surprise that during the day King Albert himself climbed the steep stone steps and watched through his binoculars the artillery duels raging some 12km away.

At the edge of the Tervaete Loop, the 8th de Ligne managed to hold on to Tervaete hamlet until 12:00 and then it, too, had to withdraw through the open fields towards Vicogne Farm. From there the front line now ran to the village of Stuyvekenskerke and then towards the Schoorbakke Bridge, leaving the entire bend in enemy hands.

Maurice Duwez, pen name Max Deauville, who was medical officer with the 1st battalion/1st Carabineers and treating many wounded in a lean-to on a farm in Stuyvekenskerke wrote later:

> . . . All those with whom we have spend such hard times, we have seen them return mutilated, bleeding and with torn uniforms. Almost the whole battalion has been wiped out. Three of our officers have been left on the battlefield. Among them the elderly commander who always had this ironic smile on his face. . . . And the procession continues, the vast plain will always surrender its victims.

A few kilometres further north, in the village of St Georges, the 7th de Ligne Regiment had been resisting the German shelling with heavy calibre grenades for four days but unfortunately all along the front, exhaustion was taking its dangerous toll.

As a result the Deputy Chief of Staff informed Colonel Brécard at 18:15 that:

. . . all efforts have been made to restore the line or to limit the retreat. Because of the exhaustion of the troops and the lack of reserves, it is to fear that an enemy attack made tonight or tomorrow morning will widen the gap and completely break the Belgian centre. If this happens we face a retreat.

In the late afternoon Major Le Clément was at the locks again and explained to Lieutenant François a new hydraulic manoeuvre he would have to execute during the night. The guard detachment would have to lift the five double gate paddles at the Ypres Lock simultaneously at ebb tide in order to create a strong current in the narrow canal. It was hoped that this sudden suction would destroy the enemy footbridges across the river by pulling them from their moorings. Later in the evening Le Clément sent François the following order:

The manoeuvre to be executed by means of the gate doors on the canalized Yser, as I explained to you at 17:00, cannot be realized yet. Continue to study and prepare it. You will receive the executive order in due time, either directly from General Headquarters, or by my intermediary. 19:45. October 23.

Back at General Headquarters Colonel Wielemans, in the evening added to his earlier statements to the head of the French Mission, that a French offensive on the left flank looked quite risky. Instead he recommended that an energetic action by the largest number of troops of the 42nd in the Tervaete Loop could re-establish the

Belgian lancers on the beach at high tide, awaiting further orders.
Thys Family Archive.

now precarious situation and '. . . transform into a success that tomorrow could, on the contrary, become a rout'.

Shortly afterwards an intelligence message arrived in Furnes from Foch's headquarters putting the enemy strength in the Tervaete Loop at five and a half battalions. This persistent tendency to belittle the Belgian military effort and the repeated refusal to send any large reinforcements was now more than the king could take. He dictated a strong worded dispatch destined for French High Command. In his message the Commander-in-Chief recalled the events of the previous days and the role his army had played in resisting the German advance without any French help. He also reminded the Generalissimo about the promises that had been made and as a result of which the Belgian Army had now used up all its reserves. He protested against the constant French practice, since the beginning of the war, of downplaying the forces of the enemy facing the Belgians.

It is interesting to note that although the monarch also referred to the British forces, he did not mention them by name. He clearly wanted to aim solely for the French High Command's high-handed attitude. Now that the situation had again become uncertain, perhaps he regretted his earlier decision to stay on national soil instead of embarking for the United Kingdom.

Fortunately for everyone concerned the message was never sent, for Colonel Brécard arrived with the news that General d'Urbal had finally given in to the repeated Belgian requests. He had ordered General Grossetti to leave one brigade of the 42nd Division in Lombartzyde and take the other two, including all divisional artillery, to the village of Pervyse in front of the Tervaete Loop. There he was expected to launch an attack, together with Belgian troops, early next morning.

At 23:30 Foch cabled Joffre that the 42nd had taken Lombartzyde. Trivializing the Tervaete Loop debacle he continued:

> . . . Tomorrow this division will send a detachment to stop the Germans that have crossed the river south of Schoorbakke. Situation good. Tomorrow the attacks will be reopened with the 42nd Division and the 9th Corps.

Sometimes one gets the strong impression that Ferdinand Foch 'fed' Joffre a self-censored version of the situation. The *bigourdan* was a smart man: not only did he know how to deal with his subordinates and get the best out of them, he also knew how to approach his superiors. The situation in the north was indeed shaky so the next day he himself visited Furnes to evaluate the conditions firsthand.

An hour and a half later Colonel Brécard sent in his daily report to the Generalissimo. His assessment of the situation was more down to earth:

> . . . In the centre the enemy has progressed significantly. He arrived at 500m off Pervyse and now occupies Schoorbakke and Stuyvekenskerke. As I judged the situation as serious, I referred to the Generals Foch and d'Urbal. It has been decided to proceed this morning with a counter-attack on the Yser bend by the 42nd. Four 120-mm batteries arrived yesterday night.

The Belgian artillery itself got a much-needed boost by the French. In the *Carnet des Officiers d'Ordonnance* [AKP #AE 530/1] we read for that day:

A great deal of French artillery (120-mm guns and 155-mm howitzers) is put at the disposal of the Belgian GHQ.

The same evening Major Maglinse, Head of Operations told Captain Commandant Nuyten to stay at the disposal of General Grossetti. As such Nuyten, shortly after midnight, accompanied the French general to Pervyse by car. One and a half kilometres before reaching Pervyse, immediately after they had crossed one of the main vaarts of the region, they turned north onto a muddy farm road and reached the headquarters of the First Army Division. It was 03:00.

Here, at Vogelsteen Farm and in the dead of night, Grossetti discussed the tactical situation with his Belgian counterpart, General Baix. Grossetti estimated that he could only spare four battalions and six batteries to send to the centre. Moreover, he was interested to know what forces the Belgians could add to support his action. After consultation, High Command agreed to release the only Belgian reserves left: the four battalions of the Second Army Division that had been withdrawn from the Nieuport bridgehead when the French had arrived. After the meeting Grossetti dictated his orders for the coming attack and had them immediately distributed to his units.

Chapter X

The Railway Embankment

In the morning of Saturday 24 October the overall situation looked grim. Despite the fact that they had been bombarded the whole night by French and Belgian artillery, all the infantry of the German Sixth Division had crossed into the Tervaete Loop. Due to the relentless Franco-Belgian shelling however, no German guns had been ferried across.

In anticipation of the arrival of the French 42nd Division the Belgians tried to put back some order in the arrangement of their units facing the attackers in the bend. But gradually the dislodged troops had to retreat. The First Army Division, on the north side, fell back on the winding Great Beaverdyke Vaart, the main drainage canal in the polder. The Fourth Army Division had to let go of the Yser embankment south of Tervaete, in the process losing the hamlet of Stuyvekenskerke.

At General Headquarters all the staff officers were pessimistic about the final outcome of this breach in the front line. It seemed time to prepare an alternative line of defence. In this respect a telephone message was sent out to both cavalry divisions at 08:20. The First Cavalry Division, billeted in the village of Alveringhem was ordered to reconnoitre possible bridgeheads on the Loo Canal near the localities of Oeren and Steenkerke (see map p.171). The Second Cavalry, stationed at Hoogstaede, was to do the same with bridgeheads at Loo and Forthem. These investigations were aimed at preparing the potential crossing points by building field works so they could be manned at first notice by a couple of cavalry squadrons.

Two hours later First Cavalry Headquarters received further instructions. Its company of *pionniers-pontonniers cyclistes* had to move to Forthem in order to double the crossing capacity by throwing a second bridge across the canal at this point. It also had to build the necessary access roads and infantry footbridges. An engineers company of the Sixth Army Division would reinforce the *pontoneers*.

At 15:00 the report of the cavalry scouting mission arrived in Furnes. It showed the *pontoneers* had put in a hard day's work. The Loo Bridge was ready but no bridge-head had been prepared since the hamlet was straddling the approach route to the bridge on the east side. At Forthem a bridgehead, large enough to accommodate a battalion, had been organized around the existing bridge, a pontoon bridge and a foot-bridge. At Oeren Bridge the *pontoneers* had built two bridges and established a bridgehead while at Steenkerke the defence of the crossing had been prepared with earthworks.

Despite the unyielding shelling of Dixmude by the enemy, Belgian forward observers noticed that the main danger lay more to the north, between km 14 and 14.5 where the

Germans were crossing the river in large numbers. Apparently they were fortifying Den Toren Farm, 200m from the river levee and 900m due east of Old Stuyvekenskerke.

Since Admiral Ronarc'h's left flank in Dixmude now became extremely exposed, he sent one of his battalions north to reinforce the defence of Old Stuyvekenskerke. But by the time the fusiliers made their approach at 13:00 the hamlet was just falling into German hands. Helpless, the marines could only stop at Rode Poort Farm, a kilometre south of the hamlet.

By now the troops of the French 42nd had arrived from the Nieuport bridgehead, passed west of Pervyse and turned east to hold the village on their left. In the early morning Grossetti, still accompanied by Nuyten had set up his headquarters at a farm a few hundred metres south of Pervyse, on the road to Oostkerke. Shortly after dawn Colonel Tom Bridges, the British liaison officer, joined both men at their field headquarters. While the French troops were digging in more to the east the German artillery was, for some inexplicable reason concentrating its fire on the village of Pervyse itself.

Following the troops the three men hiked through the soaked fields towards the railway line running east of Pervyse. This single railway track on a low embankment ran straight from Dixmude to Nieuport. On top the officers would have a good overview of the battlefield.

In time Grossetti, sitting on his legendary camp chair, Nuyten and Bridges watched the French marines moving slowly away through the open fields towards the Vicogne Farm and the enemy.

Closer to Nieuport, in front of St Georges the situation for the 14th de Ligne Regiment became untenable. Being exposed to heavy frontal German shelling and having lost touch with the First Army Division on its right it too had to fall back on the Great Beaverdyke Vaart.

The same day, 100 kilometres south of Dunkirk in Doullens, officers and soldiers of the staff were packing up General Foch's headquarters to move it north to Cassel, a town 16km north-east of St Omer. Here Foch would be halfway between Sir John French's HQ and that of his own immediate subordinate, General d'Urbal.

Leaving all the tribulations of this packing to his staff, Foch left and shortly after lunch arrived in Furnes to investigate the seriousness of the situation for himself. He had already met with d'Urbal in Rousbrugge and had then continued to Dunkirk. There he had encountered Baron de Broqueville who had taken the opportunity to accompany Foch to Furnes. After a meeting with Grossetti at the French Mission he proceeded to Belgian General Headquarters where de Broqueville, Colonel Wielemans and General Hanoteau awaited him.

Since General Harry Jungbluth had left for Le Havre to join the government in exile, Élie Hanoteau was the highest-ranking officer in the Military Cabinet of the king. In this role he was the face that had to defend the Royal Grand Strategy in front of the French and British war leaders. After the war Hanoteau reflected upon his role to his brother-in-arms and historian, Professor Henri Bernard:

Every time there was an unpleasant message to be delivered to our allies, for example in October 1914 to tell them that we were tired out, . . . Wielemans, very diplomatic and Galet, eager to stay in the shadow, always asked me to take the lead under the pretext that a lieutenant general would have more weight than they would. So, innocent as I was, I did . . .

143

After the customary formalities Hanoteau was quick to take over from the always-conciliatory Wielemans, developing the ideas put down by the king the previous evening. Foch was flabbergasted. Did these people not understand what the term résistance *à tout prix* meant? Colonel Maxime Weygand, Foch's Chief of Staff and witness to the encounter, later described the 'unforgettable terms' Foch used:

> All you talk about is the past. What is important now is the present. – Concerning reinforcements, I am not the master over it. – You held out for eight days; you will still hold for another eight days.

With his by now well-known gestures the French general underlined his phrases: 'One needs energy, and more energy. One does not talk about retreat when it comes to the very existence of his country . . .'

When he got over his rhetoric outburst Foch's pragmatic side re-surfaced. Now that the winding Yser River had been lost as a front line he was willing to fall back on an alternate defence. Consulting his ordnance map Foch pointed to a railway line running straight from Dixmude to Nieuport, some one to two kilometres west of the river. Would this straightforward line on the ground be worthwhile to be considered? Of course he had never seen the railway so he did not know but he thought it would be worth contemplating.

After all his pomposity — and presumably eager to get to his new headquarters — Foch prepared to leave without meeting with His Royal Highness, thereby flouting protocol. But the Belgian Commander-in-Chief was upstairs and having been informed, expressed the wish to meet the French general. Subsequently both men had a short and apparently rather formal conversation. Upon the remark by Foch that the Belgians should not think that they were the only ones suffering severely in this immense conflagration the king responded politely: 'You are right.'

After taking leave Foch and his officers descended the hard stone spiral staircase. At the bottom Foch turned around and said to his interpreter, Lieutenant André Tardieu:

> Someone, who is not a part of our [official military] Mission, has to stay here. Missions are only a reflection of the high commands with which they work. You will stay. You will take care of two things: organize the installation of the Territorials and see how the floods are 'set', as the engineers use to say.

Historians have sometimes taken this last sentence, later quoted by André Tardieu, out of context. For these – often French – authors, it proved that General Foch was the man behind the idea of the Belgian floods along the Yser. We hope by our exposé to have brought Foch's so-called 'intervention' into perspective.

First Foch referred to the French Territorial Division he was sending to the Belgian front. Then of course he talked about the French flood he had ordered the Governor of Dunkirk to set that same day. To prevent the flood from spreading over Belgian territory the French engineers had to block several border-crossing waterways. Obviously his junior staff officer was to supervise these French manoeuvres from the Belgian side of the border. Besides, back in Cassel, Foch cabled Joffre: 'I have ordered, this evening, that the floods on the eastern front of Dunkirk should be set. The remainder will follow, if necessary.'

144

Back on the Market Square, when Colonel Wielemans had closed the door to Foch he turned to Tardieu and said in an admiring and tactful tone: 'The determination of your General is an extraordinary thing . . . really extraordinary!' . . .

It was also on this occasion that Colonel Bridges had his first encounter with Foch. He described the General perhaps quite accurately:

> At first sight a horsey-looking little man chewing a cigar which he constantly tried to light, and with a little stick that he always carried. He was a model of simplicity, directness and apt criticism, helped out by expressive and frequent gesture. One soon began to feel that fiery spirit within, which would never allow that France could possibly be beaten . . .

The Field Marshal of the BEF meanwhile was quite worried about the strategic dangers emanating from this divided command in Flanders. This was indeed the central issue of the French, the British and even the Belgians. Although everyone was fighting a common enemy, three independent high commands – each with their own agenda – were now converging on Dunkirk.

The divided command held the biggest risks, especially for the British. The BEF was the only force that was not fighting on its own soil and it had had the explicit orders not to endanger its existence. With the move from Soissons on the Aisne River to the north the BEF had indeed dramatically shortened its supply lines on the continent but

The British Royal Engineers were always very interested in the Belgian inundations. Here is a high-level visit: in the foreground to the left Lord Athlone, brother of Queen Mary, in the middle (with white scarf) Colonel Tom Bridges, to the right Lieutenant Colonel A.C. Macdonald. Notice also the large, upright osier mats to the left and right used as a screen against enemy observation. During the Second World War Lord Athlone would be Governor General of Canada. *Nieuport 1914-1918, R. Thys, 1922.*

145

the ultimate goal, getting back on the extreme left flank of the Western Front, had still eluded its commander, Sir John French.

Perhaps it was still acceptable that the Belgians were now holding this enviable position – was it not for them that the BEF had been sent to the continent? But French divisions, now sent anew to be inserted in the north, thwarted the British plans. The tactical situation in Flanders remained precarious and the field marshal still took into account an eventual retreat towards the Channel ports. With the king of the Belgians he could, quite possibly, reach an agreement but the French troops in the coastal region could literally cut off such a move.

Sir John French had indeed reason to be worried. Not surprisingly then that a few hours after Foch's visit to St Omer, he himself went to see General d'Urbal of the DAB in Rousbrugge to enquire about French intentions.

In the dunes north-east of the Yser Mouth the French 42nd Division was making progress, albeit not at a fast pace. Some units had reached the outskirts of Westende and in the morning started an additional line of advance in the polder along the Bruges Canal towards Bamburgh Farm.

Admiral Hood was also back, off the coast with his vessels. Two old cruisers and a variety of smaller vessels now supplemented his two monitors. He had sent the monitor *Severn* home for repairs, but besides the gunboat *Bustard* now had *Brilliant* and *Sirius* at his disposal together with two sloops, eight British and five French destroyers. They bombarded the targets indicated until about 15:00 when word came to cease fire as units of the 42nd, having occupied Bamburgh Farm, were about to push into Westende.

As the French were seemingly making good progress along the coast it was decided in London to wait a day or two before wrecking the quays and docks in Ostend. Nevertheless, orders went out for Hood to steam up to the city and shell the railway station and deal with any naval activity in the harbour itself. But by the time the message reached Hood the weather had turned bad so the instructions could not be carried out.

From the railway levee east of Pervyse, Grossetti and Nuyten followed the French advance towards the river. Grossetti, also a reliable disciple of *l'offensive*, had confidence in his troops: they would swiftly deal with the Germans and throw them back across the Yser. But Nuyten, used to the reality of constant retreat, could not share his

The author crouched down behind the railway embankment near Pervyse. A recumbent infantryman would indeed have some relative cover while still enjoying a decent field of fire. Closer to Nieuport the levee was even higher, providing better cover. As such soldiers would soon build numerous improvised shelters along it.
Author's photo archive.

optimism. Instead he tried to plan a secure alternative line of defence.

In fact, as the day progressed, it dawned on him that the railway embankment itself, slightly elevated above the empty plain, could serve as a new line of defence. Here, near Pervyse, the levee gave enough protection to a kneeling rifleman while still allowing an adequate field of fire without too much dead depression. It was not much of an entrenchment but it could serve as an alternate line of resistance until, with reinforcements, something better could be established.

While studying the ordnance map another advantage caught his eye. Along the winding Yser front from Nieuport to Dixmude the infantry had been exposed to flanking fire in many locations. With a repositioning as he now saw it, the 17km long exposed riverfront would be cut down to a straight 12km defence line, at right angles to the enemy advance. With continuous loss of manpower and equipment, such a reduction would be quite welcome.

By day's end Grossetti's predictions had not materialized. The French infantry, pinned down by the German machine guns had suffered heavy casualties. As a result they too had to fall back on the soggy and shallow Belgian rifle pits, hastily dug along the Great Beaverdyke Vaart.

Most of the French rank and file were not that impressed with the offensive spirit of

The gates alongside the Ypres Lock see from upstream, just before the war. To the left, behind the median wall, is the lock chamber. To the right, in the background, one can see the gantry of the lift gates. These waterways were excellent fishing grounds.
City archive Nieuwpoort

their superiors. As a more down-to-earth Commandant Delage of the Marines wrote in his *carnet de campagne* after a rigorous inspection by Grossetti in Dixmude:

> Seen General Grossetti. Ideas about the Belgian Army and the mission of the French Army. The offensive.

At the guard detachment in Nieuport in the late afternoon, Second Lieutenant François received the following order from Captain Commandant Borlon:

> Will you please immediately open the lock doors of the canalized Yser in order to provoke a violent current in the river and as such get the result Major Le Clément requested yesterday.
>
> You will let me know if you have been able to carry out this order. That is to say, if the tide is at a sufficiently different level than that of the Yser to incite the desirable current.
>
> You will send me immediately by messenger complete information on the situation.
>
> Major Le Clément being ill, I replace him as commander of the battalion. October 24, 1914.
>
> P.S. If the tide permits you to get a noticeable result the order has to be carried out whatever the danger. The situation of our entire army can depend on it. The lift gates and lock doors must be opened to obtain a maximum flow. You will warn the lieutenants Rotsaert and Anciaux by messenger.

Shortly afterwards François did get some additional information:

> I think it would be best to drain the Yser during two (possibly three) consecutive ebb tides in order to obtain a sufficiently low water level.
>
> One can then raise the level during three or four high tides. Evidently, when you lower the water level, you will have to close the doors at rising tide and vice versa when you want to raise the level. You will please study attentively the question of how many ebb tides you will need in order to achieve a sufficiently important lowering so that the first flood that we will use to raise the water level will create an important upstream tidal wave.
>
> Password: Liège 24-25. 17:00, October 24, 1914.

By 21:00 François and his men [1] were at the Ypres Lock and started to prepare for the upcoming manoeuvre.

No further details of the draining and subsequent accelerated flooding of the riverbed as executed on 24 October have been found. We have nevertheless found a description of a similar action taken at the same lock the following month. It is this written account that we have used to make a reconstruction of the events of 24 October. The Ypres Lock – unlike the Spring Sluice – was never designed to be used as an inundation lock. Therefore such a manoeuvre did entail great hydraulic risks and was something every lockkeeper would strongly condemn – not to mention Gerard Dingens!

Since the three navigation locks in 'The Goose Foot' complex end up in the tidal Yser Channel, they all have ebb- and flood doors. So with the flood doors closed during rising

Geeraert, dressed in military uniform and wearing his medals. He certainly must have felt very uncomfortable at that moment! *Historical prints collection Callenaere-Dehouck.*

tide François and his men opened and locked the ebb doors in their recesses. Then with strong ropes they rigged the flood doors in such a way that they would not automatically open once the receding tide was lower than the canal water level. As a result, by the time low tide arrived, around 22:15, the flood doors were under some 70cm of 'reverse' water pressure from the canal side. A situation the heavy wooden doors were never designed to undergo.

Then came the critical moment: the five double lift doors beside the lock chamber were raised simultaneously and the ropes holding the two double flood doors were cut with axes. A dangerous manoeuvre indeed: the sudden release of tension on the severed ropes could easily have cut off someone's feet. Brutally the heavy doors opened and the canal water began to rush seaward like a violent mountain river. This was not the time for anyone to fall in.

As Captain Commandant Borlon had asked, we suspect that this procedure was repeated a few times during the ensuing tidal cycles. Unfortunately there is no account left of the practical results of these hazardous manoeuvres. A month later in December, it seems several enemy footbridges and even larger pontoon bridges were carried off by the sucking action and ended up entangled in the gate structure or, for the ones that had passed through the lock chamber, in the downstream channel. We also do not know if the water level in the river was raised as abruptly as Captain Commandant Borlon had requested.

Perhaps the reader can imagine what could have gone wrong with such a reckless procedure:

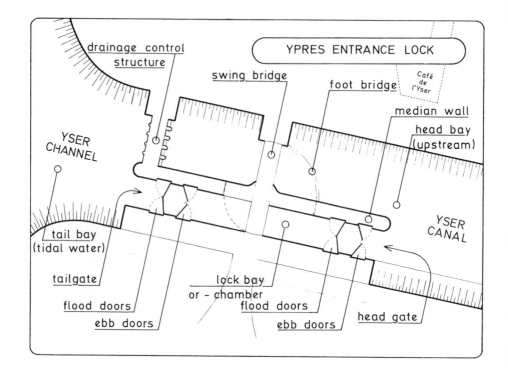

1. The flood doors, under enormous reverse pressure, could have separated from their hinges, opening up the river to tidal oscillations that would have weakened the levees and eventually would have flooded thousands of hectares of polder.
2. The cables under traction and/or the impromptu tie-downs could have snapped prematurely thereby making a second attempt impossible.
3. The unusual water pressure on the brick and hard stone structure could have forced the water to try to find an alternate route, for instance under the foundation floor, thereby making the structure unstable and perhaps blocking the free movement of doors.
4. All these strange goings-on around the lock finally could have alerted German observers, which would have resulted in a devastating bombardment.

It was indeed a last-ditch attempt by the Belgians to stop the enemy steamroller.

After his day at General Grossetti's side in Pervyse, Captain Commandant Prudent Nuyten returned to General Headquarters in Furnes. With the French not having surpassed the Belgians in the Tervaete Loop and having seen the situation firsthand Nuyten had only this advice for his superiors: 'If tomorrow, twenty-fifth, all commanding officers and all staff officers do not get on the battlefield to help, by their example and their energy, to keep the troops in place we can expect the worst.'

Later that night, at General Headquarters Report, a verbal order was given in this sense to all representatives of the major units. Nuyten's firm attitude later earned him the nickname *gendarme du Grand Quartier Général*. As Nuyten himself later wrote:

. . . given by one of these gentlemen, no doubt still ignorant about the essential importance of supervising on the spot, the execution of orders given in critical circumstances.

Simultaneously, in the Army Orders for the next day, issued at 20:00 was written:

The positions held [to the east of the railway from Nieuport to Dixmude] will be held as much as possible. One will hold, in any case and at any price, *on the line of the railway Nieuport-Dixmude.* [Our italics]

Earlier in the day Foch had suggested as an alternative, and in fact purely based on a line drawn on a map, to hold on to this little-known railway. It so happened that during the day Captain Commandant Nuyten had come up with a similar view but his personal knowledge of the terrain and his firsthand experience that day obviously led High Command to accept this proposal.

In the morning, and despite fierce opposition, the Germans had captured the village of St Georges, 2km east of Nieuport. Since the Belgian 14th de Ligne Regiment had suffered heavy casualties in the fighting, their commander ordered a retreat south-west, across the Great Beaverdyke Vaart. In the late afternoon the 6th de Ligne got the order to recapture the village. Lieutenant Marcel Corvilain recalls:

In the early evening two recce platoons (2nd Company/2nd Battalion/6th de Ligne) are sent to St Georges: one along the main road and one along the Yser levee. They are spotted by the enemy at the intersection (km 34) and have to retreat under heavy German rifle fire. After the reconnaissance the different platoons are sent forward for the attack. Again they are spotted but now they dig in.

The captain tells me that our artillery will bombard the western edge of the village and that afterwards we will advance. 'If we can still do that at least', I reply pessimistically. Bang! There goes the signal. Bang! Bang! Bang! In front of us St Georges is torn to pieces. Hendiau, with his platoon on the left side of the road gets angry and everyone starts to shoot. The captain and I have our soldiers dig in on the right side of the road.

Bullets whistle over our heads and the reinforcements that arrive dig in. When the artillery barrage stops we send patrols forward. But the Germans keep firing. At least twenty times we try to advance through the maze of smoke but twenty times we have to retreat under the hail of bullets fired at us. Then a message arrives that tells us that to our right troops are advancing along the North Vaart. When we get shot at our backs, we regroup. At 20:00h we get the order to return to the intersection with the road to Ramscappelle under cover of the 3rd and 4th battalions. At 23:00h the assault is cancelled.

With the capture of St Georges the Germans had gained a second strong foothold on the left bank. The village could now only be approached via the Bruges Road or the Yser levee. But every move on the levee could be seen for miles and a few well-positioned sharpshooters could defend the almost straight Bruges Road. Only an infantry attack behind an advancing artillery barrage could possibly dislodge the enemy from the village. But that was something the Belgian gunners could not deliver anymore.

On the Belgian right too, soon after nightfall, the Germans attacked the bridgehead of Dixmude. Four Belgian battalions and four Marine Fusiliers companies were entrenched at the town perimeter while the remainder of the French Marines held the trenches on the west bank of the river. Between Oostkerke and Caeskerke the Belgians kept two battalions of the 11th and three of the 2nd *Chasseurs à pied* in reserve.

That night the German 43rd Reserve Division of the 22nd Reserve Corps made twenty-six charges against the 12th de Ligne Regiment and one battalion of the 11th de Ligne. Several times the attackers reached the parapet of the trench, turning the fight into a man-to-man struggle with bayonet and rifle butt. Miraculously each time the assault could be repelled. Although three of the Belgian battalions involved had been in the trenches for over sixty-seven consecutive hours, they would only be relieved, totally worn out, two days later.

To reinforce the southern flank, Belgian High Command at 22:45 ordered the horse-drawn artillery to be at the disposal of the Fifth Army Division next morning in Oostkerke and the battalion of cyclists to prepare an alternate position for the Marine Fusiliers in the rear near Caeskerke.

Apparently on his journey back to Cassel, General Foch had taken the time to evaluate the overall situation in the north since during the night some good news arrived at Belgian General Headquarters. Foch informed the Belgians that the DAB would be reinforced, within four days, with two Senegalese battalions, sixteen cavalry regiments and two divisions.

Eventually though these French reinforcements were not all to go towards the Belgian Nieuport–Dixmude front. The Senegalese for instance were transported by car to Ypres and the cavalry regiments were being detrained in Hazebrouck. The 31st Infantry Division was also on its way to Ypres. To relieve the pressure on the Belgian front Foch had suggested to d'Urbal attacking north from Ypres in the direction of Dixmude.

To halt the Germans in the north Foch obviously only counted on his Dunkirk Fortified Place, his marines in Dixmude and the Anglo-French forces concentrated around Ypres.

NOTE

1. We assume that it was the same team that worked the Spring Sluice three days earlier. Since Henry Geeraert had stayed with the detachment we suspect he was also one of them.

Chapter XI

Nieuport, a Nautical Knot

Allow us return for a while to the joys of water management in the Yser River basin. Earlier we briefly recounted the workings of the drainage system on the right bank of the river, including the narrow strip of land squeezed between the Bruges Road and the straight stretch of canalized river. As the reader will remember, originally the latter had been part of the Old Yser – renamed Nieuwendamme Creek – drainage area. South of the road/dyke known as Bruges Road lay a much larger polder with a more intricate waterway system.

For a better understanding of the next pages we should first of all emphasize that the whole region has two separate, superimposed waterway grids. The higher one is the navigation layer while below are ditches and vaarts that constitute the actual drainage basin. Over time the navigation canals per se have been embanked and their water level has been raised vis-à-vis the vaart water level.

Inland shipping along the Flanders coast connects Bruges and Ostend with Dunkirk and Ypres via Nieuport and Furnes. In both the latter several canals link up. As mentioned earlier, from the north-east comes the Bruges Canal to Nieuport. Its water level, being fed by the Scheldt river in Ghent, is independent of the other local canals. South of it is the canalized Yser with a water level of +3.25m. [1] This level can be rather unsteady since a few days of heavy rain in the catchment area can quickly overwhelm the discharge capacity of the five sluice gates adjacent the Ypres Lock at the Goose Foot.

At a site called Fintele, 31km upstream of the river, the Loo Canal branches off to the north. This canal can take any excess surface water from upstream Fintele and divert it towards Furnes. Here the Loo Canal turns north-east, changes its name to the Furnes Canal, ending in Nieuport at the Yser Mouth through the Furnes Lock. This lock has been built as a mirror view of the Ypres Lock except that it has only four sluice gates. In Furnes itself a navigation lock branches off the above canals giving access westward to Dunkirk via the Dunkirk Canal.

Since it played a role in the French floods around Dunkirk we finally mention the smaller and winding Bergen Vaart that comes from France and ends in the Dunkirk Canal near Furnes. The French used this canal, called Colme Canal in France, to flood the eastern side of the Dunkirk perimeter, along the border with Belgium. At the border crossing a small lock separated the French canal section from the Belgian side. So initially these French flooding manoeuvres did not influence the Belgian polders. But, as we will soon see, Captain Commandant Nuyten thought otherwise.

In fact these canals are part of a 200 kilometre long inter-coastal waterway connecting Calais in the west to Antwerp in the north-east. It was only in Nieuport that barges still had to transit through the tidal tail bay in order continue their journey inland. This unusual procedure at the Goose Foot was inevitable because of the need to evacuate the large amount of surface water from the different underlying drainage vaarts ending in Nieuport [2].

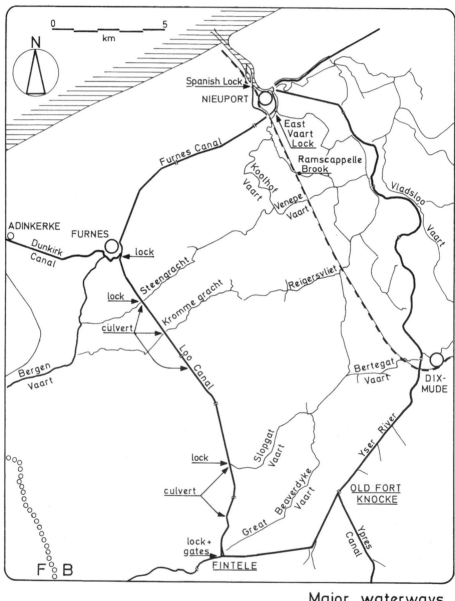

Major waterways

The responsibility for the maintenance of the drainage in the Furnes-Ambacht was entrusted to the Furnes North Watering[3]. Today this work is still accomplished through an elaborate network of ditches, brooks and vaarts. The western part of the water drains through the Steengracht (Stone Brook) into the Koolhof Vaart. The southern part, including the eastern polders between the winding river and the railway embankment, drain into the Great Beaverdyke Vaart. There is almost no gradient and on top of it

The lock on the Bergen Vaart near Houthem at the French border. In October 1914 this lock prevented the French inundation water from flooding the Belgian Army's encampments behind the railway embankment.
Nieuport 1914-1918, R. Thys, 1922.

In front left, the Koolhof Viaduct under the railway and, in the back, the Koolhof Weir, at the beginning of the war. Seawater, coming from the front right was held back by the closed and heightened weir and thus pushed underneath the railway viaduct.
Nieuport 1914-1918, R. Thys, 1922.

The weir on the Great Beaverdyke Vaart was heightened during the war, not only to contain the inundation (right), but also to act as a back up in case the German artillery destroyed the North Vaart Gates and the tidal water invaded the polder. In the background Nieuport. In the foreground left Lord Athlone, colonel Macdonald and Tom Bridges. On the right the typical brick shed where, in peacetime, the stop planks would be stored.
Nieuport 1914-1918 R. Thys, 1922.

both vaarts are interconnected. Both the Koolhof and the Great Beaverdyke end up in the North Vaart at 1,000 metres from a set of eight lifting gates with the same name at the Goose Foot complex.

Importantly, just upstream of their confluence with the North Vaart both vaarts had an identical weir in 1914 (see map p.188). Each weir consisted of three gates provided with a double set of grooves to allow the lowering of stop planks. These weirs allowed the Water staff to adjust the water level in the polder independent from the operations at the gate structures in Nieuport. For the vigorous growth of grass, sugar beet and other agricultural commodities the water level in the polder was kept at +2.20m in summertime. In winter, with the cold and wet maritime climate, the level was lowered to +1.90m. In practice this meant that in summer, in most spots, the water in the vaarts and ditches was barely a foot or so below soil level.

It is interesting to note that the seasonal lowering of the water level normally occurred mid-October but, due to the chaotic situation, this manoeuvre had not taken place in the autumn of 1914 when the Germans crossed the Yser. This not only hampered the movements of the adversaries in the water-soaked clay soil but it would ultimately have unexpected repercussions on the flood attempt.

As an alternative and in case of emergency the surface water could also be drained through the West Vaart. This disused canal ran around the west side of Nieuport and ended in the Yser Channel through the Spanish Lock. The vaart connected to the North Water via an old culvert under the Furnes Canal. To allow for navigation by small barges in the polder itself the vaarts and brooks were accessible from the canal system through three narrow locks. Two of them were situated along the Loo Canal, one giving access to the Slopgat Vaart in the south, the second more north on the Steengracht. The third lock, identical to the other two, was located just outside Nieuport and south-east,

The weir on the Great Beaverdyke Vaart, this time seen from the North Vaart (opposite from the previous view). The diamond shaped designs on the shed were ventilation openings to allow the (wet) stop planks to dry. From 1915 on Belgian soldiers were issued steel 'Adrian' helmets as seen on the right.
Nieuport 1914-1918, R. Thys, 1922.

in the levee separating the North Vaart from the Furnes Canal, almost in front of the mouth of the Great Beaverdyke Vaart. This lock was called the East Vaart Lock.

To sum up one can see the Yser river and Loo and Furnes canals as a belt canal around the polder of the Furnes North Water. Since the smaller vaarts in the polder could also be used for local navigation three narrow locks connected the lower polder with the higher canal water level.

Amazingly enough in 1914 everyone in the region seemed to have forgotten – or perhaps did not want to think about it – that these three small locks could not only be used to transfer barges but also to inundate the polder. In any case, although everyone knew the polder could be inundated, no local informed the military that this could be achieved by opening these three locks. It took an engineer officer on a reconnaissance mission to discover this possibility. But to a large extent the tide had already turned by then.

In spite of the enduring artillery duels, Sunday 25 October started off rather quiet along the front line although the same could not be said about the rear. In the morning Colonel Brécard called on Belgian General Headquarters and announced to the chief of operations, Major Maglinse that the Military Governor of Dunkirk was preparing to flood the perimeter of his fortified place. The Governor was taking this action upon orders from General Foch and the Governor warned that, '. . . these floods could spread onto Belgian territory and extend on a scale we are unable to determine'.

This flood with inland water had been planned for some days, as the drainage of the countryside through Dunkirk had been halted and the canals had been brought up to their maximum water level. Major Maglinse and Captain Commandant Nuyten, who happened to be present, were flabbergasted. Nuyten spontaneously retorted: 'So, under those conditions we will have the enemy in front of us and water in our rear!'

It did not take long for Maglinse and Nuyten to grasp the seriousness of this unexpected development. It called for prompt action. Maglinse immediately ordered Nuyten to collect all available information on the drainage system of the region in order to avoid a disaster on the Belgian side of the border. By then it was around 10:00 on Sunday morning and Nuyten decided to go into the town and try to find someone with technical know-how on the Furnes North Water. Besides, Nuyten was the right man for the job: not only was he was born and raised in nearby Ypres, so he spoke the local Flemish dialect, he was also billeted with his brother-in-law, local attorney Auguste Lesaffre.

While leaving the town hall, Nuyten bumped into the acting mayor of Furnes, Mr Despot and asked him if he knew the name of some engineer from the local waterworks or the Roads & Bridges Department who could advise him about the workings of the drainage system of the polders. Mr Despot said that unfortunately, due to the hostilities, all these men had left town. Asked if there was no other person in town who would be able to provide information on this issue, the mayor named Charles Cogge, a fifty-nine year old supervisor of the Furnes North Water authority. He lived on the north side of town so Nuyten had sent for him by one of the messengers at the town hall, Désiré 'Dies' Vandamme, who found that he was not home. Being a Sunday, he had gone to high mass, and as usual, would only return home after having had a beer in the nearby tavern Petit-Paris. Accustom to this ritual, his wife Marie 'Mietje' Libbrecht, went over to the bar and had her husband called outside. When Charles showed up at the door she told him that a messenger from the town hall was waiting for him at home. Back at the house Dies told him that General Headquarters wanted him. Cogge, being a conscientious employee accompanied Dies into town. On their way there they halted at the house of water engineer Degraer, for he was supposed to come too, but he was out.

Neither was he at the café Français where they dropped in next. So they both continued their walk and arrived at the town hall around 11:30.

Here Nuyten took Charles Cogge to a quiet corner of the building and, talking in their native dialect, both were quickly at ease with each other. The staff officer started by asking several technical questions about the water management of

'Official' portrait of Charles Cogge, supervisor of the Furnes North Watering (NWV). Furnes would not forget its famous citizen. Behind the Market Square, in the North Street, his bust still stands. *Kunstmatige Inundaties in Maritiem Vlaanderen 1316-1945, J.Leper, 1957.*

the large polder adjacent the French border. This 35 square kilometre polder, called Les Moëres in French, De Moeren [4] in Flemish, straddled the border with France. Almost half of the polder was on the Belgian side but was not separated by a dyke from the French part. Already in 1870, during the Franco-Prussian war, the Military Governor of Dunkirk had intended to inundate this tract of land but after the Prussian entry into Amiens they had turned back whereupon the governor had shelved his plans.

When Nuyten showed Cogge the ordnance map at a 1:40,000 scale of the area, Charles had to admit that he could not read such a complicated map. Instead he proposed to go home and return in the afternoon with his own copy of a dedicated water map. Nuyten agreed.

There exist several handwritten declarations, indeed signed by Charles Cogge but not all written by him, detailing the events described in the following pages. Unfortunately these 'testimonies', written by different people and quite spaced in time, are not all in accordance with each other. Sometimes the author of the document in question seems to mix up persons, places and/or events. In analysing these documents we got the strong impression that each writer, probably unwittingly wrote down the chain of events as he saw it, thereby getting the nodding approval of an innocent Charles. Fortunately, in

The only known, summary account, *written by Cogge himself* about his exploits in the company of the engineer officers in October 1914. This picture was taken from a copy since unfortunately the whereabouts of the original are still unknown. *Nieuport 1914-1918*, R. Thys, 1922.

159

combining these stories with the account of Nuyten and other witnesses, it was possible to paint a quite accurate picture of the crucial events that unfolded in the next few days.

Around 14:00, while an ugly autumn storm poured shower after shower on the battlefield, Nuyten and Charles Cogge crouched over a water chart in the corridor of the Furnes town hall. In the process Charles Cogge explained to the captain commandant all he wanted to know about the looming threat of the impending French floods around Dunkirk. Nuyten, in the meantime, had not forgotten the newly assigned front line of his own army. Although the railway embankment would be easier to defend against infantry attack than the winding river bank, it had one major drawback: if the German heavy artillery could get close enough, this well marked, straight line on the ground would make an easy target for the enemy gunners. With what remained of the Belgian infantry concentrated and lined up behind it, these exhausted men would be wiped out in no time. So to prevent the enemy from moving in its dreadful artillery Nuyten reasoned that the terrain in front of the railway should be made impassable to heavy equipment. The abundant rains provided the perfect conditions to prevent the Germans from bringing their guns forward across the river. But once the sky cleared it would only be a matter of days before the soil dried out and the enemy started moving again. Then the battle weary Belgians would be forced out of their country. A disaster was indeed looming.

Keeping the land wet was the solution. And there was in fact enough surface water available – in Dunkirk! If the Belgians could somehow divert the water stored by the French in the canals around Dunkirk and push it towards the front in Belgium, this plan could be the saviour of the army and the country.

From Cogge's explanation Nuyten deduced that the French were using the small, winding canal between the towns of Bergues and Furnes, the Bergen Vaart, as a carrier for the floodwater. Since the Bergen Vaart was fed with freshwater [5] from the Aa river coming from St Omer, Nuyten asked Cogge:

> Would it not be possible to inundate the polder between the railway and the Yser by using the freshwater from the Bergen Vaart in France and channel it through the Steengracht and the Krommegracht [Crooked Brook] eastward?

Nuyten and Cogge did not immediately discuss plans to inundate the land between the Yser and the railway. More likely Nuyten at first looked at ways to saturate the soil in the entire region between the river and the Loo Canal. This was a much larger area and would require the Belgians to retreat further west. But it would also increase the distance between them and the enemy's heavy guns. By just saturating the soil and not inundating it the negative effects on the land could possibly be lessened further.

Cogge had to disappoint Nuyten. He explained that the Bergen Vaart was partitioned in two canal sections by a lock at the village of Houthem, near the French border. The French reach of the canal being some 45cm lower than the Belgian section, it would be impossible to draw water towards Nieuport.

The normal level of the Bergen Vaart in France was +1.93m, in Belgium +2.37m. In this respect Charles Cogge was right. But we suspect that, in view of the impending flood Dunkirk had already raised the level in France to +2.90m as it had done in 1814, which was actually 53cm above Belgian level. So, theoretically, water could have been transferred from France to Belgium. But due to the extraordinary circumstances Cogge

160

In November 2000 Flemish television network VRT aired a documentary on the subject of this book. In it several key scenes were re-enacted. Here, in between two shootings Jef Laleeuwe as Cogge (left) and Geert Aneca as Nuyten, take a welcome break.
Author's photo archive.

was obviously not aware of this situation. Besides as he said, even if they could push water east, the discharge through these brooks was so small that it would take eight to ten days to get a reasonable result. Furthermore, there was a more important drawback. Because there was almost no measurable drop in ground level one would first inundate the whole region south of Furnes before the water would reach Nieuport.

Since fresh water from France could not be used for his plans Nuyten then asked if the locks in Nieuport could be used instead. Cogge replied that this too was impossible because the locks did not give immediate access to the polder, but that the North Vaart Gates could be used to flood the polder. After checking its location on the map Nuyten was again disappointed. These drainage gates were situated within the Goose Foot complex north-east of the city. That area was now under constant observation by the enemy and hence quite prone to enemy bombardment.

It is rather interesting to include two notes here.

First of all, Cogge was not entirely correct when he said that the locks in Nieuport did not give access to the polder in question. As we mentioned earlier the small East Vaart Lock, and its identical twins on the Loo Canal, provided immediate access from the Furnes Canal and hence the Furnes Lock at the Goose Foot, to the polder. This detail would have been quite useful to the military for in order to create a flood they preferred the use of a navigation lock to lift gates.

With a gate structure the doors have to be raised and lowered at each turn of the tide, which means that at four precise moments of the day soldiers need to work the lift mechanisms. The swing doors in a lock on the other hand can be unhooked from their

161

The small, charming East Vaart Lock connecting the Furnes Canal and the North Vaart (seen from the latter). The only, well preserved inundation lock in the region . . . perhaps in the whole of Flanders. But for how long?
Author's photo archive.

windlasses and once free these doors will then automatically open at rising tide and close again when the water recedes. As such this procedure is very simple and does not involve any further human intervention. From an army point of view it is the perfect way to conceal your intentions from the enemy.

Charles Cogge can be forgiven for this oversight since, although he was an experienced man, he had had no dealings with the locks and navigation on the canals.

It could be said that this missed opportunity deprived the military of an early start and an efficient way to flood the polder. But at that early stage in the battle this would eventually have forewarned the enemy who would have changed their battle plans accordingly and with devastating results.

The German steamroller was still in full swing and the Anglo-French front line between Dixmude and further south was not at full strength yet. So if an 'early' flood had been set, the Germans would certainly have shifted their main attack more inland, concentrating all their power south of Dixmude and thereby forcing a breakthrough north of Ypres. The Belgians would then have been taken in the flank and pushed into the sea.

Secondly, various authors have maintained that the Germans were too close to the lock system. This is indeed a misinterpretation of Captain Commandant Nuyten's words. Only the next day the French would evacuate the bridgehead and the danger of the Germans occupying the locks would become real. The main drawback as Nuyten saw it was that, as described above, by using the lift gates the gate runners would have to raise and lower the heavy paddles several times a day. For a structure with eight double doors, this meant sixty-four individual cranking operations a day. Not only did this require a lot of manpower but also the raising and lowering of the sixteen steel racks on which the doors were hung could be seen from afar. Such a rhythmic activity at an exposed location near the front line would certainly be detected by the enemy's forward observers and as a result would trigger a devastating reprisal with large calibre gunfire.

In the end Nuyten, now clearly running out of options, asked Cogge what his personal advice would be. The senior supervisor explained that, instead of the locks on the north-east side of town, they could use the Spanish Lock on the west side of Nieuport. The old and now disused branch of the Furnes Canal, better known as West Vaart, connected this old structure, built in 1820, to the polder. This vaart passed underneath the 'new' Furnes Canal by means of a culvert and then turned under the railway levee to end up in the North Vaart. But still, all the seawater would end up on both sides of the railway since between Nieuport and Dixmude several drainage canals passed from west to east under the railway.

'And if we closed all the underpasses in the railway levee?' Nuyten asked.

'That will be impossible,' Cogge replied. 'There are too many of them and some, like the Great Beaverdyke Vaart, are 10m wide and have a depth of at least two metres.'

'However,' Nuyten insisted, 'try to imagine that we could do it.'

'Then the water would stay on the east side of the railway', Cogge had to admit.

He estimated that by using the Spanish Lock they could flood the polder in eight tides, or four days. But if they opened the North Vaart Gates instead, which were a lot wider, it would only take three tides.

This conversation proved enough for Captain Commandant Nuyten. He left Charles Cogge briefly in the corridor and entered the offices of General Headquarters where he stopped Captain Commandant Galet and told him: 'I found the way to set a flood between the Yser and the railway.'

Now events started to unfold rapidly. Cogge was brought before the Deputy Chief of Staff where he again explained his ideas about a flood. Major Maglinse, Chief Operations was also brought in as well as Captain Commandant Masure, Head of the Transport Section. Masure was renowned for his encyclopaedic knowledge. He had already succeeded a few weeks earlier in organizing, within twenty-four hours, the successful evacuation of all army stores from Antwerp and all this under the unsuspecting noses of the Germans.

After all of them had discussed the feasibility of this major undertaking and weighed the pros and cons, they agreed to inform their Commander-in-Chief. The king, who happened to be at General Headquarters at that moment, listened to all the arguments of his staff and ultimately approved the project in principle.

High Command, almost from the start envisioned the project in two stages: first inundate east of the railway to stop the German infantry; secondly flood or saturate the whole area west of the railway levee and up to the Loo Canal to avoid the subsequent slaughter by enemy bombardment. Although the German heavy guns would be confined to the grounds east of the river they would still be well within striking distance of the whole area west of the railway. Clearly though King Albert at this stage only approved of a limited flood, that is between railway and river.

One of the first problems High Command ran into was the fact that at Army Headquarters no post of Army Engineer-in-Chief existed. So on the spot it was decided to create a Directorate of the Inundation Service and to call on the commander of the engineers' battalion of the Second Army Division in Nieuport, Captain Commandant Victor Jamotte to head this new service. Captain Robert Thys was assigned as his deputy.

Another vital decision to be taken was the height of the water level to be achieved.

A water level too low would perhaps leave dry access corridors in the polder that the enemy could use to press on. A water level too high on the other hand could not only provoke a breach of the railway embankment (it had never been designed to act as a levee) but it might also allow the Germans to use flat-bottomed boats and barges to launch an assault on the railway line.

Again upon Cogge's advice it was decided to set the flood level at +3.00 to +3.25m. Although according to the ordnance maps that way a rather unwished-for depth of 1.80m would be reached in the low spots but on the high ground it would at least provide the required two feet of water.

Next, orders went out to the various engineers' companies assigning them a specific underpass to block. We know the companies of the Second Army Division that were involved: the Company Borlon was to built an emergency dyke near Nieuport while the companies Spinette and Delobbe were to block the Venepe Vaart between Nieuport and Ramscappelle.

Meanwhile Nuyten had sent Charles Cogge home, but only after he had asked him if he would be willing to come on a reconnaissance trip along the railway levee. There the supervisor would be most useful: he could indicate the different culverts to block and give any practical information to the soldiers on the spot. Cogge had dutifully agreed.

Deputy Chief of Staff Colonel Wielemans was billeted at the home of the local Justice of the Peace, Emeric Feys. This gentleman was also a member of the local Water Board and he was highly interested when Wielemans told him about the impending inundation. After all, the total area of land to be flooded comprised some 140 square kilometres, hundreds of farms and over ten villages and hamlets.

Feys, as a man of the law, had one important issue he wanted to raise: did High Command realize that all the people in the affected region would have to be financially compensated for the damage to their property and crops due to the flooding?

To reinforce his argument Feys dug up an official deed from his archives, dated 15 April 1798 that he showed Wielemans. This document had been

Justice of the Peace, Emeric Feys, in Furnes pointed out to Colonel Wielemans that financial compensation for the affected farmers in the inundated polder could mount rapidly. This statement certainly influenced the decision to limit the initial flooding.
Kunstmatige Inundaties in Maritiem Vlaanderen 1316-1945, J.Leper, 1957.

164

registered by the *Département de la Lys* – Belgium was then under French rule – and acknowledged the fact that farmer Hendrik Demolder from 's Heerwillemscappelle, a hamlet west of Pervyse, would be refunded for two years of rent he had paid on 140 square units of the 172 he had rented and that had been inundated for the defence of Nieuport in 1793. Farmer Demolder had been the grandfather of Feys' spouse. A powerful precedent indeed!

This intervention by judge Emeric Feys has, in later years, often be misinterpreted. Some authors even wanted to credit the man with the initial idea of the flood. As we already have seen, the truth is evidently more complex. Certainly this financial reality must have played an important role in the final decision; perhaps it was even the deciding factor not to go ahead with the second stage of the flood, west of the railway towards the Loo Canal. Who dared to predict in what shape the Public Treasury would be after this devastating war was over?

The total area that the military wanted to inundate was indeed large. Today it would compare to twice the size of the Dallas-Fort Worth Airport or almost five times Paris-Charles De Gaulle.

Apparently Wielemans was not the only one who discussed the project with local dignitaries that day. According to a post-war report by Roads & Bridges engineer L. Bourgoignie, Captain Commandant Jamotte and Captain Thys, who were both billeted, together with two other officers, at the home of Mr Cortier in Furnes were brought into contact with Mr Van Staen, retired chief supervisor of Roads & Bridges in Furnes. Unfortunately nothing more is known about this encounter. Also the testimony of Germain Van Marcke, the school teacher from Wulpen, about his discussion with the two artillery officers from General Dossin's staff (see Chapter VI) would fit in here.

Around 16:00 Jamotte and a Captain Grégoire went by car to pick up Cogge at his home. Together they drove to Wulpen, a village between Furnes and Nieuport where General Dossin, commander of the Second Army Division, had his headquarters. Here Cogge explained the work that had to be carried out in order to strengthen the banks of the shallow West Vaart. If this were not done properly the floodwater would invade the polder west of the town.

From there they continued to Nieuport, stopping first at the railway bridge across the Koolhof Vaart. When the water had travelled along the West Vaart and under the Furnes Canal it would have to pass for some 150m on the west side of the railway levee before it would turn to pass underneath the railway track. Here the army engineers were to build a 175m long emergency dyke, two metres high, to prevent the water from again flowing westward. In this levee would be included the existing weir on the Koolhof Vaart which in turn would have to be heightened by 1.30m. But this could be accomplished by simply inserting more stop planks in the grooves. The appropriate timbers were always kept in storage in the nearby brick shed of the waterboard.

The plan was to continue north along the West Vaart to inspect the various ditches that drained into the old canal and that would have to be blocked. But the bombardment on Nieuport intensified and it was considered too dangerous to proceed. They agreed to return to Furnes and carry on with their investigation the next morning. By 19:30 they arrived in Furnes.

Off the coast Admiral Hood had a nerve-racking day. There was little he could do due to the autumn storm which prevented any air reconnaissance to locate enemy targets.

A view, taken from the railway levee in 1991. On the extreme right in the background – see the arrow – the existing culvert under the Furnes Canal, leading to the Spanish Lock via the West Vaart. From this culvert an emergency dyke was built to the weir in the foreground to prevent the seawater from reaching the Belgian lines (to the left).
Author's photo archive.

The enemy heavy batteries that threatened the Belgian positions along the Great Beaverdyke Vaart were too far inland for accurate targeting. Furthermore, the only objective that could be found brought the French positions at Westende and Bamburgh Farm in the line of fire. Every effort Hood made to close in to get in a better position was met by fierce fire from newly installed and well-concealed enemy artillery in the dunes. So in the end he decided to stand off. In the evening, to make matters worse, the gale forced the smaller vessels to take shelter and the monitors, who had steamed to Dunkirk to replenish ammunition, were unable to sail.

With the early morning announcement by Brécard about the impending flood around Dunkirk, one of the first tasks at General Headquarters had been to warn Baron de Broqueville who was in the city at the time. He in turn immediately sent a strong worded protest to General Foch. In it de Broqueville declared to Foch that, in such case, the Belgian Army would have to lay down its weapons and evacuate the last shred of country left, '. . . which means opening the door to Dunkirk for the enemy'.

Foch was quick to inform Joffre of his intentions and the Belgian reaction. At 09:00 he cabled the following lengthy report:

> I ordered the flood with seawater of Dunkirk. The operation will take a maximum of two days. My decision has raised an energetic protest from the Belgian Government.
> 1/ The flood will extend into Belgian territory. We can, it is true, avoid this inconvenience by building a dirt levee, 4km long; but this remedy will not be solid and it will not be lasting.

2/ The inundation, even limited in height, will flood the road to Furnes, Hondschoote and les Moëres, the supply route for the Belgian Army.

3/ In case of a withdrawal, there will only be one road for the French to retreat as the Belgians are operating on the Yser (Furnes-Dunkirk road).

In view of these serious objections and other minor ones (forced evacuation of the population, infection of the drinking-water wells), I decided to postpone the operation.

As we are master over the exits at the coast of the canals by which we set the flood, it is perhaps not necessary to set it at present. In three days, when the Belgians will have abandoned the Yser line, we can set the flood without the enemy being able to oppose it.

In view of these considerations, let me know if you deem this measure necessary at this moment or, on the contrary, if I am allowed to wait until the Belgian Army in retreat will have lost the Yser line, then the one on the Loo Canal on which it seems to me it can maintain itself and on which we have to try to hold it by relieving it from all concerns of its communications and supplies. (EMA: #3341)

While Foch was still rather diplomatic about the Belgian ability to resist any further, General d'Urbal wrote a more blunt assessment. In fact, half an hour after Foch had cabled Joffre, d'Urbal wired Foch that, from now on, the DAB would be calling the shots between Nieuport and Dixmude: 'I hope, with or without the cooperation of the Belgian Army (on which I don't count anymore) that the reinforced Grossetti Division . . . , today will hold the line Nieuport-Dixmude.' (EMA: #3350)

In the rear of the army, along the Loo Canal, the *pontoneers* had been working the whole day to fortify the field works in front of the canal crossings. The Second Cavalry

Another view of the (new) Koolhof Vaart Weir and shed in 1991 with the weir to the right and the rebuilt railway viaduct to the left. In 1914 the emergency dyke ran from the weir to the culvert (left out of view). This forced the seawater under the railway towards the inundation. The new weir and shed have since disappeared again to make way for a holding pond. *Author's photo archive.*

A peaceful view of the road from Caeskerke to Dixmude during the war. Notice the Decauville (narrow-gauge) railway on the left of the cobblestone road.
Ons Land, Magazine, 1919.

Division in particularly had been organizing the village of Loo and the brigade commanders of the First Cavalry had been reconnoitring the bridgeheads at Oeren and Steenkerke.

While deliberations went on in the town hall, the queen was visiting the wounded in Furnes. With the Germans being firmly established on the left bank of the Yser it was decided by the medical staff to evacuate the wounded by train to the next village, Adinkerke, four kilometres west. In all, there were over 9,000 casualties. The operation was a nightmare for the victims and the stretcher-bearers. That night the queen wrote in her diary that many wounded died during transport.

Closer to the front line the situation was even more harrowing: it was estimated that 1,000 men were being treated in pitiful conditions in poorly improvised dressing stations, or had died between Furnes and the battlefield. And nobody could even guess the number of dead and wounded still on the battlefield and the men missing-in-action.

It was a terrifying and emotional sight: thousands of poor souls were now within three kilometres of the border of their country. What was to come next?

At night Colonel Brécard sent in his daily report to the Generalissimo. He acknowledged that along the whole Yser front the various troops had held their positions but that the Belgians were exhausted. Nevertheless he wired, they would try to set a flood between the Yser and the railway.

Although during the day a south-westerly storm had been battering the men in the muddy foxholes, the German infantry had relaxed its pressure. By 20:00 the enemy made a surprise assault on the outskirts of Dixmude. The vigilance of the defenders made sure that the attackers were repulsed. Shortly after midnight the Germans tried again. Taking advantage of the moonless night caused by the heavy overcast skies, the thunder of the shelling and the raging fires, a few hundred Germans succeeded in penetrating the town. First they reached the Town Square, then the riverbank. But here an alert machine gunner got them in his sights. While one enemy column fled back in town, the other pushed on across the river and further along the main road, getting as far as the railway crossing in front of Caeskerke. By daybreak it was all over: they were all killed or apprehended in the fields south of the road.

NOTES

1. For experts only: All water levels in this book are measured against 'zero Z', the Public Works Levelling made between 1840 and 1848. To compare them with the modern 'zero D' (Second General Levelling) one must subtract 0.1065m (roughly 10 cm). One should also be cautioned that all the water levels mentioned are as used in the early twentieth century and are not necessarily the same as today.
2. In the 1980s a lock was built in the Nieuwendamme Polder connecting the canalized Yser with the Bruges Canal, thus bypassing the Goose Foot complex.
3. Maintenance of dykes, waterways and related structures in the Flemish polders was entrusted to local polder-boards, called watering (-boards).
4. *Moer* [moór]: Dutch word for marshy ground, peat bog.
5. To set an inundation for defensive purposes the military in previous centuries had always preferred to use inland water over seawater as it was deemed less damaging to the soil and thus to agriculture.

Chapter XII

The Impending Collapse

Monday morning the weather was still as bad as the previous day. The endless rain showers had let up but the wind had shifted to the west-north-west and was now blowing at a stiff, stormy pace.

At 06:00 Charles Cogge was ready again. Together with Captain Commandant Jamotte, Cogge was driven towards Dixmude for an inspection of the various under-passes. Due to the heavy traffic on the narrow, wet, cobbled roads behind the front line their itinerary took them on a zigzag pattern throughout the polder (see map).

At some point the German bombardment was becoming so intense they had to make a detour to reach the Bertegat Vaart between Caeskerke and Dixmude. This six metres wide canal had to be blocked, under the railway levee, together with some smaller culverts in the vicinity. From there they drove back north on the main road towards Pervyse. One kilometre before reaching Pervyse they took a side road and crossed the Reigersvliet Brook. Then it was walking again for a few hundred metres towards the railway and the Great Beaverdyke Vaart crossing. This underpass was even bigger, almost eight metres wide. But now they were very close to the German lines. Heavy shelling forced them to return hastily to the car. But Cogge was undeterred.

Shortly after the war Charles himself recounted his story in his own vivid language:

Monday morning we left early to check on the preparations. We drove to Schewege, not far from Dixmude, and then walked on foot through the fields towards the railway. Our soldiers were on guard in that spot and there were Frenchmen at the Old Proostdyke. We reviewed the work being done at the Great Beaverdyke Vaart and, since I got that far anyway, I wanted to check up on Mrs Allewaerts homestead nearby since she herself lived in Furnes. She was going to leave and I had agreed to watch her house. They had told us that her homestead had been set on fire already by the bombing and I wanted to see for myself if it was true. And indeed, I peeked over the levee and saw that the farm had gone.

The French soldiers looked at me but the officers who accompanied me told me they had nothing to do with me. Shortly afterward the Germans started to bombard ferociously and like that we were in the middle of a hail of steel and lead. The officers retreated quickly but I was short of breath and could not move that quickly. So I inched back towards the Reigers Brook.

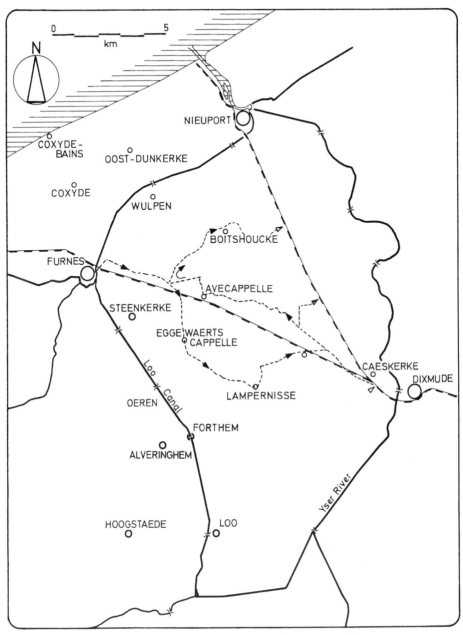

Jamotte/Cogge recce

Out there stood six guns apparently without ammo because they were not firing.

'You are retreating slowly, old man' the gunners said. 'You're lucky they didn't mow you down.'

'Bah, bah!' I replied. 'there's more room around me than on me so it would be pure luck if one of those hummers struck my head.'

But then all of a sudden I heard one of those loud whistling sounds so I quickly ducked down behind a small stable. There were all these manure heaps around us and see . . . zut, boum, bang, all these heaps flew up in the air and the manure was spread out around the field in a flash, quicker than the farmer could have done it.

'What do you say, old man?' shouted the gunners. 'Be happy you got here, eh?'

'Yes,' I said, 'but what can we do? We're in the thick of it and we have to get through somehow.'

The officers had run south and they winked at me.

'Are you going there?' the soldiers asked, 'it's dangerous you know.'

'I have to.' I replied.

'But you're too old to run like that.'

'I won't run for sure, I'll take it easy. I won't die before my time has come.'

Lieutenant General Emile-Jean-Henri Dossin, commander of the Second Army Division. In 1914 his divisional headquarters was located in the village of Wulpen, 5km south-west of Nieuport.
Guldenboek der Vuurkaart, 1937.

Because the enemy was so near, they had to take another long way about to reach the Venepe Vaart underpass near the Boitshoucke railway stop. But they did not get that far. The First and Second Army Divisions in this spot were pulling back from the Great Beaverdyke Vaart and the fighting was too intense to come near. At the farmstead of the burgomaster of Boitshoucke, Cogge explained to Jamotte what had to be done at the underpass of the Venepe Vaart and further north at the Ramscappelle Brook and the other, smaller culverts.

The exhausted soldiers that laboured to close the various underpasses used the most diverse material they could find nearby: at the Venepe Vaart for example the soldiers had only wheat sheaves from a nearby field to dam the waterway. They had to wade – at times waist-deep – through the brown water and at every bridge they were always within a few hundred metres of the enemy. The sappers had one small consolation: there was no current in the waterways. The reason for this was simple: with the lock personnel in Nieuport gone all the gates were closed and no run-off water was evacuated to sea. The drawback of course was that, with the abundant rains of the previous days, the water level in the polder had risen sharply. But this in turn would be an advantage once the gates in Nieuport were opened to start the flood.

After their exploration the two men drove back west to Wulpen to meet General Dossin and by 11:30 they were back in Furnes. Apparently Charles Cogge had enjoyed his excursion with Jamotte. This is what he recalled after the war about the time when he got out of the car on the Market Square in Furnes:

> At once some gentlemen were gathering around me, burgomaster Despot, Mr
> Pil and others and they asked how it was. I told them: 'Gentlemen, I won't

The Venepe Vaart, two kilometres south of Ramscappelle, seen from the railway embankment towards the 'own' lines. Notice the bridge of the road Ramscappelle-Pervyse in the background.
Nieuport 1914-1918, R. Thys, 1922.

deceive you, it's bad, but there are people of good will that have launched another attack and we will have to wait how this turns out.'

This news surely made the rounds in the well-to-do households in town since by the time evening rolled around quite a few of them had already left for France.

Afterwards Charles was introduced to Jamotte's deputy, Captain Robert Thys. He was the officer who would be in charge of the actual opening of the Spanish Lock and the flood in front of the railway levee.

Robert Thys was born in 1884 in Schaerbeek, a suburb of Brussels. From the first day on Robert was immersed in that special atmosphere that reigned in higher intellectual circles all over Europe in the second half of the nineteenth century: the drive for the exploration of the still uncharted territory of the 'dark' continent of Africa.

His father, Albert Thys was a career officer who, after his outstanding studies at the Royal Military Academy in Brussels, had been among the few young men who had convinced King Leopold II to launch several expeditions from the mouth of the Congo River upstream into the interior to explore the possibilities and riches of this vast expanse of tropical forests. Albert Thys, not only a bright officer but also a man with a keen eye for business, soon headed a group of companies he had founded to deal in lumber, rubber, ivory and other tropical products. But in the humid heartland of Africa it was one thing to harvest a crop, it was a far greater problem to transport it to the Atlantic for shipment to Europe. All would go rather well along the Congo River down to Leopoldville-Kinshasa but then, for some 350km, the mighty Congo rumbled and tumbled through the Crystal Mountains which effectively prohibited any shipping on the last stretch towards the wide mouth of the river. Realizing the strategic importance of this broken link, fascinated by the challenge and enticed by the major business opportunities it would generate, father Thys retained royal

assent to build a railway from Matadi, the seaport on the Congo to Leopoldville, as such bypassing this unnavigable section of the river.

By the time young Robert was in his teens his father's business activities in the Congo had boomed and other railway projects were on the drawing board. Besides his civilian career Albert Thys had in the mean time become a colonel in the Belgian Army and an orderly officer of the

For almost four years engineer Captain Robert Thys led the Sappers-Marines Company, a specialized unit dedicated to maintaining the inundation in the Belgian sector. Most officers of the company were already experienced civil engineers or young university professors before the war.
Thys family archive.

174

king himself. It seemed more than logical that the son would follow in his father's footsteps.

So at the age of seventeen Robert entered the Royal Military Academy and in 1905, barely twenty-one, he was assigned to the Engineers' Regiment. Four years later though, he resigned from active duty and after studying electricity at the Montefiore College in Liège, he joined his father's business conglomerate as an electrical engineer.

Turning away from a strictly military career was likely to have been because of his father's ambition to electrify 'his'[1] railway from Matadi to Leopoldville.

As three major mountain rivers crossed the rail line this hydro-electric potential had persuaded Albert Thys that by building dams on these rivers he would be able to produce electricity to power his locomotives. And that was where his son's engineering capabilities would come in handy.

Almost immediately Robert took off for the Congo to travel the railway and to start a preliminary study of the geography and hydrology of the region. He was a well-organized and dedicated engineer and he used a, by then, well developed invention as a tool in his investigation: a hand held camera to register his findings.

In the spring of 1913, just after being promoted to captain in the reserve forces, he married a charming young lady named Germaine Gillieaux and for their honeymoon the couple travelled to Norway. The trip in fact had a dual purpose: Robert would be able to study the Norwegian hydroelectric projects!

When, in the afternoon of the last day of July 1914, the Belgian Government mobilized its armed forces Robert Thys was in the country and the next day he arrived

Duffel. Brug in het Dorp. Pont du Village.

Uitg. V.o G. M. V. D. S.

The bridge on the Nèthe River in the town of Duffel before the war. This swing bridge was also a cable-stayed bridge as had been used in Nieuport on the original Ypres Lock, replaced in 1877. With the First World War cable-stayed bridges disappeared from the landscape until they were 'rediscovered' in the second half of the twentieth century. For large spans they are now more popular than suspension bridges.
Historical prints collection Renée Beever

at his engineers' unit, part of the Antwerp Garrison Army. Its mission was to prepare the defence of the south-eastern perimeter of the Antwerp Fortified Place. One of the many tasks was to initiate a planned flooding along the Nèthe river. Only ten days prior to the discussion in Long Street in Nieuport Thys had written in his field diary: '. . . 4 October I am sent to the town of Duffel to set a flood north of the Nèthe river by blowing up the dyke upstream from the bridge . . . the flood extends by itself north of the river and adds to the existing flooding along the south bank.'

Having made the retreat from Antwerp Thys had arrived in the Furnes-Ambacht region together with the Second Army Division. With the reorganization of the army he had been transferred to the engineers' battalion of this division on 14 October. Because of his technical background Robert Thys was the obvious choice to look after the drainage system and transform it into a weapon against the enemy.

In the French camp General Foch, who had not yet been advised by the Generalissimo of his proposal to postpone the Dunkirk flood, was uncertain about the situation in the north. The previous evening he had said to Tardieu: 'I see things far less clear than on the [Battle of the] Marne river. Meanwhile, let's inundate! Since you have been there already, return there once more!'

So in the morning Tardieu crossed the border into Belgium again to check on the progress of the preparations for the Dunkirk flood. In the late afternoon, accompanied by two Belgian lieutenants, he went to watch the rumbling water from atop a hillock.

Unfortunately, in his book published in 1939 André Tardieu was not more specific. A few questions arise, among others the rather improbable existence of a hummock in this flat landscape. It must be said that his book was written long after the facts and after a brilliant political career. Possibly he talked about the stretch of dunes west of the village of Adinkerke, the Cabourg Domain [2] near the border and the ring canal of the Moeren Polder. As we will see soon, he was quite likely supervising, as Foch had asked him to do, the French engineers while they were preparing the inundation of the Moeren Polders.

What is important to us is that his observations were certainly unrelated to the Belgian plans. The overall situation on the Belgian front was now extremely critical, especially between Ramscappelle and Pervyse. Not only had the troops of the First and Second Army Division pulled back from the Great Beaverdyke Vaart in a disorderly fashion but they also did not seem to reorganize on the railway levee. Some units were even reported as far away as Furnes, 8km from the railway. At 10:30 General d'Urbal cabled to Foch that his territorials, who only stayed in line when the regular units did so too, would lose their hold if they saw the Belgian soldiers give way. Luckily around noon the situation was restored along the railway levee by inserting a couple of battalions of the 42nd taken from the Nieuport sector. Later on, west of Pervyse two French cavalry regiments, the 6th Hussards and the 8th *Chasseurs*, arrived as a reserve for General Grossetti.

But the Belgian artillery was in bad shape. One by one the guns fell silent. They had been in continuous action since the beginning of the battle. The intensive use and lack of maintenance was now taking its toll on the gun barrels and carriages while the supply of shells was running out. Without fire support the infantry would not be able to hold on to the railway embankment, or any other line for that matter.

Both cavalry divisions, still in reserve west of the Loo Canal, were kept at high alert 'horses bridled and saddled, ready to be mounted'. At 10:10 a brigade was ordered

Belgian Cavalry somewhere in the field at the start of the war.
Onze Helden, R. Lyr, 1922.

towards Furnes to occupy the bridgehead on the Loo Canal while the battalion of cyclists was sent to the Steenkerke bridgehead. The men and horses of the Second Cavalry Division were kept close to the Loo bridgehead. Indeed, High Command feared the worst.

Although the British monitors had been bombarding the German positions in front of Nieuport since early morning, the collapse of the centre was a bad omen to the king. Contrary to his usual practice he returned to La Panne shortly after lunch and told the queen to leave at once.

The fighting was now drawing dangerously close. If Dunkirk pushed ahead with its flood and the Germans advanced on Furnes the queen and her small escort risked being cut off from the army and its protection. They would be trapped in the dunes.

The British Admiralty for its part feared a German landing between Nieuport and La Panne. The stubborn resistance of the western powers in Flanders could prompt German High Command to outflank the land battle and sail an army in between the Yser River and Dunkirk. Besides, with the fear of an approaching stalemate this might be the perfect time for the Imperial *Hochseeflotte* to engage the British Fleet in an all-out North Sea battle.

Of course there was the alternative Belgian plan for a large flood to be set east of Furnes that would push all Belgian troops onto an 8km wide strip of national soil. The modest royal refuge would then be too close to the front line. Whatever happened, the future looked definitely grim and frighteningly uncertain. But where was there for the queen to go?

The appearance of the Couthof Mansion in Proven has not changed over all these years.
Author's photo archive.

Unfortunately not many details are as yet known on this episode and its relation to the Battle of the Yser River. From excerpts of Queen Elisabeth's diary that have been published, we know that she first went to Watou, 8km west of Poperinghe, then to Proven, a few kilometres north. There she stayed at the Couthof Château for the night. Both villages were close to the French border and apparently the field hospital from Furnes had moved to Poperinghe also. One would expect the queen to have left La Panne and crossed the border into France. On the contrary, she had skirted the border and moved back inland.

Since an evacuation of the army through Nieuport harbour towards Great Britain was now out of the question, it looks as if at this point the king contemplated, in case of a collapse of the Yser front line, to pull his remaining forces out of this sector and move them southward to link up with the BEF now deployed in and around Ypres. This would also explain the king's sudden visit to the British Field Marshal in St Omer that same evening.

What did the king and queen discuss that day at lunchtime in La Panne? With some documents still not accessible to historians, we can only guess. But actions on the ground give away intentions.

With still that little bit of hope left, the king knew his spouse was not to leave the country. They decided that she would drive south, stay close to the border and try to find any suitable lodging west of Ypres. There she would be close to and behind the British lines. For the time being she would be safer on that part of the front than in the unstable situation of the Furnes area.

The queen wrote in her diary that day: 'They will open all the locks to inundate.'

In the Dixmude bridgehead the men were at the end of their physical and mental resistance. During the day two Senegalese battalions and a battalion of the Fifth Army Division could relieve only the most exhausted troops.

At 15:15 Colonel Brécard wired an alarming message to the Generalissimo:

> The Belgian Army, entirely disorganized, has not a single well-structured unit in the fighting line. Its artillery lacks all ammunition.
> Belgian High Command intended, at 15:00, to order a retreat and meant to include the French troops (42nd Division).

178

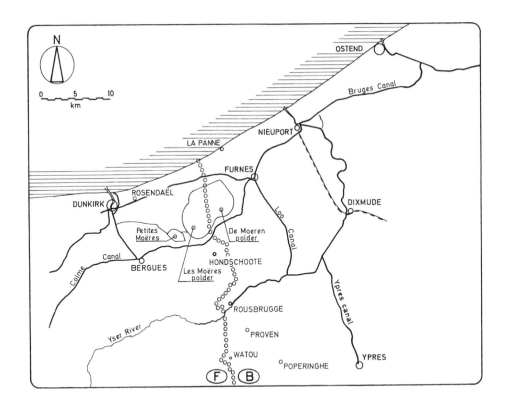

I absolutely opposed the retreat of our troops that are not under immediate command of the Belgians.

Moreover, Belgian High Command declares that it is not possible to set a flood of the Yser as was planned yesterday. (EMA: #3379)

Here two questions remain:

A. If the French opposed any retreat of their own troops, why did the last brigade of the 42nd Infantry Division on the left flank, evacuate the Nieuport bridgehead, on the right bank of the Yser, that night?
B. Why would a flood south of Nieuport be impossible all of a sudden? Perhaps there was a misunderstanding: as long as the extent of the Dunkirk flood was not known the order to inundate in front of the Belgian line could not be given.

Shortly before Brécard sent his distressing note to Joffre, Captain Thys was at General Headquarters asking Colonel Wielemans to authorize him to motor to Dunkirk to investigate the actual extent of the French flood. If indeed the Belgians wanted to retreat behind the Loo Canal, then they needed every available square metre of dry land west of Furnes. And it was of course that area that was threatened by the flooding around Dunkirk.

The Deputy Chief of Staff agreed but to give the mission an official character he

179

The Dunkirk Canal before 1914.
Historical prints collection Callenaere-Dehouck.

ordered Staff Captain Commandant Prudent Nuyten to accompany Thys into France. Arriving at the border they fortunately discovered that the French engineers had dammed up the Furnes-Dunkirk Canal at the border and had thus far only inundated an isolated polder east of Dunkirk called *les Petites Moëres*. With this promising news they did an about-turn and headed back for Belgian territory.

Shortly before their return into Furnes, at 18:00, Joffre had at last made up his mind on the Dunkirk flood. He cabled his answer to Foch: 'I approve of your proposals concerning the flood.'

With this decision the threat of a French flood in the Belgian rear had finally subsided. As soon as the news reached Furnes Colonel Wielemans ordered Thys to proceed with the flood between the river and the railway.

According to Robert Thys it seems that at General Headquarters only Wielemans and Maglinse understood that it would take many high tides to obtain a sufficiently high water level – was this perhaps with regard to the large Yser River/Loo Canal project – and that it was important not to destroy the lock doors?

Thys ends with the telling remark: 'A long discussion on the subject.'

In the evening Captain Thys drove to Cogge's house in order to ask him if he would be willing to come along on the nightly trek to the Spanish Lock. Upon arrival Thys found out from Cogge's wife, Mietje, that he was at Mrs Allewaert's. She was the lady that had fled to Paris. Charles and Mietje lived at Claeyssensoever but due to the approaching hostilities Mrs Allewaert, who owned a beautiful mansion in the Zwarte Nonnenstraat [Black Nuns Street], had asked them to take care of her house during her absence.

When Captain Thys invited Mietje to take a seat in his car to drive over there the good woman categorically refused. She would not have anything to do with such a newfangled invention and walked in front of the car towards Mrs Allewaert's residence.

Upon hearing what the captain had in mind Charles agreed but Mietje started

180

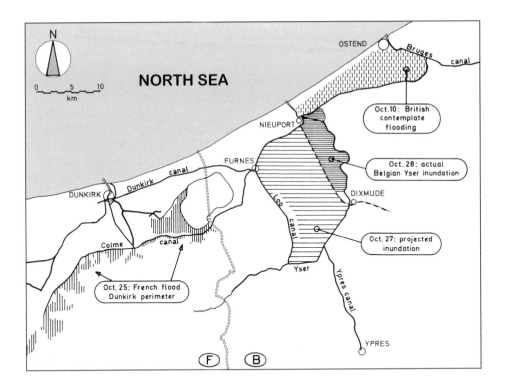

lamenting. Her elderly husband had already made two dangerous excursions with the military and, suffering from bronchitis, he had bouts of severe coughing. She feared that at the lock, in the middle of the night and almost under the nose of the Germans he might attract the enemy's attention and risk being killed. Apparently their daughter Clementine was also present, vigorously supporting her mother's views. There was nothing for Captain Thys to do but to return to General Headquarters and to consult with Colonel Wielemans. With the help of a few soldiers Thys could indeed easily open the lock doors but in all the mayhem the brave supervisor was the only one who would be able to figure out the most practical way to get to the disused and isolated lock on the west side of the city.

After talking to the Deputy Chief Thys returned to the Cogge family with the promise that Charles would get 2,000 francs and a medal for services rendered.[3] Mietje, presumably realizing the futility of her protest, finally gave in.

In the afternoon at the Goose Foot, Second Lieutenant François was informed that he had to follow the orders of the French Lieutenant Colonel Claudon in connection with the destruction of the Furnes Lock Bridge. Shortly thereafter Claudon himself appeared and ordered François to prepare for the demolition.

While performing this mining operation some tense moments passed when a nervous soldier, unrolling the electrical wires, inadvertently pulled the detonator from the charge. But undeterred by intense enemy bombardment, Sergeant Henry still managed to crawl under the bridge and restore the situation. Once everything was ready and François wanted to proceed with the destruction, a messenger from Claudon arrived

Lieutenant François did a good job when blowing up the swing bridge on the Furnes Lock on 26 October, 1914. The iron structure ended up on the gate side of the lock, out of sight and out of use for the enemy. The bridge was not wide: one lane for vehicular traffic with a raised pedestrian path on either side. It is doubtful nevertheless if this destruction would have held up a determined enemy long enough.
Nieuport 1914-1918, R. Thys, 1922.

and warned him to wait until the Colonel himself showed up. When this eventually happened Claudon told François that upon an order from High Command he should wait until midnight before blowing up the bridge. As a result François had the mining tools collected again. At night the three battalions of the 42nd Division that had remained in the Nieuport bridgehead at last evacuated their positions and withdrew across the lock system. With Lieutenant Colonel Claudon at his side François finally destroyed the swing-bridge at 23:00.

With this action any hope of a fast and reliable flood via the wide North Vaart evaporated. It must be said though that, because of the German advance south-east of Nieuport, the bridgehead had become untenable. Nevertheless to the Belgians the bridgehead was vital in the control of the water management and flooding of the whole region. Conversely France's main concern was Dunkirk which had its own access to seawater.

Back in Le Havre, where the Belgian government and most of its administration was now residing, something was reverberating concerning the proposed flood in Belgium. Baron de Broqueville, still in Dunkirk, had cabled George (Joris) Helleputte the Minister of Public Works, informing him of the project and the complaint by the military that all personnel of Roads & Bridges had disappeared. As a result the minister ordered three of his engineers, Mr Bourgoignie, Mr Hainaut and Mr Brichet [4] to travel to Dunkirk and contact the Minister of War.

In the early evening, while Robert Thys was heading towards Furnes to contact

Charles Cogge, King Albert accompanied by his advisor, Galet, and the British Colonel Bridges, left the town en route for the French border. It was an extreme gesture by the Royal Commander-in-Chief to leave Belgian soil at such a critical moment in the struggle for the nation. But so much was now at stake that a visit to the Commander of the BEF in St Omer did warrant the risk.

Not 15km inside French territory, the motorcar passed through the town of Bergues. At a roadblock, not far from Fort Suisse, nervous French territorials asked for the password. Captain Commandant Galet, embarrassed at his ignorance, was forced to reveal the identity of his royal companion and fortunately the baffled sentries let them proceed without further inconvenience. The 25km drive through wet darkness was mostly spent in silence. Occasionally Colonel Bridges would divert the gloomy thoughts of both his companions by briefing them on Field Marshal Sir John French, the man they were about to meet for the first time.

Sir John French was a soldier's general, popular with the troops. Tom Bridges, who had worked under the field marshal since the outbreak of the war, could not suppress a smile when he elaborated on the ebullient character of his short, mercurial superior. Most of the time though, it seemed the king and Galet did not hear Bridges' stories.

Around 20:00 the car with its royal passenger arrived at the outskirts of St Omer. The shadows of the many cobble stoned streets with manor houses didn't catch the

The Headquarters of Field Marshal Sir John French in St Omer in 1914, as it looks today. An apparently rather run-down manor house that doesn't even have a commemorative plate to recall that for one and a half years during the Great War this was the BEF's headquarters. *Author's photo archive.*

183

attention of the Sovereign as he was too absorbed by the tremendous uncertainties his country was facing.

St Omer was another of those picturesque small towns that dotted *le plat pays* of Flanders. In 1678, through the Treaty of Nijmegen, the Spanish Netherlands, or Flanders, had been forced to turn over this town on an isolated mound to the French but a lot of ordinary folk here still spoke Flemish.

The field marshal's headquarters was set up in a stern-looking, three-level, stuccoed manor house at number 37 in the rue St Bertin. Upon entering British General Headquarters it was as if the three men stepped into another world. The portly field marshal greeted King Albert with his omnipresent Irish charm and, as a surprise to the monarch, immediately invited him and his small party to the dinner table. In the mess room, surrounded by his complete staff, it seemed as if the horrors of war were the last thing on Sir John French's mind.

A month before Sir John had turned sixty-two. With his heavy, white moustache and thin white hair he was another of those military leaders who was many years King Albert's senior. But his disposition towards the king of the Belgians was entirely different from that of the French generals. Here was a man with an intense devotion towards his own monarch, first King Edward VII and, since 1910, King George V. This entrenched philosophy together with his warm-hearted nature immediately translated into a mutual, unspoken affection.

In his long career as a brave cavalry officer Sir John had seen a lot of galloping action in the vast expanses of the British Empire. On the contrary here on the European continent, his forces had faced a well-organized, disciplined and massive aggressor. The bloody battles and subsequent retreats since August had made him uneasy about British involvement in the whole affair. As a man of action he had always favoured operating on an open flank where he could manoeuvre his troops at will, but in the present situation he feared that the flexible front was slowly being transformed into a ruinous war of attrition.

After dinner Sir John, his chief of staff and King Albert withdrew to an adjoining salon for a tête à tête. Of the subjects discussed at this private meeting, nothing is known. Relying on the available information and indications on the ground, we have tried to reconstruct the likely topics.

The two commanders recognized that they were both facing an identical tactical situation. Their respective forces were exhausted by a difficult and dangerous retreat and both men were looking for a safe area to rest and reorganize their troops before any new attack could be ordered. Contrary to their wishes nevertheless, the French Generalissimo had been constantly asking for offensive action in an effort to turn the German right.

To avoid a collapse of the overstretched front line the field marshal had been contemplating for some time setting up an entrenched camp around Calais and Dunkirk if his forces had to again give way under German pressure. There, behind the fortifications and floods the BEF could then more comfortably be reinforced from England. With a short supply line across the Channel, protected by the British Fleet, it could await the opportune moment to debouch into the German flank. Up until that moment it would be a painful thorn in the German side. In fact, such a manoeuvre would keep the front moving for a while and buy time to reverse the odds. The French on their part could then withdraw deeper into France, allowing them to shorten their front and supply lines considerably as well.

As the field marshal pointed out on a wall map, a retreat of the French left flank on the Avre/Somme rivers for instance would shorten the front line by no less than seventy kilometres.

King Albert on the other hand was determined to hold on to whatever was left of his kingdom, as long as a British soldier was on Belgian soil. Here the monarch thought he had found a common interest: perhaps the whole Furnes-Dunkirk-Calais area could be transformed into an Anglo-Belgian fortified camp? He went on to explain to the British commander that the situation for his troops was now desperate. Perhaps the field marshal could send some help? Even a battalion or so of British troops joining the Belgians in their trenches would give at least the morale boost that was now so desperately needed.

Sir John had to disappoint the monarch. His own Expeditionary Force was now stretched to the limit and he had to keep a watchful eye on the area between Ypres and Dixmude. Two French territorial divisions and four French cavalry divisions were the only troops that now covered a potential retreat for the British towards the coast. These meagre French forces faced Houthulst Wood where he suspected the 3rd German Reserve Corps was assembled in preparation for an attempt to turn his front. If this manoeuvre succeeded the BEF would be cut off from the Channel ports, its supply and escape route.

He told King Albert that he had talked to General Joffre five days earlier and that the French Commander-in-Chief had informed him that the 9th French Army Corps was due to arrive in Ypres, with more troops to follow later. In the meantime he, unfortunately, could not spare any forces.

The Royal Consort's separate and sudden journey inland and the simultaneous low-key visit of the king to Sir John French cannot be called a coincidence. Undoubtedly King Albert also broached the subject of the queen's trip that evening. Queen Elisabeth's personal diary could possibly give more clues, but it was not accessible at the time of writing. So for now we can only voice our strong assumptions.

The king went on to explain to Sir John that, due to the precarious situation along the Yser front line, he had asked his spouse to leave their provisional residence at La Panne in the afternoon and motor inland, towards the British held sector. The king asked the field marshal to provide the queen with an armed escort if necessary and, in case the BEF had to withdraw towards the coast, to give her safe passage to the United Kingdom. Sir John F. replied that he was extremely honoured by this request and that he would take every step possible to secure the safety of Her Royal Highness the Queen Consort.

Due to the highly sensitive character of this personal agreement and perhaps even the disastrous impact this news could have on the morale of the Belgian soldiers, it was agreed that this discussion would be kept secret at all costs.

For the local inhabitants of the polder the perils of war were of a more practical nature. A village schoolmaster from the Furnes-Ambacht region wrote in his diary that night: 'October 26: There is talk about opening the sluices. Centuries ago, when there were no locks yet, this region was often submerged. But who will prevent the water from receding at ebb tide?'

The news of the monarch's secret visit to the BEF Headquarters could not be kept quiet, at least not at the highest military level. The next morning at 09:00 Colonel Brécard at the French Mission sent the following warning to the Generalissimo: 'I learned that the king has visited Field Marshal French yesterday evening to ask that the Belgian Army be relieved and put in second line.'

NOTES

1. Halfway between Matadi and Léopoldville a town was established along the railway called Thysville, today Mbanza-Ngungu.
2. Six months later – and within three weeks – a 500-bed army hospital, made out of prefabricated buildings, would be erected here.
3. For more details of Charles Cogge's rewards see Appendix III: 'A royal treatment'.
4. For a critical review of the actions of these engineers see Appendix II: 'Roads & Bridges Mysteries'.

Chapter XIII

At the Spanish Lock

Around midnight the rain let up and slowly a black, star filled sky unfurled. Earlier Captain Thys had taken Charles Cogge from Furnes to Nieuport. Before entering the town, at the Pelican Bridge across the Furnes Canal, Thys had left the car and had sent Cogge with a gendarme [1] as an escort, on foot the half a mile through the fields towards the Arch Bridge across the West Vaart. He himself had walked through the mud to the weir at the Koolhof Vaart where the emergency dyke was being built, to pick up a few soldiers to assist them at the lock.

Because of the fierce bombardment Cogge and his companion, upon arrival at the West Vaart took cover behind a small dwelling near the bridge. While waiting there, bundled up in their greatcoats, both were surprised to discover that they knew each other. The constable, a man from the village of Forthem near the Loo Canal had at one time worked as a cabinetmaker for Cogge!

The Koolhof Vaart Weir in October 1914 while it was temporarily being heightened with sand bags to counter the seawater. In the background the railway levee. Later a more permanent modification was built in brick.
Nieuport 1914-1918, R. Thys, 1922.

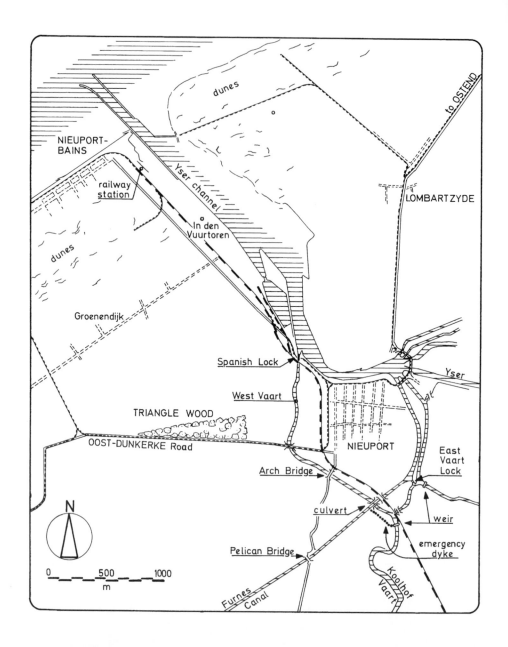

For two hours the shelling prevented the captain from joining them at the Arch Bridge. Finally, during a lull, Thys and some troopers arrived and together they continued along the West Vaart towards the Spanish Lock where they arrived at 02:30. Along the vaart Cogge had stopped in a few places to indicate some ditches that emptied into the vaart and needed to be blocked off.

Once at the lock, on top of the west bank of the Yser Channel, they were now in full view from the opposite side. Since the French had evacuated the bridgehead on that side

188

The Arch Bridge on the West Vaart. While waiting for Captain Thys, Charles Cogge and his *gendarme* had to take cover here in the early hours of 27 October.
Nieuport 1914-1918, R. Thys, 1922.

only hours before, there was a good chance that the Germans had moved in. In that case the enemy would spot any movement of lanterns or be alerted by any unusual noise. Hence all the work had to be done quietly and in the dark.

On the tidal side the flood doors were locked with a chain and padlock. Cogge had expected to find the key to the padlock in the lock shed nearby but they couldn't find it there, nor any tools they needed. Presumably all useful equipment had been pillaged during the previous days. After some struggling they managed to open a link in the chain with a crowbar. They then opened both sets of flood doors and pulled them into their recesses.

Originally – that is before 1870 – this lock had been used as a navigation lock for barges travelling to and from Furnes, the West Vaart originally being the Furnes Canal. With the building of the new Furnes Lock and canal on the east side of town, the West Vaart had been cut off and the lock was now solely used to drain water from the polder. For this purpose only the small gate paddles in the doors were raised and lowered while the swing doors themselves remained locked. With the building of the railway line towards Nieuport-Bains, over the head gate, the lock had also lost its upstream ebb doors. The remaining downstream ebb doors had been replaced with so-called 'set-doors'. This type of door that cannot be manoeuvred but that moves freely with the current, is only wood-cladded at the lower part of the frame, up to a well-determined height. The reason for this unusual construction was simple. If in a normal setting the flood doors in a lock are secured in an open position then the polder will gradually flood since the ebb doors will automatically close at each low tide, thereby trapping the surplus water in the polder.

189

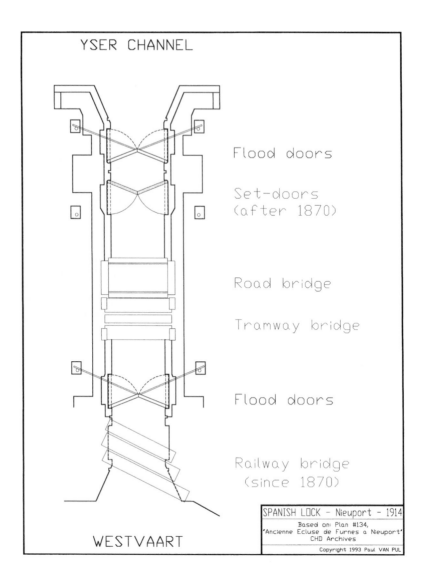

YSER CHANNEL

Flood doors

Set-doors
(after 1870)

Road bridge

Tramway bridge

Flood doors

Railway bridge
(since 1870)

SPANISH LOCK – Nieuport – 1914
Based on: Plan #134,
'Ancienne Ecluse de Furnes a Nieuport'
CHD Archives
Copyright 1993 Paul VAN PUL

WESTVAART

But if the ebb doors are replaced with set-doors then the excess water will return to the sea over the top of the closed part of the door. As such one will maintain a constant, preset water level in the polder.

This peculiar set-up was of course not installed to protect the polder from flooding – for that purpose one had the flood doors – but it was meant to inundate the polder and to automatically maintain a well-determined water level in it – just the kind of action Captain Thys wanted to initiate.

Since they had no tools available, including the metal racks to crank open the doors, the soldiers had to push the heavy doors open by hand and this could only be done once the water level on both sides of the doors was equal. Then all they could do was wait.

190

An example of a set-door in an inundation lock. Only the lower part of the doorframe is boarded. This type of door could swing freely in the lock chamber and was not operated by a capstan like the flood door in the background.

'The water rose . . . and it would not go faster than nature wanted it to go,' Cogge said some years later.

As long as the tidal water in the channel was lower than the water level of the vaart the set-doors stayed shut under the inland water pressure thereby preventing any loss of polder water. But after some time the rising tide slowly reached the top of the closed section of the set-door. At first seawater rippled over the top in a thin trickle, then, as the water flow gradually increased, the set-doors slowly opened up. But with the rising water flow a distressing situation developed.

When the lock had been discarded as a navigational structure forty-five years earlier, the retaining rings for the doors had been removed as a precautionary measure. This simple procedure, evidently unknown to Cogge and Thys, now prevented both men from anchoring the doors with their proper gate hooks in their recesses. With the rising tide the drag slowly increased and the soldiers were having a hard time holding the doors back. By 03:45 the situation was becoming dangerous, to such an extent that the men had to let go of the doors for fear of being thrown into the deep, narrow lock chamber to a certain death in the treacherous rising waters. Distraught and helpless they all watched the doors close! With the water pressure steadily increasing there was no way that the doors could be opened again before the next low water. The flood attempt, at least for the time being, had failed.

To save at least some of the effort Captain Thys decided to raise the small gate paddles in each door. This allowed for an opening of two square metres, the best they could do for the time being. Depressed the men walked back along the West Vaart to

View of the Yser Channel from the Spanish Lock, shortly after the events of October 1914. The opposite bank – and possible German sharpshooters – were not far off.
Nieuport 1914-1918, R. Thys, 1922.

the Pelican Bridge where the motorcar was still waiting. From there they drove towards Wulpen where they reported to General Dossin and later continued towards Furnes where they arrived around 07:30.

Once back in Furnes Thys conferred with lockmaster Kemp, the man in charge of the locks in town. Since he was apparently the only nautical expert in the region still at his post, Thys had talked with him the previous evening. The lockmaster had warned him about using the Spanish Lock, but only because in his opinion the capacity of this structure was too small for the undertaking the military envisioned. Now Kemp suggested the only option left: open the doors at low tide and insert wedges under them. But this would make the undertaking a lot more complicated: they would have to carry a lot of extra tools, descend into the lock chamber, install the wedges blindly under water and hammer them in place. That would be time consuming and dangerous. On top of it there was always a chance that the wedges would have the wrong dimensions and that the doors would still shut due to the water pressure. A second failure was unacceptable. They needed another solution.

At High Command Thys discussed the situation with several staff officers, including Prudent Nuyten. Seventeen years later, General Brécard (Head of the French Mission in October 1914) wrote about that day: 'On several occasions I met with Captain [sic] Nuyten of the Belgian Engineers [sic] who handles the question [of the flood] from the point of view of its realization and the repercussion on the positions occupied by the troops SW of the railway.'

With a tidal cycle of over twelve hours the next opportunity to open the lock doors would be in the late afternoon. That was an extremely dangerous time: all activity

The Spanish Lock, later in the war. In the foreground, left the upper part of the inundation door (set-door). Notice also that woven osier mats have been installed to disguise any movement from enemy observation.
Nieuport 1914-1918, R. Thys, 1922.

would be highly visible by enemy observers. Therefore it was decided to wait until the next night to make a new attempt.

To speed up the flood however there was perhaps still another avenue: tapping into the pool of freshwater now stored by the French in the canals around Dunkirk. Charles Cogge had told Nuyten that the Bergen Vaart was unusable for such a purpose but it seemed possible that water could be 'pushed' from Dunkirk through the Dunkirk and Furnes canals instead. If that were to be done someone, quite possibly Cogge, proposed to rupture the southern dyke of the Furnes Canal, somewhere between the railway embankment and the small East Vaart Lock. The level in the canal being a foot higher than in the vaarts, the water would rapidly invade the polder east of the railway.

After two cold, miserable weeks of heavy rain, alternating with showers, drizzle and fog, daybreak on 27 October promised a relief: an open sky finally allowed a low, rising autumn sun to project long shadows on the rich, gleaming clay soil and waterlogged grasslands. It seemed even the enemy was taking time off to enjoy the bright day: the shelling was less severe and more sporadic, concentrated mainly on Nieuport, Ramscappelle, Pervyse, the Rode Poort Farm and Dixmude. The assaults were scattered, small scale and lacking vigour. It was a welcome relief for the weary Belgians.

During the night two enemy attacks had taken place on the railway levee, one towards the Boitshoucke halting place, the other on Pervyse station. The Boitshoucke attack was repulsed by the 4th de Ligne Regiment, the one on Pervyse station by the 1st Grenadiers. Later on some reconnaissance troops were spotted in front of Ramscappelle.

Taking advantage of the apparent lull in the fighting the Belgians feverishly strengthened their new defence line along the railway embankment. Simultaneously the French, still holding the isolated village of Stuyvekenskerke 2km in front of Pervyse, agreed to withdraw on the railway levee. With this move the front line now coincided with the railway from Nieuport up to almost 2km south of Pervyse. From here the line slowly wandered off towards the south-east, reaching the Yser in the bend at km 16. [2] Engineer units meanwhile laboured stubbornly to finish off the closing of the culverts under the railway and the building of the emergency dyke along the Koolhof Vaart.

With this shortening of the front line the Belgians were able to withdraw most of the Third and Sixth Army Divisions from the front and put them in reserve. As both cavalry divisions had been the only major reinforcements available for a few days this move at once offered High Command some breathing space.

The restructuring came at a price however. Between Nieuport and Dixmude, somewhat considered the 'Belgian sector' of the front, the French had now engaged their 42nd Infantry Division, three cavalry regiments, the Marine Fusiliers Brigade, two battalions of Senegalese and the *régiment d'infanterie territoriale de Dunkerque*.

Furthermore, on the extreme northern end of the front, between the coast and Nieuport, the French detachment of Colonel Costet consisted of one battalion of the 162nd Territorial Regiment, the 3rd *Chasseurs d'Afrique* and a battalion of the 6th Territorial Infantry Regiment.

At 14:00 a relatively insignificant incident happened in Furnes: three enemy shells exploded on the railway station, causing quite a few deaths. But its impact was far more psychological than physical: with the front line at least 8km away, let alone the closest enemy gun positions, the immediate threat of another German advance became perfectly clear to the army top brass assembled in the Flemish county town.

It is not inconceivable to assume that this incident – and perhaps others of the kind – once diligently reported by the French Mission in Furnes to the Generalissimo, convinced the French that in the end it would be safer to rely on the defences of the Dunkirk Fortified Place rather than pushing precious water to Nieuport.

In the morning the British flotilla was back in action off the coast. Admiral Hood had received a sizable reinforcement by the addition of the old battleship *Venerable* in which he now flew his flag. This London-class battleship, built in 1902, carried a formidable punch: four 305-mm guns, twelve 152-mm guns, sixteen 12-pounders and six 3-pounders.

The assigned targets included Westende, Slype and Lombartzyde. But by this time

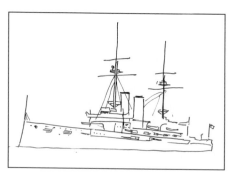

HMS *Venerable*
Author's photo archive.

Breach in the dyke between the North Vaart (right) and the Furnes Canal (left) later in the war as a result of a too high water level in the inundated polder. In all probability this incident happened in the same spot as where the levee was blown up in the afternoon of 27 October, 1914.
Nieuport 1914-1918, R. Thys, 1922.

the Germans had so many field guns positioned in the dunes that Hood's vessels could not venture within 4km of the coastline, thus greatly reducing their accuracy and field of fire. During the day the situation gradually grew worse: the Germans were able to zero in on the squadron with a heavy gun while one of the attending destroyers reported the sighting of a German submarine. This double threat forced Hood to retire to Dunkirk.

At first the French response to the Belgian request for flood water was positive. The Dunkirk authorities agreed to open the temporary dam in the Dunkirk Canal at the border and they promised to open the gates in the harbour at the next rising tide. Upon this news the engineers of the Second Army Division were ordered to blow up the canal dyke east of the railway as proposed earlier. Captain Grégoire and Second Lieutenant Adam subsequently installed 250kg of tonite in the levee separating the Furnes Canal and the North Vaart and sometime after 17:00 a sizable breach was created, thereby connecting both waterways. 'French' water could now enter the polder.

Why the military choose such a drastic and rather ineffective solution will perhaps forever remain a mystery. As mentioned earlier it is assumed that Cogge had made the proposal to the engineers. But then it is quite unlikely that he was unaware of the fact that not 200 metres away the East Vaart Lock connected the canal with the polder. That the opening of this lock would have been a lot more efficient, would have been less likely to attract the attention of the enemy and most importantly, would have allowed them to retain control of the operation is something Charles Cogge must have known. Was he perhaps emotionally too overpowered by the exceptional circumstances?

195

Going by his earlier reactions and his comprehensive knowledge of the subject, we suspect that Captain Thys did not agree with this turn of events. But his was only one voice and he had no decision in the matter. As we will see later the order to blow up the dyke most likely came from Captain Commandant Jamotte, the Head of the newly created Inundation Directorate. So possibly not Cogge, but Jamotte himself came up with this strange idea. The High Command was now desperate to get water in the polder.

The previous evening, at 17:00 the three engineers of the Roads & Bridges department had left Le Havre for Dunkirk. Their mode of transportation is unknown but it appears they were not in a hurry: for some inexplicable reason it took them 21.5 hours to cover the 316km that separate Le Havre from Dunkirk, or an average of 15km an hour.

There could be an explanation though: since the whole region from Le Havre to the front line in the north had been put under (French) military control it is quite possible that these civilians had to rely on Belgian military transport to travel to Furnes. This recently improvised shuttle system consisted of requisitioned vehicles that drove certain interconnected routes. So if a passenger arrived at the 'terminal' shortly after the car had left it was quite possible that the person would have to wait until the following day for the next departure towards Furnes.

Upon arrival, the next day at 14:30, the engineers first called on the office of Baron de Broqueville. The Minister of War had been forewarned by his colleague, the Minister of Public Works now in Le Havre, of their impending arrival but the Baron had left and was in Furnes at General Headquarters. So instead the engineers met with his secretary, Captain Commandant Louis Chabeau. Although intelligent and hard working, Chabeau was one of the most unbearable of officers in the close-knit de Broqueville 'court' and quite possibly he was not too happy with these civilian snoopers. The secretary advised the engineers to proceed to Furnes but first to contact the Chief Engineer of the Waterways in Dunkirk, Mr Bourgeois. It had been brought to his attention that High Command in Furnes had asked Bourgeois to urgently execute certain hydraulic manoeuvres on French soil.

Arriving at the office of the Chief Engineer the three men got a more detailed explanation of the manoeuvre requested by the Belgians. They were informed that Belgian High Command had decided to try to halt the German advance by inundating part of the Furnes-Ambacht region between Nieuport and Dixmude. Subsequently it had advised Bourgeois that it was impossible to operate the lock doors in Nieuport because of the enemy bombardment and perhaps even because of the close proximity of the Germans to the structures. As a result the Belgians had asked Dunkirk to open their seaward gates and push saltwater towards Furnes. Bourgeois declared that the operation would be executed, or was being executed, during the next rising tide. As next high tide in Dunkirk was at 19:15 the seawater must have already been rushing towards Furnes at the time of their meeting. 'But,' Bourgeois added, 'this operation impeded or suspended certain measures being taken by the French Roads & Bridges Service to set certain strategic floods in the French Moëres polder region.'

This declaration gave rise to a discussion in which it was agreed that the manoeuvre requested by Belgian High Command was an extreme measure that would have quite a slow effect – only exceptional circumstances could justify this action. Furthermore, from a technical point of view, the engineers agreed that the operation had a major drawback: the north side of the Dunkirk Canal not being embanked, the canal could only support a rise of one foot. Otherwise a large tract of land between the canal and the dunes, from Dunkirk to Nieuport, would be flooded unintentionally.

Apparently this statement was not quite true. According to Joseph Leper, who was director at the Furnes North Water during the Second World War, in 1944 the Germans ordered the water board to inundate the same polder, this time as a measure against an Allied invasion. For that reason the water level in the canal was subsequently raised over two feet whereby, between Adinkerke and the border, only twenty hectares – fifty acres – were accidentally flooded. At that time certainly on the Belgian side of the border the situation had remained unchanged since 1914.

The three Belgian engineers told Bourgeois that they would continue on to Furnes to investigate the matter and that they would return the following morning to report on the situation. Leaving Dunkirk at 15:40 engineers Bourgoignie, Hainaut and Brichet then covered the 21km to Furnes in forty minutes. Baron de Broqueville not being available, they were met by Colonel Wielemans who in turn advised them to contact the Head of the Inundation Directorate, Captain Commandant Jamotte.

Jamotte, who was on an inspection mission along the Loo Canal, arrived shortly afterwards. From him the engineers learned that in fact the military did not want to submerge the land completely but that they rather wanted to soak the soil with water and make it waterlogged. This would hinder the movement of the enemy, hamper the relocation of guns and impede the supply of ammunition and other vital material. Perhaps, Jamotte said, it would be sufficient to fill the various vaarts and ditches to the brim, allowing for some local shallow depressions to fill with water. Eventually the same procedure could be repeated for the whole region east of the Loo Canal. For the time being though only the land between the railway embankment and the Yser river would be affected.

During his afternoon trip along the Loo Canal the Captain Commandant had verified that the doors of the flood locks on the Slopgat Vaart and the Steengracht were in working condition and that the stop planks on the culverts under the canal had been lowered. These measures were, of course, critical. If, in the present circumstances, the whole polder east of the Loo Canal was to be inundated the Belgians would need all the water they could get from Dunkirk. And this water could only be channelled through the Loo Canal and the locks on the Steengracht and the Slopgat Vaart. But to prevent that water from escaping back to the west, the culverts under the canal had to be closed beforehand.

Bourgoignie informed Jamotte about the meeting with Engineer Bourgois in Dunkirk. He also warned Jamotte that the water from Dunkirk had to be brought in cautiously in order to prevent cave-ins on the water face of the levees along the canal. Even the total collapse of a dyke segment was not inconceivable. The civil engineer was also of the opinion that the water influx would be slow as the three flood locks had a relatively small cross section and were quite far from the water intake. The lock of the East Vaart near Nieuport for instance was some 35km from the Dunkirk tidal water gates.

To counter this argument Jamotte answered that, if necessary, he planned to breach the southern dyke of the Furnes Canal just west of the East Vaart Lock by means of explosives.

When Bourgoignie indicated that the most direct and efficient manner to inundate the polder would be to lift the gate paddles of the North Vaart in the tidal bay in Nieuport, Jamotte responded that this structure at present was inaccessible. Therefore it had been decided to use the Spanish Lock instead.

Jamotte spoke of the failure at the lock the previous night but said that a new attempt would be made the following night. Since the situation on the Belgian front line had become extremely alarming High Command meanwhile had requested the help of the Dunkirk authorities.

Bourgoignie continued in his report in 1920:

> After being informed about the inconvenience for the defence of Dunkirk of this flow of water from France to Belgium it is agreed that Commandant Jamotte will join us tomorrow morning at the office of the Chief Engineer Bourgois. He will then inform us about the result of the new attempts made at the Spanish Lock and we will talk the situation over together with Mr. Bourgois.

Apparently Chief Engineer Bourgoignie took the French point of view. From a pure tactical standpoint it seemed more logical for everyone, including a lot of well-meaning Belgians, to retreat within the prepared defence of Dunkirk. But this overlooked the constitutional consequences.

After their meeting with Jamotte the three engineers went on to meet Baron de

A detail of the iron rack hooked to a vertical pin mounted at the top of the lock door in order to open it. On the platform the rack runs along a gear wheel mounted at the bottom of a capstan.
Author's photo archive.

The paved road from Nieuport to Nieuport-Bains (today the Albert I Avenue) before the war. The local railway originally followed the railway track, which was closer to the Yser Channel. Only later, but still before the war, the narrow gauge railway would be moved next to the road. *Historical prints collection Callenaere-Dehouck.*

Broqueville. As there was no lodging available in Furnes they left the town at 17:50 for Dunkirk where they arrived at 18:30.

Meanwhile Captain Thys was already back on the road. Around 16:00 Thys picked up Charles Cogge again at his home in Furnes. First they drove to the canal lock in Furnes in order to retrieve some spare racks from the office of lockmaster Kemp. These could come in handy at the Spanish Lock later that night. Then they drove to the local police station and continued on to General Headquarters where they met Colonel Wielemans and Captain Commandant Nuyten. They then went on to divisional headquarters in Wulpen where they picked up the lieutenants François and Rotsaerts. Since Second Lieutenant Adam had blown up the Pelican Bridge on the Furnes Canal near Nieuport, they were forced to take an alternate road to reach the Spanish Lock.

The Pelican Bridge was an important north/south link. That the bridge was destroyed is another indication that High Command did intend to inundate the whole Furnes-Ambacht polder. The only canal crossing left near Nieuport was now the railway, but this access was, for the time being, essential for the work being carried out by the engineers on the emergency dyke near the Koofhof Vaart.

Instead of following the Furnes Canal towards the Pelican Bridge they crossed the canal near Wulpen and headed for the village of Oost-Dunkerke. From here they drove parallel to the coast the 3km to the Groenendyke settlement and on to the Yser Mouth. By now they were getting close to enemy territory. They left the car at an isolated inn, most likely the tavern In den Vuurtoren [In the Lighthouse], between Nieuport-Bains

199

and Nieuport, not far from the Yser Channel. From there it was only a mile hike to the lock. As it was getting late in the evening, they decided to rest at the inn and prepared some soup and meat for supper.

The inhabitants of the tavern, also farm folk, had apparently fled just before their arrival since there were potatoes still boiling on the stove. The men eagerly took advantage of this unexpected treat and quickly passed the hot pot around.

Being too early in the evening and to avoid any unnecessary activity in the vicinity of the lock Captain Thys decided they all should have some sleep. The driver of the motorcar was assigned to guard duty and to awake the group at 00:30. Thys and one of the lieutenants each laid down on the two available palliasses and Cogge made himself comfortable in an armchair by the stove. After a while the driver, being perched over a book he desperately tried to read by a flickering candle, nodded off. Fortunately the elderly Charles stayed awake.

At 00:15, after he had made a pot of coffee, Cogge woke everyone up. The men enjoyed the strong, steaming brew, then, close to 01:00, they took off accompanied by a corporal and a soldier carrying strong ropes, machetes, pickaxes and other equipment. Charles and the captain carried the small tools.

When, under an open sky and a full moon, they had almost reached the lock they met a gunnery captain with a crew and a 75-mm gun. Upon questioning him Thys found out that the officer, Philippe Tahon, had been sent by General Headquarters with written orders from Captain Commandant Jamotte to destroy the lock doors. This would of course be a disaster. Thys turned him away, as well as a lieutenant of the engineers who had been ordered, in case the destruction with the guns failed, to blow

A view from the dunes onto the cobblestone road from Nieuport-Bains to Nieuport (in the background). To the left, some hundred metres behind the greenery were both railways. Left and right of the road are rider trails. Far right a paved path for pedestrians.
Historical prints collection Callenaere-Dehouck.

A groove in the hard stone wall between both flood and ebb doors was another simple device to transform a navigation lock into an inundating lock. By lowering stop-planks in the grooves, either a salt water or a run-off water flood could be set.

up the lock doors. Brute force would only compromise any flooding attempt. Once the doors were destroyed there would be no way to control the tidal stream and achieve a stable flood. Thys was confident this time his scheme would work.

Obviously Captain Commandant Jamotte was by now desperate to get water into the polder. After Thys had left on his expedition in the late afternoon, and engineer Bourgoignie was again en route for Dunkirk, word had arrived at High Command that the French would no longer provide seawater through Dunkirk. So only the Spanish Lock could now provide the salvation of the country.

Once at the lock, around 02:00, they got to work immediately. The soldiers dug a few foxholes on each side of the structure and the ropes were tied to the head of the flood doors. Rotsaerts and François blew up the iron rack that prevented one of the doors on the east bank from opening. Then came the anxious waiting for the rising tide to reach the vaart level. The flood doors were now open, held in their recesses by the ropes. The men huddled in their foxholes, the open end of the ropes tight in their cold hands.

Charles Cogge explained: 'It was all fire, the sky was red and along the channel people were still fleeing. It was awful to hear all the noise, the crying, the lamenting and then the shooting and the explosions'

Captain Thys was lying on the freestone near the still closed set-doors. Occasionally he would measure the water level on both sides of the door.

'Charles', he would whisper, 'it's taking so long.'

'Yes, yesterday the weather was rough, but today it's calm. That could make a difference of two hours. But don't worry, it will come.'

The captain's thoughts slowly drifted off to the days of his long sea voyages to Africa. When the legendary *Congo Boat* slowly ploughed its way through the choppy waters of the English channel towards the Gulf of Biscay, the *colons* [3] got one last chance to catch a glimpse of the old continent. On port, through the mist and the drizzle produced by the foaming wave tops, the passengers could still distinguish the monotonous flash of the Casquets' lighthouse, a few rocky outcrops twenty-two nautical miles west of Cherbourg. From then on Europe, the mother country, family and friends became a dream, for years, for some even forever. At this moment these thoughts floated through the captain's mind. When would they all be able to return to their families again? Would it also take years? Would they even survive this murderous clash of arms? There was an even more ominous message locked into these memories. What did Victor Hugo write in his *L'Homme qui rit* [*The Man Who Laughs*]?

> To a ship under full sail, rigged with all its tackle and comfortable to handle to its pilot, the beacon of the Casquets is valuable. It shouts watch out! It warns about the cliff. To a ship in distress it is only terrifying. The hull, paralysed, lifeless and without resistance against the mad buckling of the sea, can only go where the breath takes it. It is defenceless against the forces of the wind, as a fish without fins or a bird without wings. The lighthouse shows it the ultimate spot, signals the vanishing point, indicates the shrouding. It is the candle of the sepulchre. (*The Man Who Laughs*, Part 1, book II, XI)

Had the king navigated the right course for his country? Would this old lock be the beacon that would guide them all through these dark times and finally bring them into a safe port? Or was the country adrift, out of control and would this lock be the beginning of the end? Would the nation strike a rock, founder and carry everyone to their graves?

Repair, with sandbags and pickets, of the breach in the levee between the North Vaart (left) and the Furnes Canal (right). The water flows from the inundation towards the canal, whose water level in normal times would be higher than the water in the polder. *Nieuport 1914-1918, R. Thys, 1922.*

The clear night was eerily quiet. In the distance they could hear guns thunder occasionally and machine guns rattle angrily now and then. Several fires burning unchecked lit up the town.

Since there was no reason for Cogge to wait for another few hours in the cold autumn night, Captain Thys decided to send him back to the abandoned tavern and the waiting car. He had taken Charles along merely as a local guide so there was no need to have him endure another perilous and sleepless night within easy range of the enemy.

As they were within 200m of the opposite, presumably hostile riverbank they could but whisper and move around bent down or on hands and knees. Finally, at 06:15, the set-doors slowly swung open and the seawater started to roll inland. This time there were no surprises. The influx increased but the soldiers held the flood doors in their recesses. For the officers there was no more to do. They left the corporal and soldier to watch over the doors and walked back to the car.

With a detour by the Groenendyke settlement they returned towards Nieuport and the railway bridge across the Furnes Canal. While an exhausted Cogge stayed in the vehicle the officers crossed the bridge on foot to reach the Koolhof Vaart. Here they inspected the construction of the emergency dyke and the solidity of the closed and heightened weir.

Meanwhile daylight had slowly settled in. A light south-westerly breeze was blowing under a cloudy sky. Satisfied with the work, the officers returned to the motorcar on the north side of the canal and, via Oost-Dunkerke and Wulpen, drove back to Furnes where they arrived shortly before noon.

NOTES
1. Some post-war authors made it appear as if Cogge was under surveillance by the constable, as if he was untrustworthy. On the contrary. The whole area was now practically deserted by the local population and instead bristling with mainly foreign military personnel. As such the *gendarme* acted as a uniformed escort for the elderly civilian.
2. This exposed location was kept in Belgian hands throughout the war. It became known as the 'Trench of Death' and a portion of it has been restored as a memorial.
3. *Colon*: French abbreviation of colonial; A Caucasian of the mother country who makes a living in the colony.

Chapter XIV

The Bargee is a Daredevil

On Wednesday morning, 28 October, while Captain Thys and Charles Cogge were on their way back from Nieuport to Furnes, Captain Commandant Jamotte was heading for Dunkirk. There he met with Chief Engineer Bourgeois and the three Belgian engineers of Roads & Bridges.

Bourgeois had to announce that during the night he had been asked to stop the flow of water towards Furnes and that he had no idea where the countermand originated. Apparently Jamotte had an explanation: various installations of the Belgian Army in the vicinity of Adinkerke were being flooded by the rising water level in the Dunkirk Canal, overflowing its northern bank.

Jamotte's remark leaves the impression that the counter order came from Belgian High Command. However, no evidence of this has been found. Besides, as we have seen earlier, only a small portion on the Belgian side of the border could be inundated in this way. The damage on the French side conversely, where a similar topography existed, but over a length of some 13km, must have been far greater.

Besides, Jamotte continued, the second attempt to open the Spanish Lock had succeeded and they could now manoeuvre the lock doors whenever needed. He also indicated that the flood would be limited to the land between the Yser and the railway embankment and gave a description of the preliminary works that had been carried out.

The old culvert under the Furnes Canal being in a rather precarious state, Roads & Bridges engineer Bourgoignie urged Jamotte to try to use the North Vaart Gates as soon as possible. It was now a few days from full moon, which meant that each high tide the water level in the West Vaart would be some 10cm higher. Subsequently the dynamic pressures on the culvert abutment wall, with only a submerged opening of five square metres, would get bigger and bigger, enhancing the danger of collapse.

After their meeting with Bourgois, the three Belgians called on Baron de Broqueville telling him that with the approval of Captain Commandant Jamotte they considered their mission completed and that they would return to Le Havre. They left Dunkirk at 14:30 and arrived in Le Havre the next day at 16:10.

Along the front line itself a rather calm day passed by. A lot of men in uniform wondered if the enemy too was exhausted or if it was just the calm before the storm. At night the Germans had launched an attack on the railway near the village of Ramscappelle but it had been repelled. Later during the day a few short but violent bombardments erupted here and there which were followed by a few unsupported attacks. All of them were swiftly repulsed.

Admiral Hood and his squadron were again on the scene off the coast. The supply of shells and loads was running low but, with the impending flood, he was allowed impulsive fire for the next forty-eight hours. With the *Venerable*, his three monitors and the gunboat *Bustard* he pounded away at the usual targets in and behind the dunes. This time though he got targets as far inland as St Pierre-Cappelle as the morning air reconnaissance had located a heavy battery and a group of four artillery positions in the vicinity.

The Germans had realized that this daily fleet bombardment was one of the main factors for them being bogged down in their coastal advance and they were gradually building up their coastal artillery against this annoying and devastating threat. For his part it became clear to Hood that his flotilla was becoming the main target of the enemy heavy batteries and as a consequence his squadron began to suffer more than it had done since the beginning of the operations along the Belgian coast.

Shortly after noon the destroyer *Falcon*, on anti-submarine patrol north of Westende, came under heavy and accurate fire from shore batteries. She kept up her assigned patrol path but at 14:00 a direct hit on the foremost six-pounder instantly killed the captain and seven crew members, wounding another sixteen. Out of action she limped back to Dunkirk. The other ships also took hits but were able to avoid serious injury by altering course every so often. Under these conditions of enforced movement and constant turns, indirect return fire was becoming extremely difficult. Moreover, during the afternoon the sighting of a German U-boat again interrupted the shore bombardment. During the subsequent chase *Venerable* ran aground on one of the numerous sandbanks off shore. Fortunately she was out of range and as the tide rose she refloated with the assistance of the cruiser *Brilliant*.

Queen Elisabeth, still lodged at the Couthof Château of the burgomaster of Proven, was irritated by the inactivity she had been confined to. The previous day she had written a few letters in the early morning then at 09:00 her husband had briefly visited accompanied by General Hanoteau. This time the monarch had been more optimistic. He had told her that the situation between Nieuport and Dixmude was improving. The French 120 and 155-mm guns had been pounding away on the Germans the whole night.

After his visit the queen strolled in the park surrounding the castle with her two lady companions, Countess de Caraman and Viscountess Colienne de Spoelbergh [1]. Later

The destroyer HMS *Falcon*

on they found some distraction in knitting socks for the soldiers and in the afternoon the young Doctor Paul Derache dropped in to discuss the problem of the ambulances.

Derache had been appointed as chief surgeon of the Hôpital Fort Louis not far from Dunkirk. This 30-bed hospital had recently been put at the disposal of the Belgians by the French authorities. Mrs Marie Curie-Sklodowska had donated the radiological equipment and the American Embassy had equipped the operating theatre.

In the evening, before going to bed, the ladies chased the mosquitoes that had invaded the rooms and during the night they were woken by the artillery duels between British and German guns in the distance to the east.

The tidings arriving in Proven the next day were more hopeful: the railway levee was now firmly held and the intended flood would result in a reduction of the front line thus allowing the re-establishment of reserves. On this reassuring news the queen got on the road again heading back for the coast. From Proven her small party drove to the French border near Rousbrugge from where they continued towards Bergues and Dunkirk. There they visited the wounded soldiers in the hospital at Rosendaël [2], near the canal to Furnes. At 17:00 the commander of her *gendarmerie* escort, officer Blanpain informed the queen that they would return to La Panne and they reached the Maskens Villa at 18:30.

The queen would never return to Proven for a night's stay. For the rest of the war the royal couple remained in La Panne, except for part of 1917 and 1918 when they alternated between La Panne and the Ste Flore Farm in De Moeren polder, a few miles south-west of Furnes.

In the evening Colonel Brécard had a long meeting with the commander of the 42nd Infantry Division. Usually confident and with a high morale, Grossetti was all of a sudden pessimistic and considered the situation very serious. He figured that his division was walking a tight rope: heavy losses had thinned the ranks and the survivors were exhausted, not to mention that two battalions of his division, together with eight batteries of 75-mm and one cavalry regiment had been withdrawn from the Belgian sector by French High Command to be deployed behind the Ypres Canal.

Admiral Ronarc'h for his part felt the same: his marines in Dixmude would not hold

The Maskens Villa, seaside this time, in the dunes of La Panne. Throughout the war many famous Allied political and military figures visited the Belgian king here. As a souvenir, the queen, an avid photographer herself, would take a picture of their illustrious visitors, often on the steps of the small deck. *Historical prints collection Callenaere-Dehouck.*

206

Generalissimo Joseph Joffre pays a visit to the Belgian king at La Panne. From right to left: King Albert in a typical posture, General Joffre and Queen Elisabeth. In the background the Maskens Villa.
Mémoires du Maréchal Joffre, 1932.

out much longer. Together with the deplorable state of the Belgian guns this made for quite a distressing situation. As a result Brécard cabled the Generalissimo at 23:30 the following dispatch:

> The morning has been rather quiet but since 14:00 very violent bombardment between Pervyse and Dixmude with 21 and 32 [cm calibre guns]. The flood between the Yser and the railway is not yet complete, but its effect makes itself already felt up to Pervyse.
> Belgian High Command and General Grossetti think that tomorrow the Germans will launch an attack north of Dixmude. The situation is being aggravated by the insufficiency of the Belgian artillery of which many guns are fouled and lack ammunition.

Earlier in the day he had already sent a message concerning the actual strength of the Belgian Army and the widespread lack of ammunition. He had also said:

> . . . I advised to economize [on shells] but this is difficult to accomplish for only the artillery has enabled the Belgian Army to hold out and endure.

In the late afternoon and evening a second high tide was now surreptitiously pushing its way inland. But the results were not that encouraging. Although the Spanish Lock had a width of 5.60m, quite acceptable an opening to provoke a flood in reasonable time, the shallow West Vaart narrowed in three spots. First, 700m upstream of the lock, the bridge on the Oost-Dunkerke Road brought the cross section back to 4.50m. The same happened a second time at the Arch Bridge, another 400m upstream. Finally, a mile from the lock, the water had to pass through the old culvert under the Furnes Canal. Where the West Vaart had not been subjected to tidal water for many years now all of a sudden the rising tide carried along a mishmash of nets, kegs, broken boards, jolly boats and whatever other floating debris a constant bombardment can produce. All these objects collected against the culvert abutment wall, hampering the flow rate.

The weir on the Great Beaverdyke Vaart partly collapsed during the war as a result of the excessive water pressure. This picture was taken shortly after the disaster. The water level of the inundation was now quickly dropping, over time opening the possibility of a large-scale German attack on the Belgian front. Left, the weir and in front the North Vaart which leads to the tidal gates. The row of trees marks the levee between the North Vaart and the Furnes Canal. From here they run parallel to each other towards the Goose Foot complex. *Nieuport 1914-1918*, R. Thys, 1922.

In the interwar years it has been argued by some that due to the lack of maintenance in the preceding years, one or more of the openings would have been completely blocked. From a recently resurfaced report from Captain Thys however, we learned that in May 1916 divers from his *pontoneers'* company inspected the four channels of the culvert and they did not find any obstructions.

Another, more important obstruction however, unbeknown at the time, was the weir on the Great Beaverdyke Vaart, a few hundred metres upstream from the culvert. Similar in construction to the weir on the Koolhof Vaart (which was heightened since it formed part of the emergency dyke), the stop planks in the dam had not yet been removed for the winter season. The military engineers, unfamiliar with the local situation, were not aware of the existence of this structure nor had Charles Cogge mentioned it. As a result the rising water at first began to fill up the adjacent wide North Vaart and the ditches in the fields along the railway embankment towards the paved road to Ramscappelle. So with hindsight it is no surprise that in the evening at the closed underpass of the Venepe Vaart, only 5km south of Nieuport, the water level was still unchanged. But to the military at the time this news was quite distressing: they had to flood an area of some 30 square kilometres and stretching as far back as 12km inland in the shortest possible time.

After the war, critics have often argued that this blockage prevented a swift inland advance of the seawater. Conversely, with the abundant rains of the previous two weeks the weir had held up a considerable amount of surface water, thus 'saving' water for the upcoming flooding manoeuvres. Anyway, this would explain the surprisingly positive

After the collapse the weir on the Great Beaverdyke Vaart was sealed off from the inundation with a cofferdam made out of sandbags to allow for reconstruction. Here we get a good idea of the size of this 'small' structure. We should not forget that all activity in no man's land could only be carried out with manpower and simple tools.
Nieuport 1914-1918 R. Thys, 1922.

effect over the whole area two days later after this rather discouraging slow start.

Strangely enough Charles Cogge has always remained silent on this matter. It has been mentioned by some authors that he was responsible for the seasonal placement, and removal, of these stop planks but that is highly unlikely. Cogge lived in Furnes and the weir was near Nieuport. Quite probably someone from the Water Board in Nieuport, or perhaps even the lock personnel at the Goose Foot, were responsible for the proper workings of the weir.

A similar weir existed a mile upstream, the Great Beaverdyke Vaart at Ketelersdam, not far from St Georges. Strangely Captain Thys only learned about the existence of both weirs on 2 January 1915. Subsequently, in a daring nocturnal excursion by shallop – by then the polder was no-man's-land – he managed to open the first weir on 4 January. Ten days later, in a similar action, he discovered that the weir at Ketelersdam was open.

Certainly totally frustrated by the lack of progress was Henry Geeraert, the bargee who had assisted Second Lieutenant François at the Spring Sluice with the flood of the Nieuwendamme Creek on 21 October. After this exploit Geeraert had somehow managed to stay in Nieuport, close to the locks and the Belgian *pontoneers*. With them he lived in the small vaulted cellars of the deserted, crumbling town. Now that it looked

The North Vaart Gates seen on the tidal (downstream) side. At low tide a visual inspection is made of the piers, the columns and the lift doors. Notice the inland water jetting through the cracks. Slowly throughout the war the doors and columns, one after another, would be dislodged, then destroyed by enemy bombardments. In the company shop near Furnes, heavy flap doors would then be constructed which, during a lull in the fighting, would be installed on site.
Nieuport 1914-1918, R. Thys, 1922.

as if the enemy was going to overrun the Belgians in the final hours before the flood would reach its full extent, Geeraert was definitely upset.

Regardless of the risk, he was absolutely convinced that the quickest way to flood the polder was to lift the eight gates of the North Vaart. But to open these gates the military needed the appropriate windlasses to operate the gearboxes and he was the only one still around who knew where they were stored.

With all his jovial persuasiveness Henry somehow managed to convince Captain Commandant Borlon, commanding the engineers' battalion in Nieuport of the urgency of the matter. And so, late in the evening of 28 October Borlon had a small detachment organized. Accompanied by Geeraert and led by himself, Borlon and his men cautiously headed for the locks. As the bridge on the Furnes Lock had been destroyed they crossed the structure one by one, running stooped across the narrow lock doors on their way to the North Vaart . . .

With the flood work gaining momentum, it was impossible for Captain Thys to direct all the fieldwork alone. As a result High Command appointed a second assistant to Captain Commandant Jamotte at the Inundation Directorate: Captain Fernand Umé.

The appointment of Umé was not unexpected. Umé and Thys knew each other already quite well. Although two years older than Robert Thys, Fernand Umé graduated from the Royal Military Academy in the same class as Thys. In 1905 they were both assigned to the Engineers' Regiment but, while Thys left active service in 1909 and went in the reserves, Umé stayed in the army and moved on to head the *Pontoneers'*

At the company bomb shelter in La Panne. Captain Umé is the man with his hand over his eyes. *Nieuport 1914-1918, R. Thys, 1922.*

Battalion of the Liège Fortified Place in 1912. A year later he graduated as an electrical engineer at the Montefiore College – today the Liège University – probably again in the same class as Thys. After the outbreak of the war Umé made the retreat from Liège to Antwerp with the Third Army Division, then on to the Yser River.

Now, on the evening of 28 October at 23:00, Thys travelled from Furnes to Nieuport to explain to his comrade-in-arms what he had already accomplished at the Spanish Lock and what the plans were for the next days.

Upon his arrival at engineer's headquarters in Nieuport Thys heard to his amazement about the improvised attempt being made by Borlon and Geeraert in front of the friendly lines. This was an alarming development. When Second Lieutenant François had blown up the Furnes Lock Bridge two nights earlier the French troops had abandoned the whole Goose Foot lock complex. Since then it was not known if the Germans had occupied the structures or not.

During the daytime the defenders of Nieuport still had some visual control over what happened in front of their line but it was quite possible that the previous night the enemy had deviously occupied the locks' platform and the houses of the lock staff dispersed in between. Even if they had not done so yet they would now be close enough to detect any movement, day or night, on the Five-Bridges Road. If one man of the detachment was taken prisoner, or if the Germans just made the right deductions, the whole enterprise could be ruined. Within a short time the road to Dunkirk would be open for the enemy. Or to paraphrase Victor Hugo: the wind would blow the Land of the Belgians onto the cliffs.

The enemy, once master of the North Vaart Gates, only had to open the gates at ebb tide to drain all the water that Thys had so secretly managed to let in. With its superior

211

drainage capacity – 16m wide versus the 5.60m of the Spanish Lock – the Germans could actually drain three times more water from the polder through the eight lift gates than Thys would ever be able to let in! Immediately Thys phoned High Command and before Borlon and his team could start their work the daring escapade was called off.

Once the dust had settled over this unexpected event Thys could finally bring Umé up-to-date about the ongoing flood procedures. Then he could call it a day. Having been on his feet for almost sixty hours Thys badly needed some rest. He returned to his billet in Furnes where he went to bed and slept until 13:30 the next day.

In the early hours of Thursday, 29 October a heavy fog blanketed the Flanders countryside. At the Spanish Lock a third high tide was streaming vigorously through the deep, narrow lock chamber lined by the tall freestone walls. The results inland, visible once the mist had lifted, were still not encouraging: officers and men peeking across the railway levee at Ramscappelle started to discern some sloughs on the land in front of them but once past the village, Pervyse way, the fields were definitely still dry.

After heavy shelling between Boitshoucke and Pervyse the Germans launched yet another assault on the First Army Division but the 4th de Ligne Regiment, holding the line in that spot, was able to throw the enemy back. In the afternoon an even more vigorous attack followed, this time accompanied by a diversionary charge on the Second Army Division near Ramscappelle. The 3rd and again the 4th de Ligne managed to fend off the attackers a second time. Several German batteries were now confirmed as being

The North Vaart Gates, this time seen from the polder. Taking advantage of an unusually low water level in the polder – for that to happen both upstream weirs needed to be closed simultaneously – the foundation floor is checked for cracks. The engineers were always afraid that the numerous explosions in and around the locks would undermine the structures, which would in turn create water seepage and eventually cause a massive cave-in.
Nieuport 1914-1918, R. Thys, 1922.

on the Yser left bank, offering close artillery support to the infantry. It was obvious that the enemy was attempting to break through the Belgian lines more inland, away from the threat of the British Fleet and still far enough from the Pervyse/Dixmude area, where the Belgians were firmly supported by French troops.

Hood's flotilla was ready to take on more distant targets. With the temporarily extended liberty regarding the use of ammunition the Admiral put the 305 and 152-mm guns of the battleship *Venerable* to good use, especially on the German gun positions between St Georges and Schoorbakke. The sight of the bombarding vessels left a momentous impression on the few troops in reserve relaxing on the beach and in the dunes. The queen best described the fire by the *Venerable*:

> Awful bombardment the whole day, especially by the British ships. We follow the gunnery with binoculars. A new warship has arrived. It looks magnificent in the sun. Its fire is heavier than that of the others and shakes the whole house. Everything is illuminated in the evening by the firing guns.

At 12:30, like the previous day, the station in Furnes received three hits, apparently by 150-mm rounds. More devastating was the bombardment on Pervyse with 320-mm grenades.

On the Nieuport/Dixmude front the French contingent was now being reinforced by three battalions of the 38th Infantry Division. This division had arrived from Dunkirk

A pre-war view of the Furnes Lock Gates. Coming from the right Captain Umé, Geeraert and their helpers first needed to cross the gate structure, then the narrow lock doors (hidden from view behind the stairs on the left) and then continue towards the North Vaart Gates. All this at night, in single file and only lightly armed.
Historical prints collection Callenaere-Dehouck.

in the Loo area the previous day but the bulk of its forces was now being directed to the south-east of Loo, across the Ypres Canal.

General d'Urbal for his part expected the Marine Fusiliers Brigade, together with the 3rd *Chasseurs d'Afrique*, the 8th *Chasseurs à cheval* and the 6th Hussars to attack from Dixmude and south of it, towards Thourout. The tall General had certainly not lost his aggressive attitude! He still had misgivings about the results of the Belgian flood attempt though and, for that matter, the Belgian military effort in general:

> To prevent being halted in his offensive by an adventure on the lower Yser, the general commanding the [DAB] army ordered the establishment of a second line of resistance towards the French border. This line, starting at the coast near Coxyde, will join the line of the Loo Canal, which it will subsequently follow.

With the looming threat of a German offensive south of Nieuport on the one hand and the poor results of the flood through the Spanish Lock on the other, High Command at 16:00 finally gave in to the ever increasing pressure from everyone to attempt an opening of the abandoned North Vaart Gates regardless the danger of detection by the Germans.

So after dark, at 19:30, Captain Umé and Henry Geeraert crossed the Furnes Lock atop the slippery, narrow doors and made their way to the North Vaart in short spurts, taking cover and halting every so often. With them they again had Corporal Ballon and the soldiers Cop and Van Belle, the three men that had been part of the team that had opened the Spring Sluice on the 21st. To protect the party against a sudden German encounter in no man's land a platoon of forty Carabineers-Cyclists of the First Army Division, led by Lieutenant Lupsin, had fanned out in front of them and were now hiding in the hedges between the locks. One of the carabineers had at first created some anxiety since he had slipped on the lock doors and had ended up in the water, luckily without serious injury.

With high tide at 21:10 there was no time to waste. The rising water in the channel had already surpassed the vaart level, enabling them to raise the eight double sliding doors immediately. Every move had been discussed beforehand. Geeraert quickly found the windlasses and soon the five men started their nerve-

Henry Geeraert, in greatcoat and with cane, posing at a gearbox on the North Vaart Gates. Soon rows of fascines were installed along the railings to conceal the workings on the lock platform from prying enemy eyes. Later on these were replaced by steel sheet pilings, which gave better protection against enemy rifle fire.
Nieuport 1914-1918, R. Thys, 1922.

Geeraert, this time in uniform with medals and kepi, poses at the North Vaart. The protective sheet piling did apparently not stop every projectile as can be seen in the foreground. *Historical prints collection Callenaere-Dehouck.*

racking work. In the dark they moved from gearbox to gearbox, each time popping the square keyhole of the heavy handle over the corresponding, well-greased shaft protruding from the cast iron box, after which they started cranking frantically.

Once in a while they whispered a word, then they anxiously looked around. It was hard labour since it took two men to operate one handle in order to lift a door. So each time they stood facing each other, handle in between them and four hands alternately grasping the large stock. Sixteen times over again they repeated the same procedure, slowly raising each door. With their hearts in their mouths and gasping for air they expected the Germans to open fire out of nowhere at any moment.

The gear assemblies worked smoothly but in their excitement the soldiers, sweating in spite of the autumn cold, had the impression that the noise they created could be heard for miles around. Undoubtedly the enemy would realize what was going on and would react fast and furiously. Even though the whole operation took only twenty minutes, to the men on the dark and deserted locks it seemed like hours.

Amazingly no counter-attack erupted

In the next four years the doors of the North Vaart would still be raised and lowered numerous times. Left, Henry Geeraert, in the middle, Hector Billemont (killed on 25 June, 1918) and on the right, Sergeant Emile Derouck (wounded 27 November, 1917). *Nieuport 1914-1918, R. Thys, 1922.*

215

Today the North Vaart Gates at night project an almost enchanting vista. In October 1914 it was a place where behind every corner or bush death loomed. In the background on the right, we see the imposing King Albert I monument, erected after the war.
Author's photo archive.

from across the river. How many German eyes were following every move? Where was the boche?

As each door was raised the water in the North Vaart started to move faster and faster until, over the full width of the structure, the blackish seawater was gushing angrily inland. As swiftly as they had arrived the brave Belgians now retreated through the low vegetation, across the lock doors and lift gates on the Furnes Canal to the relative safety of the friendly lines. The carabineers followed one by one.

With the raising of the doors the entire manoeuvre was not yet finished. Before the tide started to recede the whole procedure had to be reversed, the doors had to be lowered again. For six hours the five 'inundation sappers' waited anxiously in the cellar of the abandoned tavern A la nouvelle écluse chez Lobbestal, right in front of the Furnes Lock swing bridge.

Many questions went through their minds. What if the Germans noticed the rushing water? Would they grasp what was happening? Would they retaliate and level the whole area? If the enemy did not react now, would he have set up an ambush when they returned? Even if none of the above happened, would the gear mechanisms work properly to lower the doors safely? Wouldn't there be a door that would suddenly come crashing down?

Captain Umé himself later confessed: 'We were sitting there, pale with fear.'

Shortly before midnight the men returned to the North Vaart. Lowering the doors was hopefully somewhat easier since gravity would lend a hand. And from the enemy

216

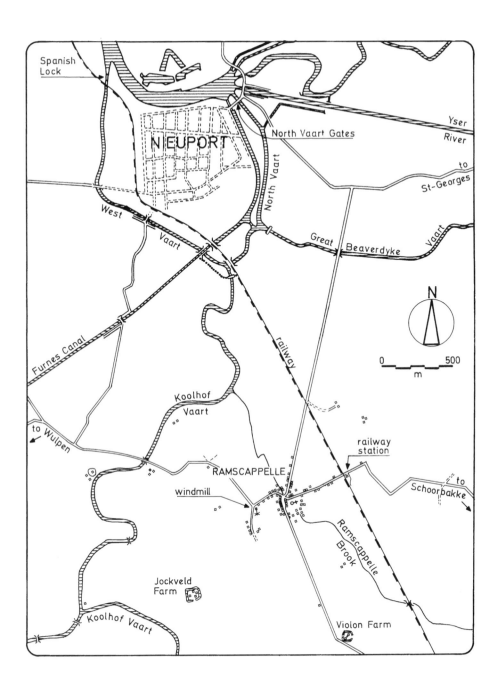

Spanish Lock

NIEUPORT

North Vaart Gates

North Vaart

Yser River

to St-Georges

West Vaart

Great Beaverdyke Vaart

Furnes Canal

N

0 ____ 500
m

railway

Koolhof Vaart

to Wulpen

railway station

RAMSCAPPELLE

to Schoorbakke

windmill

Ramscappelle Brook

Jockveld Farm

Koolhof Vaart

Violon Farm

217

there wasn't a whimper. But when Captain Umé was about to give the order to start Geeraert, standing on the landside of the structure, suddenly held him back. He threw a chunk of wood in the water and, noticing it still floated inland he whispered: 'Captain, wait . . . not a drop can be enough for those bastards!'

Then one by one the doors were lowered. One after the other the men released the pawl from the ratchet of each gearbox and slowly winched each two metres wide, four metres high, heavy wooden leaf back down.

A massive amount of seawater was trapped in the polder.

NOTES
1. For the rest of the war Colienne would volunteer as a hospital nurse. She would be one of a few brave nurses that would even venture out into the trenches herself to collect the wounded. For lots more on the Belgian Medical Service during the Great War visit Dr. Patrick Loodts' website: *Médecins de la Grande Guerre* www.1914-1918.be (in French).
2. We suspect that the queen, in her diary talked about the newly established Fort Louis Hospital, headed by Dr. Paul Derache.

Chapter XV

The Final Rumble in Ramscappelle

On the morning of 30 October pictures taken by aeroplane revealed a first, large slough being formed east of Ramscappelle. It was high time! The whole night the Germans had been bombarding the entire line of defence. Before daybreak eight German regiments attacked on a 10km wide front, from Nieuport to halfway between Pervyse and Dixmude. The blow was especially violent in front of Pervyse and Ramscappelle.

At the level crossing near Pervyse the entire 13th de Ligne Regiment, one battalion of the 10th and a battalion of French *Chasseurs* resisted gallantly. During the morning hours the failure of the German assault in this spot became apparent by the capture of over 200 prisoners.

Near Ramscappelle the news was not as good. At 07:00 the Germans had reached the railway in force and soon a couple of machine guns had the line in enfilading fire. At the same time the Belgians learned about, and endured, a new terror: hand grenades. With a renewed effort the enemy jumped the tracks and dashed the 400m along the narrow cobblestone road leading straight towards the village church. Here, in the cluster of houses, they were halted by a counter-attack of the remnants of the 5th and 6th de Ligne and the 151st French Regiment.

From 11:00 on an amalgamation of four battalions [1] tried to regain a foothold in the settlement but their initial momentum was broken at the outskirts of the village. Two hundred and fifty metres west of the steeple, past the last house, the Germans had captured a windmill and had immediately installed machine guns in the few small windows and on the garret. Now they could cover a vast area west of the railway with deadly fire. Together with the machine guns, hidden in the houses along the perimeter of the village, a frontal assault in daylight became impossible.

In the cellars of the Jockveld Farm, 700m south-west of the windmill, the French colonel of the 16th *Chasseurs* was in charge of organizing a counter-attack. The main problem was that the winding Koolhof Vaart encircled the windmill at a distance of 1,000m. This would force the attackers to concentrate and cross the waterway at the few available narrow bridges. It was an extremely vulnerable point of departure.

The loss of Ramscappelle and the fierce fighting near Pervyse did not boost the king's morale. The combination of the use of the railway embankment and the flood east of it had seemed a quite viable idea to protect his army and a meagre stretch of national soil from the claws of the invader. Anxiety was once again taking over: was there another retreat in the making? Would he have to leave Belgian territory after all? What

219

would happen to his soldiers once in France? And how would the German Emperor treat the compatriots he had been forced to leave behind?

Admiral Hood meanwhile kept up the shore bombardment. In honour of the French cooperation in the naval force Hood transferred his flag to the brand new French destroyer *L'Intrépide*. This was in fact the first time in history that a French warship acted as an English flagship without having first been captured!

L'Intrépide and its sister ship *L'Aventurier* had originally been destined for the Armada Republica Argentina but had been taken over by the French Navy on the wharf on 9 August 1914. They had both joined the French naval complement under the orders of Hood off the Belgian coast in October.

By now the position of the squadron was more precarious than ever. Owing to the batteries that the Germans had concealed all along the occupied coast, it was increasingly difficult for the vessels to get any appreciable results from their fire. Solely by constantly keeping on the move at high speed could heavy casualties be avoided. Also the threat of submarine attack was growing daily.

Sensing the importance of this successful and certainly undisturbed opening of the North Vaart gates Captain Thys immediately asked High Command to have the Five-Bridges Road and the lock complex re-occupied.

It is not clear though if his request was fulfilled right away. We should keep in mind that, from the coastline up to and including Nieuport, French units had taken over the front. Only at the Goose Foot, Belgian engineers still had some control over the situation. This improvised patchwork of various units from different nationalities did not simplify the chain of command. Somewhat later a French soldier apparently captured

Maintaining the flooding and at the same time keeping the Allied lines dry was the main role of the inundation company. Here we see a temporary grave for a fallen soldier in the water a few metres behind the railway embankment, just south of Nieuport in January 1915. *Nieuport 1914-1918, R. Thys, 1922.*

The flood seen from the church tower in Nieuport, early in the war. One can see the sharp line between the water (left) and the dry land behind the railway (see the arrow). *Nieuport 1914-1918, R. Thys, 1922.*

sixty prisoners in the lock house near the Bruges Canal, north of the Yser which indicates that the French had at least moved onto the lock platform.

Later in the day, with a better understanding of the changing hydraulic conditions, Thys proposed to speed up the flood by also opening the Furnes and Ypres locks. But in his book he rather cynically commented: 'They do not want to act too quickly.'

As said earlier, the military engineers preferred to use locks doors to lift gates to attempt a flood in the battle zone. The choice of the Furnes Lock was a logical and feasible proposal, especially in combination with the East Vaart Lock or through the ruptured dyke along the canal. His suggestion to also use the Ypres Lock – the one on the Yser – looks less obvious to us. Unless the captain had another plan in mind.

Since the opening of the levee between the Furnes Canal and the North Vaart had now become useless with the cancellation of the push of water from Dunkirk, the ruptured dyke would be repaired in the following days.

Around 12:00 sloughs started to appear in the fields across the railway between Ramscappelle and Pervyse. The Germans occupying Ramscappelle, when looking back, realized that they were being cut off from their own lines by slowly rising water. Captain Otto Schwink, an officer of the Imperial German Staff wrote:

At 11:30 however, a General Staff Officer . . . reported that the attack could not be continued owing to the constant rising of the water. What had happened? On the morning of the 30th the advancing troops had been up to their ankles in water; then it had gradually risen until they were now wading up to their knees, and they could scarcely drag their feet out of the clay soil. . . . The rise of the waters was attributed to the torrential rain of the previous few days, and it was hoped that on approach of dry weather the excellent system of canals would soon drain it off. But the rising flood soon prevented the movement of wagons . . . the green meadows were covered with dirty, yellowish water and the general line of the roads was only indicated by houses and the rows of partly covered trees. It soon became evident that the enemy must have blown up the canal sluices and called in the sea to his aid.

In the late afternoon the water emerged in the trenches still held by the Belgians across the railway south of Old-Stuyvekenskerke, 11km from the Spanish Lock. While the North Vaart Gates had only been opened once, by now five tides had automatically passed through the Spanish Lock.

In the evening, encouraged by the success of the past night, Captain Umé, Geeraert and their three assistants repeated their endeavour on the North Vaart Gates structure. This time the covering Carabineers detachment was under command of Lieutenant Penneman. Amazingly enough, again they carried out their work without being detected by the enemy.

Finally the Germans had to concede defeat. During the night General von Beseler, commanding the Third German Reserve Army Corps, ordered the bulk of his troops to withdraw from the west bank back across the Yser River. A few small detachments were left behind in Ramscappelle and near Pervyse.

At 06:00 on 31 October, the Franco-Belgian assault on Ramscappelle, supported by French artillery, was renewed: to the north and north-west two Belgian battalions, one of the 14th and one of the 6th de Ligne Regiment, to the south and south-west the French 16th *Chasseurs* Regiment, reinforced by the two other battalions of the 14th and 6th and eight Senegalese companies.

Marcel Senesael, an Yser veteran himself, described what the men of the 6th de Ligne endured south of Ramscappelle:

> As always, having started off before breakfast, the men had to fight on an empty stomach. In the heavy, soaked clay soil they lost their clogs that had replaced their worn-out shoes. Each dash forward was more demanding than the previous one: the fire got more concentrated and the tiredness increased. At

The Nieuport Road – now Ramskapelle Street – at the railway crossing in 1914. Today the E40 freeway from Brussels to Dunkirk passes here high above on a massive, modern-day embankment.
Nieuport 1914-1918, R. Thys, 1922.

about ten o'clock the officers allowed the men to take a break in the shelter of a water filled ditch. Suddenly, from behind Jockveld Farm, loud voices reverberated across the wet killing fields. Agile like cats, a row of unfamiliar soldiers crossed the Koolhof Vaart, fanned out and took up positions nearby. Wide trousers, slim stature and red headgear on a brown face: these were Zouaves.

As it happened these southerners were on their way to take up positions south-west of Violon Farm.

Around 14:00 the exits of the village were again in Franco-Belgian hands and soon afterwards the last remaining Germans were killed or chased back into the muddy waters across the railway. Meanwhile, further south the troops had also regained control over the entire length of the railway embankment. Near the Pervyse station sixty Germans surrendered to the French. Around Old-Stuyvekenskerke though, where the water had not yet attained critical levels, the enemy still tried to mount an attack south-wards to cut off the Franco-Belgian stronghold of Dixmude but again they failed.

The threat of German submarines off the Belgian coast was becoming more menacing with each passing day. The seaplane-carrier *Hermes*, which had arrived in Dunkirk the previous day, sailed again for Dover but around 10:00 she was torpedoed and sunk eight miles west-north-west of Calais. This incident raised the question whether the risk the Dover Patrol was now running was worth the results it could still achieve. The enemy batteries were now so well concealed in and behind the dunes that shore bombardment was becoming practically useless. The battleship *Venerable* was there-fore ordered to return to England and instead the old battleship *Revenge* was being prepared at Portsmouth as a bombardment vessel.

The old *Revenge*, would later on still serve well on the extreme left flank of the Western Front. Completed in 1894 the ship floated a formidable array of firepower: four 343-mm guns, ten 152-mm, sixteen 6-pounders and twelve 3-pounders. In Portsmouth in October 1914 bulges were fitted as defence against mines and torpedoes, together with an early form of minesweeping gear. While operating off the Belgian coast in 1914-15 she was often heeled by flooding one of the bulges to increase the elevation of her guns. When the stocks of 343-mm shells ran out her guns were relined to 305-mm that increased their effective range to 14.6km. In August 1915 she was renamed *Redoubtable* but soon afterwards the vessel was decommissioned.

The situation around Ypres meanwhile, 25km to the south, was becoming acute for the BEF. General Foch visited Sir John French at 02:00 on 31 October to discuss the situation. The Field Marshal was again pondering this 'Dunkirk option'. He wrote in his memoirs *1914*:

To me, indeed, it seemed as though our line at last was broken. If this were the case, the immense numerical superiority of the enemy would render retreat a very difficult operation, particularly in view of the fact that Ypres and the river Yser lay in our immediate rear.

That night Captain Umé and Henry Geeraert lifted the gates of the North Vaart for the third time, amazingly again without enemy interference.

The next day, All Saints' Day, was a Sunday. The royal couple went to mass at 08:30.

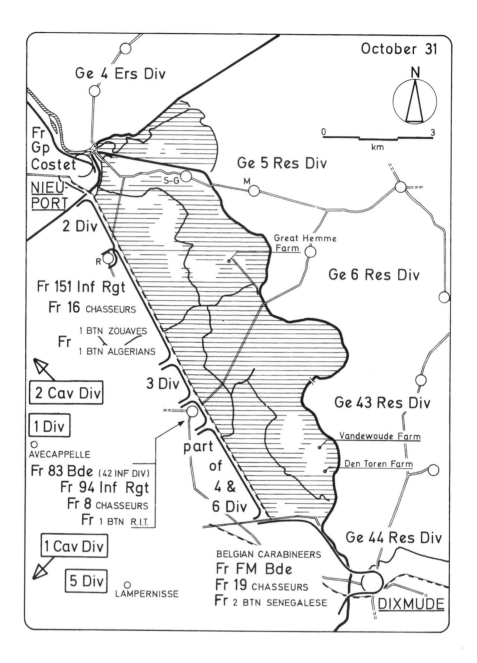

October 31

N

Ge 4 Ers Div

Fr
Gp
Costet

Ge 5 Res Div

0   3
km

NIEU-
PORT

S-G   M

2 Div

R

Great Hemme
Farm

Ge 6 Res Div

Fr 151 Inf Rgt
Fr 16 CHASSEURS

Fr   1 BTN ZOUAVES
    1 BTN ALGERIANS

3 Div

2 Cav Div

Ge 43 Res Div

1 Div

Vandewoude Farm

AVECAPPELLE

Den Toren Farm

part
of
4 &
6 Div

Fr 83 Bde (42 INF DIV)
Fr 94 Inf Rgt
Fr 8 CHASSEURS
Fr 1 BTN R.I.T.

1 Cav Div

Ge 44 Res Div

5 Div

LAMPERNISSE

BELGIAN CARABINEERS
Fr FM Bde
Fr 19 CHASSEURS
Fr 2 BTN SENEGALESE

DIXMUDE

Contrary to what they had experienced during the previous months, the air was filled with calmness, no war sounds could be heard. Occasionally the sun managed to break through the clouds, bringing some welcome relief from the sharp cold brought on by a stiff south-easterly breeze.

In spite of the fact that the German bombardment started around eleven o'clock, the enemy was now in full retreat: north-east of Pervyse they blew up the bridge across

The Noble Rose restaurant in Furnes. A shell hit the upper floor while Robert Thys was having dinner downstairs. The historic house, built in 1572, was restored a first time in 1890. In 1906 the German poet Reiner Maria Rilke stayed here, while during the Great War the French nuclear physicist, Marie Curie, visited briefly.
Nieuport 1914-1918, R. Thys, 1922.

The Noble Rose today. The famous inn was restored after the war while a third restoration took place in 2000. Since the war the American Allen family have been godparents of the building.

the Great Beaverdyke Vaart, as such cutting the road Pervyse-Schoorbakke. By nightfall they only held on to a few sites west of the river: the village of St Georges and the Union Bridge in the north and the Great Hemme Farm and the Schoorbakke Bridge in the centre. In the south they stuck to the higher ground around Den Toren en Vandewoude farms.

With the *Venerable* gone and the *Revenge* not yet having arrived there was not much firepower left to Admiral Hood. So as the front was rather calm he decided to give his sailors a break and kept his flotilla in port.

While Captain Thys was having lunch at the Noble Rose Restaurant in Furnes at 13:00, a 150-mm shell suddenly came in through the façade above the main entrance and exploded on the first floor, blowing out windows and roof tiles. After that every five minutes or so a shell landed somewhere in town until 16:30. All in all twenty-five shells of 105 and 150-mm calibre were counted. The attack caused a lot of nervous excitement and created a new wave of refugees fleeing in the direction of Adinkerke and

La Panne. As the closest German lines were still 11km away everyone wondered how a German gun could fire that far. The panicky atmosphere did quieten down somewhat with the arrival of King Albert. The monarch stayed the whole afternoon at General Headquarters.

Because of the still rising water the last German troops around Old-Stuyvekenskerke too were forced to retreat across the river.

Again – and this would be the last time in order to achieve the set flood level – Umé and Geeraert opened the North Vaart Gates in the evening.

On All Souls' Day, 2 November, Belgian reconnaissance patrols on the inundated polder confirmed that the Germans were still occupying some farms west of the river. These were apparently being fortified with several machine guns each. Other patrols, the next day, were able to reach Lombartzyde and St Georges; some men even crossed the Yser and reached as far as Mannekensvere.

As a result of this encouraging news Belgian troops quickly re-occupied the locks and the immediate vicinity. Until the end of the war this bridgehead was to stay in allied hands.

A few days later the Germans would deal a last major blow to the Belgian Yser front. On 10 November 1914, in a murderous battle the exposed and indeed fragile bridge-head of the town of Dixmude was lost to the enemy.

With the coastal route to Dunkirk firmly locked by the floodwater the enemy shifted his attention more to the south. The next major access road to the Channel ports passed through the Belgian town of Ypres, an unassuming, quiet, Flemish locality until then mainly known for its imposing and beautiful thirteenth century, gothic Clothmakers' Hall. The Germans would now focus all their strength on this communications centre in order to force a breakthrough.

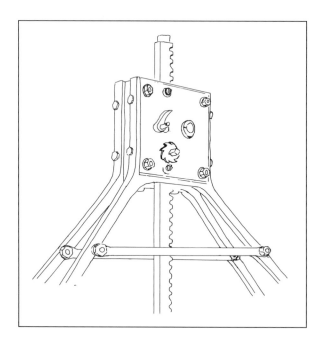

Detail of the lift mechanism of one of the doors of the now abandoned gates of the Nieuwendamme Creek on the Yser. Only the lockkeepers could lift the doors as they carried the handles with them.

But the BEF was waiting for them. While the Belgians had secured one small part of their country, Sir John French was not going to disappoint their king. He would hold on to that other parcel of Belgium that was still free: Ypres.

And the rest is history.

NOTES

1. One battalion of the 14th de Ligne, one battalion of the 8th Algerian Tirailleurs, one of the 4th Zouaves (French light infantry) and the 16th Battalion chasseurs.

Chapter XVI

After the Battle

Detracting from its strategic importance the Battle of the Yser River is better known to the outside world as 'The First Phase of The First Battle of Ypres'. When on 3 November 1914 large tracts of land had disappeared under water the front stabilized between the North Sea and Dixmude. But it had all come at a tremendous high price for King Albert's small conscript army: almost one third of the infantrymen that had gone into battle two weeks earlier were now killed, wounded or missing. As always total figures vary somewhat but historian A. Peteau gives a figure for 31 October:

> But the losses for the Belgian Army had been considerable: they could be estimated at 14,000 men killed or wounded. The infantry had been reduced from 48,000 to 32,000 rifles . . . .

For the remainder of the war the Germans stayed east of the Yser, seemingly comfortable with the status quo in this sector. The Belgians were physically in control of the drainage of the region but the enemy would quickly vent his anger over measures taken at the Goose Foot that did not suit him by bombarding the locks angrily and ferociously.

The next four years Captain – later Captain Commandant – Robert Thys led a specialized company of *sappers–pontoneers* that maintained the floods. Thys surrounded himself with a handful of officers, in civilian life experts in hydraulics and mathematics. Together they succeeded in extending the flooding considerably, mainly east and south of Dixmude, always into German occupied territory.

Along the 33km stretch of flooded no man's land bordering the Yser River and Ypres Canal a unique pattern of brown water warfare developed: an intricate system of well-camouflaged listening posts was established by both sides and daring nightly raids in flat-bottomed boats were conducted regularly to capture prisoners, collect information or silence annoying enemy positions.

In spite of frequent artillery bombardments the *pontoneers* kept the drainage control structures in Nieuport operational throughout the war. In 1918 though, before the final Allied offensive, the Germans practically obliterated all the sluices and locks.

After the war Robert Thys returned to civilian life building a career first in the Belgian Congo, later on in Belgium. He was promoted lieutenant colonel (Reserve) in 1934. Four years later failing health forced him to resign from military duty. With mischievous enthusiasm and full of geniality he could talk about the more picturesque side of his

In November 1914 Captain Umé managed to create another large flood east of Dixmude. He opened the Ypres Lock at spring tide in Nieuport and pushed water through the Yser all the way past Dixmude by way of the Handzaeme Vaart. Here we see the Handzaeme Vaart in more peaceful times in the centre of Dixmude.
Historical prints collection Renée Beever.

role in October 1914, as if it had been one adventurous hunting game. But when it came to 'my men' he would invariably stress their heroic devotion to their work. Besides, his men would have gone through hell for their commander. For all of them he was like an older brother who not only looked after their physical well-being but also their social and cultural wants. Until his death in 1964 he would chair an annual reunion of 'his' *sappers-pontoneers* in Nieuport.

Captain Fernand Umé left the Inundation Service shortly after the events to head various telegraph units. In 1920 he was appointed Professor of Electricity at the Royal Military Academy, a post he held for the next thirty-two years. In 1945 he was promoted lieutenant general (Reserve).

After October Charles Cogge, the elderly supervisor of the Furnes North Water withdrew to his home in Furnes. He had informed Nuyten about the workings of the drainage in the region, he had guided Jamotte along the railway embankment and had brought Thys to the Spanish Lock in the middle of the night. He had accomplished his duties.

At the age of fifty-one Henry Geeraert, the daring bargee, stayed with the *pontoneers* and manoeuvred the locks for the rest of the war. He became known to the soldiers as 'father Henry' and worked with them as an equal, under the most dangerous of circumstances. Already during the war he became the legendary symbol of stubborn, civilian resistance to the Boche. Like tens of thousands of others he paid dearly for his life in

(above) The bust of Charles Cogge on a high pedestal in North Street in Furnes. *Author's photo archive.*

(left) Henry Geeraert, too, got his bust. Perhaps not quite inappropriately placed above a tavern in front of the Furnes Lock in Nieuport. Oral tradition has it that here Geeraert, Umé and their platoon waited anxiously to return to the North Vaart that fateful night of 29 October. *Author's photo archive.*

the trenches. He passed away in an asylum in Bruges in the afternoon of 17 January 1925. Early the next morning King Albert himself alighted at the home to salute his deceased compatriot.

In the early 1950s a last national tribute would be paid to this cherished folk hero: his effigy appeared on the 1,000 francs banknote, back to back with the other Belgian legend of the Great War, King Albert himself.

After the war lockmaster Gerard Dingens returned to his locks to supervise their reconstruction. As retired Head Lockmaster he was back at work from August 1919 onwards. He passed away in Nieuport in 1926. Perhaps due to his authoritarian character but certainly because of his strong but honest, personal views on the military situation in 1914, he had lost out in becoming a national hero.

The Belgian Army, although seriously decimated and technically cut off from its recruiting base, managed to make an impressive comeback. During the war 30,000 young men managed to escape from occupied Belgium and volunteer for their own army. These journeys were a courageous exploit in themselves. Often dressed in rubber suits and equipped with wire-cutters, guides at night brought these daring patriots

In 1950 the Belgian Central Bank printed a 1,000 franc banknote with on one side King Albert
I and on the back a tribute to the 'saviour of the country' Henry Geeraert and the flood along
the Yser River. Buisseret's design was a composition of Geeraert's bust as seen on a picture
earlier in this book and in the background an engraving after another picture taken by Captain
Thys. On the right we see part of the Furnes Lock gantry and a view of the tidal bay. At the
time when the picture was taken, the land abutment of the gantry had been washed away due
to repeated shell bursts. These bank notes were withdrawn in 1958.
Historical prints collection Callenaere-Dehouck.

through the live, electrical barbed wire set up by the Germans along the Dutch-Belgian
border. Then travelling undercover through Holland they still had to make it to England
before they could enlist in the army. By 1918 the Belgian Army was back at its pre-war
strength. It guarded a front line of over 30km, from Nieuport-Bains on the coast to
Langemarck, just north of Ypres. In September 1918 the Belgian 'Army on the Yser'
comprised almost 170,000 men. At the outbreak of the war the total strength, including
the Garrison Army, had been close to 190,000 men.

Even more important, it was now better trained, better equipped and better led than
ever before.

King Albert, who was to become known and revered by his fellow countrymen as
the King-Soldier, never relinquished his supreme command of the Belgian Army in
favour of an Allied Commander. Quite the reverse happened. For the final Allied offensive in 1918 then Marshal Ferdinand Foch, Supreme Allied Commander, honoured
King Albert by presenting him with the command of the Army Group Flanders. This
temporary formation was composed of the Belgian Army, the French 7th Army Corps,
the British 2nd Army and the French 2nd Cavalry Corps. It would be the first and only
time in history that a king of the Belgians would command a large foreign army group.

Through careful and compassionate management of his precious human resources
the king had been able to avoid the so bloody and most of the time senseless offensives
that had been ordered by French and British commanders in the field.

Only recently historians came to reveal a totally different side of this beloved

The North Vaart Gates at the end of 1918. Only two of the original eight gates were still usable. The tower on the right is what remains of the reinforced concrete observation post established at the strategically located Café de l'Yser.
Nieuport 1914-1918, R. Thys, 1922.

In the autumn of 1919 the Belgian royal couple embarked on the USS *George Washington* for an official, almost triumphant visit to the United States where they visited both the west and east coasts. Here we see King Albert (left, in uniform) and Queen Elisabeth (lady on the right) in Central Park in New York where no less than 22,000 children cheered them on.
Ons Land, magazine, 1919.

232

To close the so-called 'Visé Gap' north of Liège, which the Germans had used to get quick access to central Belgium in 1914, a new fort was built at Eben-Emael in 1932. Perhaps it was impregnable to ground troops but in 1940 it was no match for German paratroopers who landed right on top of it. Here we see German soldiers gathered around the cross of remembrance which they erected on the roof of the complex to honour their comrades fallen during the operation.
Author's photo archive.

monarch: that of the king-peacemaker, or a man far ahead of his time. All through the war, he secretly tried to open up a diplomatic channel for talks aimed at an all-encompassing peace based on a 'no victors' concept. Unfortunately his relentless efforts never paid off.

Two of the king's close advisors from early on, Prudent Nuyten and Émile Galet, continued their promising military careers after the Great War.

Galet, as Lieutenant General, became Army Chief of Staff in 1929, succeeded in 1931 by his comrade-in-arms, Nuyten. At that moment dark war clouds were again gathering over Europe. Unswervingly Galet and Nuyten expressed their far-sighted ideas and practical proposals for a mobile defence of the country. But their voices were silenced in the political jungle of the inter-war period. Instead more taxpayers' money and reinforced concrete was poured into ever bigger and presumably 'better' fortifications.

After four years in the front line the town of Nieuport – now the city of Nieuwpoort – was totally levelled. In 1919 a massive reconstruction project was started and within a few years the city and its famous locks had risen from their ashes.

The Yser Mouth, once the extreme northern end of the Western Front, now boosts the biggest marina in northern Europe. In the shadow of the locks, untouched by today's hustle and bustle of the many gastronomic bistros lining the fisherman's wharf, *Café de l'Yser* is now a restaurant and small, charming, county town hotel. Also *Chez Lobbestal* is still there as a typical local tavern.

We have a practical message for those readers that want to visit the Spanish Lock in Nieuport today: *do not trip over one of Great War's little mysteries.* Indeed on the lock platform adjacent the lock chamber are several cast iron rings treacherously sticking out of the pavement! Who placed them there and why they are still there after such a long time is still unknown. For convenience sake we call them *'Thys' Rings'* since their purpose is quite obvious.

When on that historic night of October 26 to 27, 1914 the flood doors prematurely closed under the pressure of the rising tide it was clear that in the future such an occurrence was to be prevented at all cost. As a matter of fact up until the Second World War this inconspicuous lock still figured prominently in the military defense plans against another invasion (from the east).

Re-installing the typical door hooks (see picture p.131) was risky: any malicious passer-by with some tools would then be able to open the doors and cause a disaster. Keeping the doors open manually with heavy cables – as had been done that night – would still be the simplest option. But that did indeed require unbridled, raw manpower. A more "elegant" solution to bring the water pressure under control was found with the installation of two heavy, cast iron rings alongside each flood door. In case of another inundation attempt in the future a cable could then be strung from the door, through the rings (see the arrows). Friction on the rings would lower the tractive force so one sapper would be able to operate the flood doors. *Author's photo archive.*

Chapter XVII

Questions That Still Fascinate

Up to now we have told the story of the floods in the Belgian Sector of the Western Front at the beginning of the First World War. All the witnesses to this historic epic that survived the war have meanwhile set off to join the thousands of their comrades that by 1918 had found their grave in that waterlogged region of Europe. To the researcher this brings serenity to the investigation but also an enormous lack of personal contact with the main actors. All that is left are barely noticeable traces on the old battle-field and thousands of yellowing documents.

This predicament, as we have seen, sometimes leaves us with unanswered questions; uncertainties that linger in the historical haze. Some details have been absorbed by time and certain controversies will perhaps never be explained.

Luckily the story does not end there. October 1914 was in Belgian history an unprecedented period. The population at large was fleeing from a brutal invader, the politicians were busying themselves to go into exile and a demoralized, conscript army under direct orders of its monarch was trying to find its way along the land, without any preconceived and democratically accepted strategy. Unsettling times indeed.

Four years later, in the flush of victory, a series of fundamental questions of this early period were left unanswered. 'Why bother,' our forefathers must have thought, 'in the end we did win, didn't we?' Having been fenced off from their homesteads our boys – at least the ones who had survived this ordeal – could finally return home to their loved ones. What could be more important?

In the following pages we will try to untangle a few of those lingering questions that are so important to historians. A definite answer though will perhaps never be given.

Appendix I

The Elusive Keeper of the Locks

The (non) involvement of lockmaster Dingens and the engineers of the Roads & Bridges Department in the October 1914 floods has been a controversy for several decades.

After the war the lockmaster accused the military of forcing him and his staff to leave while Lucien François claimed they had fled after Le Clément de Saint-Marcq and Thys had visited the lock complex. Also according to Dingens he had left all the equipment to manoeuvre the locks in place. In a post-war affidavit François nevertheless maintained: '. . . in spite of us insisting [they left] without handing over the tools to manoeuvre the lock gates.'

As the reader will have understood the situation around the locks in October 1914 was a nasty and confusing mess. After the war each party tried to justify its own 'patriotic' behaviour. As often happens we suspect that the truth lies somewhere in the middle. Unquestionably the locks men did not flee at the first crack of the gun but they were not exactly driven off by the guard detachment either. The ever-increasing pressures of the approaching hostilities simply forced Dingens to lay down his responsibilities.

In 1920, in a lengthy interview published in two Belgian newspapers Gerard Dingens told his version of the events of October 1914. Although a valuable document, several points in the story, as told by both journalists, do not fit in.

A. Hans, in his article in the Flemish *Het Laatste Nieuws* newspaper of 18 June 1920 hinted that Dingens, after the investigation by the British officers on 10 October, then explained to them the idea of inundating the area between the Yser and the railway Dixmude-Nieuport. As such Dingens claimed to be the creator of the ultimately 'miraculous' flood. Strangely enough, the other journalist, G. Paquot in the French-language, sister newspaper *La Dernière Heure* of 5 June 1920, did not allude to this suggestion. Anyway, if one has a closer look at Dingens' allegations one has to come to a different conclusion:

At the time of the meeting with the British officers on 10 October, the area between the Yser and the railway did not have any tactical value whatsoever to the British in their defence of Ostend. It was 16km away from Ostend and the area Dingens would have suggested was sitting perpendicular to the coastline, a situation that would not even contribute to the defence of Nieuport, let alone Ostend. Just by the nature of his position Dingens must have known this.

Unfortunately, after all these years, no report on the matter has yet surfaced, written by those British officers that talked with Dingens on that day. For instance, relying on

Probably a post-war portrait of lockmaster Gerard Dingens. A personality that indeed radiated authority and, in normal circumstances anyway, must have commanded respect.
Historical prints collection Callenaere-Dehouck.

the intentions of the British – that is isolating Ostend from the mainland – we suspect that they had similar conversations with other lockkeepers in the Ostend region, like at the Slijkens Locks just east of the city and perhaps even in Zeebrugge. Their statements could put things in a different perspective.

As the British officers must have felt, there were a couple of discrepancies in the lockmaster's explanations. Dingens did stress the fact that it would take a long time to inundate the polder towards Ostend because the Nieuwbedelf Gates openings were too few and too small. But apparently he never mentioned to them that the same polder could simultaneously be flooded by using the Caemerlynck Sluices on the opposite end of that polder, namely in Ostend itself.

It was also irrelevant for him to mention that the roads would still surface: this was exactly what the British wanted! This procedure would give them control of the roads and preclude use of the adjoining land. In any case, his statements did not exactly convince the officers as we read about their doubts in the ensuing days.

The next day, 11 October, when the Francophone Belgian lieutenant and sergeant arrived on the scene another problem arises. One can ask the question why, at that moment, no higher ranking public servant from the lockkeeper's own administration of Roads & Bridges, showed up or, perhaps more logical, why did Dingens himself not try to contact one of his superiors to complain about the behaviour of the troopers? Although in the next few days the leading engineers of the department would leave the coastal region, on 11th they were all still supposed to be on duty, some even in Nieuport itself. We can only suspect that Dingens' own pride prevented him from calling superiors to his assistance. According to G. Paquot, when Captain Commandant Nuyten visited the lockmaster on 13 October, apparently Dingens reiterated 'his idea' on inundating between the Yser and the railway embankment.

After the initial discussion, according to Dingens, he went on to say that in fact only one particular polder would be easy to inundate: the area to the west of the Yser River, between this river and the railway embankment Dixmude-Nieuport. One would only have to carefully obstruct the various culverts under the railway. Special care would have to be taken though, in blocking the nine-metres wide, so-called Koolhof Vaart viaduct on the southern edge of Nieuport. Dingens underlined his explanation by showing the various stages on the ordnance map. He explained that this flood could be set rapidly by using seawater although, he declared, this would affect the fertile clay soil.

For two reasons this mere 'suggestion' by the lockmaster – if he ever made it – was of no interest to Nuyten: first of all this polder was well away from Ostend . . . and then we refer back to the discussion with the British earlier on, and secondly, his own General Staff had chosen this region to assemble the army!

On this second point, there are two more reasons why Dingens' version of the meeting is unreliable at certain points:

1. The initial intent of High Command, as discussed in Eecloo on 9 October, was only to use the Furnes-Ambacht region simply as a staging area to regroup. The Yser had been mentioned as a physical marker on the ground to act as the perimeter of this 'safe haven', of which only its exits would have to be guarded. The Anglo-French forces under General Rawlinson were understood to make the front east of the river and as such shelter the Belgians from direct German attack.
2. Even if, at that time, the Belgians had the intention to really defend the Yser line, the polder indicated by Dingens was located west, or behind the river, the intended line of defence, not in front of it.

Besides, how would Dingens have known about a decision taken at the highest level, behind closed doors, only a few days before? With the tactical situation evolving so rapidly and the enemy clearly having the initiative nobody could predict how the conflict was going to develop, either in the long or the short term.

So, when Dingens in the 1920 interviews mentioned 'his' idea to G. Paquot and/or A. Hans it was more of a well-constructed afterthought on his part, expressed in an attempt to defend his behaviour in October 1914. After all, his personal motives might have been noble – a fact that nobody in the region at the time seems to have appreciated – his actions could not be excused in the post-war era of veneration for a victorious King and Army. Unfortunately it looks as if both journalists exploited the lockmaster's skewed views to serve a more political objective.

In the interview Dingens also complained about Captain Commandant Nuyten not having given him his name nor informing him about which army unit to contact if the need arose. This was of course an essential part of his story.

For the information Nuyten was most concerned about, that is the physical condition of the roads and bridges, there was no need to reveal his identity. And about the army unit to contact, i.e. the service that was dedicated to floods as such, it did not exist yet.

In a detailed retort by then Major Fernand Umé, published on 26 June 1920, the major regretted that Dingens had not offered his services to the engineers, even at a later date.

According to G. Paquot, the lockmaster, then living in Coxyde, had indeed offered his collaboration, notably through Engineer Captain Vantrooyen and his superior,

Throughout the war the discreet lockmaster Victor Kemp in Furnes acted as a valuable expert on the waterways of the Furnes-Ambacht region. The military engineers could always count on his unbiased advice. After the war his contribution to the war effort has always been overshadowed by the actions of Geeraert and Cogge.
Christiane Kemp.

Engineer Major E. Lefêvre. The latter had apparently phoned from Wulpen to General Headquarters on 3 or 4 November. But Captain Commandant Jamotte had indicated that they did not need the assistance of Dingens since High Command was satisfied with the means at its disposal.

Of course at that moment the nautical expertise of Dingens was not critical anymore: the tactical situation had stabilized, the engineers had the hydraulic problem under control and lockmaster Kemp from Furnes could give them all the advice they needed.

Lockmaster Receiver Victor-Cyrille Kemp in Furnes is a man who has often been overlooked in history. He was born in Boesinghe on the Ypres Canal, a few miles north of Ypres in 1860. At the age of twenty-nine he started his career as a Lockmaster Third-Class at the lock in Boesinghe itself. In 1907 he was promoted to Lockmaster Second-Class when he moved to the Dunkirk Lock in Furnes. At the same time he became a receiver in order to collect toll rights at that location.

During the war he never abandoned his post and unswervingly served the Allied cause. Since the canals in the region were less prone to damage from German bombardments they were used to transport large quantities of goods from France to free Belgium. As a result Kemp often locked through thirty barges a day in Furnes. He got a final promotion in 1919 when he moved to Bruges as a Lockmaster First-Class. He passed away in Bruges in 1940.

On 18 or 19 October 1914 an officer, possibly Major Le Clement de St-Marcq but certainly not Robert Thys, got in touch with lockmaster Dingens at the Goose Foot in Nieuport to discuss the idea of inundating the Nieuwendamme Creek and to get his advice. Dingens was not in favour of using seawater to inundate the polder because this would have an adverse effect on the arable soil and contaminate the fresh water supply of the farmers and their livelihood, its cattle. Also the brickworks, located behind the sluice and the only major industry in the region, would be severely affected.

More than likely he offered an alternative: 450m upstream of the Yser Lock the

The Nieuwendamme Gates on the Yser in 1991 as seen from the creek. Top left the five gearboxes to lift the doors. As can be seen from the lowered racks, all the doors are closed, hidden behind the installed stop planks. This outmoded structure is the oldest original weir in the region.
Author's photo archive.

Nieuwendamme Creek touched the Yser Canal levee. In that spot the Nieuwendamme Gates, built into the dyke connected the Yser with the creek. Lifting these gates would allow the military to flood the creek with fresh water from the Yser.

From other information from Dingens, concerning the high water levels and the expected spring tides in the Yser Mouth, Le Clement learned that in the next two or three days the high water curve would be peaking, i.e. a series of spring tides was approaching. Back at the command post, after having reviewed all the figures and the information from Dingens, the idea was further discussed.

Although the use of the Nieuwendamme Gates would have less impact on the polder environment, there were a few important tactical disadvantages. These lift gates, being isolated and exposed on the north bank of the Yser, would be a nightmare to operate: each time a sapper would have to cross the Yser or he would have to run the enemy gauntlet for 400m along the naked northern Yser levee.

A seawater flood through the Spring Sluice could be set faster, better and simpler than opening the Nieuwendamme Gates and letting fresh water fill the polder. Finally, after getting back in touch with the lockmaster, Le Clement de St-Marcq asked him for his assistance with the undertaking but the man refused.

In essence Dingens did not want to be blamed by the peasants of the polder, nor the Furnes North-Water Board, nor the directors and factory workers of the brickwork, in a week when the battle would be over, that he had ruined their lands, water and industry.

Soon after the war which had lasted four years instead of one week, when he noticed

The 140-year old gates of the Nieuwendamme Creek as seen from the Yser River. This outdated hydraulic gem is set in the northern levee of the Yser, a few hundred metres east of the Ypres Lock.

that he had lost out to a simple, unlettered bargee in becoming a national hero, Dingens had to 'adjust' his account of events in order to justify his behaviour.

In 'When Can Memories Be Trusted?' (*Time Magazine*, 28 October 1991) Ulric Neisser, psychologist at Emory University, is quoted as saying: '[Clarence] Thomas [1] is a rigid person who insisted on the prerogatives of his position, such people can be 'good repressors' of unpleasant memories.'

Perhaps Gerard Dingens was a man who fitted that category.

NOTE

1. In 1991 appointed Justice of the U.S. Supreme Court after a much publicized congressional hearing involving the accusation of sexual misconduct by law professor Anita Hill.

Appendix II

Roads & Bridges Mysteries

We read in Chapter XII that on 26 October three engineers of the Roads & Bridges Department left Le Havre for Dunkirk. They were dispatched by their boss, the Minister of Public Works, George (Joris) Helleputte.

The reader will remember that, upon receiving the request from Baron de Broqueville, it took almost twenty-four hours before the engineers left Le Havre and then again, it took those three gentlemen an unusually long time to travel from Le Havre to Dunkirk. Looking at their whereabouts even more closely the reader will discover that they spent exactly one hour and a half in Furnes, the prime centre of all the activity. Considering all the urgency and the tremendous importance of the project for the survival of their country it seems as if these experts on the coastal waterways showed little enthusiasm for their assignment.

We know already that lockmaster Dingens opposed any floods for the commendable reason that he did not want to compromise the livelihood of his fellow countrymen in the flood plain. Engineer L. Bourgoignie, also a man from the coast, was the Head of the Coastal Service of Roads & Bridges in Ostend. On the one hand it stands to reason that in that capacity he personally knew the lockmaster in Nieuport rather well. Evidence of that exists today.

On the other hand, from the technical remarks he made to his different interrogators, we get the firm impression that Bourgoignie opposed a flood in Furnes-Ambacht just as adamantly as Dingens; he just used more diplomatic language. There is another document that raises questions in this regard. Historians Marie-Rose Thielemans and E. Vandewoude published the original of a cable, written by Captain Commandant Galet and dated 26 October. The cable is addressed to 'J.H.' in Le Havre and signed by King Albert. It reads: 'Answer: Return and resume your work.' Thielemans and Vandewoude suppose that the terse response by the king involved a cable on a rather trivial matter of exiled Antwerp municipal employees. This earlier dispatch, of which the exact subject(s) and wording seem to be unknown, had been sent to the king's orderly officer in Furnes. Thielemans and Vandewoude suspect 'J.H.' to be General Harry Jungbluth, the king's long time mentor. Besides the fact that the initials then would have to be 'H.J.' it is highly unlikely that a Francophone high-ranking officer would have been involved in a local Flemish and purely civilian public sector dispute.

Contrary to what both editors suspect, we argue that this cable was most likely addressed to the Minister of Public Works, George (Joris in Flemish) Helleputte. This pro-Flemish politician used to initial his documents 'J.H.'

A group picture of the lock staff, a few years before the war. In the front row on the right sits lockmaster Dingens and next to him we see chief engineer Bourgoignie from Ostend. Shortly after the war, and by order of Minister Helleputte, Bourgoignie would write a detailed report of the events of October 1914. In it Bourgoignie was very critical about the work of the military engineers.
Historical prints collection Callenaere-Dehouck.

On 26 October Bourgoignie and his assistants left their minister 'J.H.' en route for Dunkirk and Furnes. From his own account we understand that Bourgoignie apparently only met with people, either indifferent to the Belgian cause, like the French Chief Engineer Bourgois, or people who were more or less loosely associated with the Broqueville-clan: Chabeau, Wielemans, Jamotte and de Broqueville himself. The three of them certainly never met with people like Galet, Nuyten or the military engineer par excellence in the field, Robert Thys. One would expect those civilian experts to roll up their sleeves and do something in Furnes or Nieuport but apparently they 'came, saw and left'. Was this lack of initiative and action due to personal unwillingness or was it upon higher order to 'Return and take up your duties again'?

In our long research of this story we were unable to retrieve any information on the personal files of any of the Public Works employees mentioned in all of the previous pages. What we did find however were several letters indicating that Lieutenant Colonel (Reserve) Robert Thys in 1960 had already conducted a similar search for the files of the lock personnel from Nieuport in 1914. Unfortunately the initial question(s) by Thys could not be retrieved although his original request should still be available in Public Works Archives. But we do possess a copy of the answer by the then Deputy Chief of the Cabinet at Public Works. In it the man admits that:

243

'. . . after long research in the archives . . . it is not permitted to find documents related to the events that happened in Nieuport in 1914 during the Battle of the Yser.' Peculiar wording indeed.

The next day Robert Thys did sent a telling reply: 'I thought as much that it would be impossible to retrieve any documents on the subject of the lockkeepers of Nieuport in 1914. Excuse me for causing any inconvenience but *I wanted to make really certain. . . .*'. [Our italics]

Did Thys suspect someone in higher office of having removed the files of the lock personnel after the war? Could that someone have been Bourgoignie himself?

From one letter by Thys to Lucien François in June of 1960 we learned that he had prepared what he called a 'File Dingens' and that he was to question the burgomaster of Nieuport on this matter the next month. As Thys spent most of his later years in Nieuport – he passed away in this city in 1964 – he was well known here and a meeting between him and the burgomaster on this subject must certainly have taken place. Nevertheless upon our written enquiry to Nieuport officials in 1994 they responded that they too had been unable to retrieve any information on the matter.

Another mystery that was never solved was the sudden departure of all higher personnel of the Coastal Service on 13 October (see Chapter IV).

After the series on 'The Legend of the Lockkeepers of Nieuport' in *La Flandre Liberale* in which the question was put – 'Where were the Roads & Bridges personnel?' – a letter to the editor was published on 16 June 1920. In it one of those public servants who wanted to remain anonymous, wrote: 'We left in the morning of October 13 on orders from the higher administration.' One wonders if it was not Bourgoignie himself,

An idyllic view in a time of war: the weir on the Great Beaverdyke Vaart some time after the abutment pier collapsed. In the background war ravaged Nieuport.
Nieuport 1914-1918, R. Thys, 1922.

a native of the coast and part of that higher administration, who had ordered their departure in October 1914.

One can argue that the Roads & Bridges personnel were pulled out because certain individual(s) in the administration considered the whole Belgian war effort a lost cause. In giving them their marching orders the administration certainly deprived the invader of the technical know-how to inflict serious damage, like floods, to the local infrastructure. It would in a way explain the lack of enthusiasm when the engineers returned to Furnes as advisors on 26 October.

Appendix III

A Royal Treatment

After the war a lot of criticism was aired concerning the fact that Charles Cogge was paid for his trip with Captain Thys to the Spanish Lock. The strong patriotic feelings that swept the country after the Armistice dictated that the man, as a public servant, should have volunteered his services for the good of the country. According to some, High Command had 'bought' Charles, while others maintained that the man had simply solicited money for something that they considered simply his duty as a civil servant. Putting aside such criticisms one should take into account the rough, pre-war welfare situation.

The social and financial conditions in the Cogge family were certainly not bright. As a young mother Mietje had lost ten of her twelve infant children and now, at the age of fifty-nine, her husband was an ailing man. Mietje did have good reason to worry about their future. On the other hand, for Captain Thys it was more than imperative that the feeble supervisor accompany him on that important trip. Charles knew the polder, with its tens of vaarts and hundreds of brooks, like the back of his hand. He was the only man still in Furnes who would be able to direct the engineers, in the middle of the night, via the shortest, quickest and safest way to the Spanish Lock. Since it was quite likely that the enemy had now reached the opposite bank of the Yser Channel, Thys and his men could only open the heavy doors under the cover of darkness. If Charles did not join them the operation would have to be postponed for at least another twenty-four hours. That was something the army, and the nation, could not afford anymore.

Captain Thys knew that Mietje's objections were genuine and that they were irrefutable. But he also knew that Charles as breadwinner had to provide for the daily bread on the table. So the Cogge family needed money. That was the only argument that would persuade Mietje to give up her protest.

On 1 November Charles was recommended to be knighted in the Order of Leopold. Three days later King Albert personally pinned the medal on him. The story goes that, lacking the proper medal, the king used Colonel Wielemans' own Knight's Cross as a replacement. The remuneration of the 2,000 francs though was another story.

Since after the war all authors, except one, mentioned that 200 francs had been promised to Charles we at first assumed that this was correct. Only M. Nevejans wrote that he had received 2,000 francs, which we therefore assumed as being a misprint. But during ongoing research after the publication of the Dutch version of this book in 2004, we unexpectedly came across two original, carbon copies of documents, written in July

1916 and both signed by Robert Thys, in which he reminded High Command that it still had to pay 2,000 francs to Cogge. Our discovery emphasized the importance of the operation. While 200 francs seemed to be a decent reward for Charles' contribution to the survival of the nation, 2,000 francs was simply royal treatment.

Subsequently we made some enquiries into the practical value of such an amount of money in those days. As a result Guido Demerre, retired principal of the Saint-Bernardus High School in Nieuport and local historian, told us that the grandfather of his spouse, who was a principal in Alveringhem during the First World War, received a yearly salary of 2,000 francs.

Whether or not the outstanding 2,000 francs were finally paid out in 1916 remains a mystery to this day.

After the war King Albert enjoyed enormous popularity. He prematurely died, according to official documents, from a climbing accident in 1934.
Ons Land magazine, 1919.

Appendix IV

German Ignorance

How was it that the Germans ignored the fact that the whole coastal area could be inundated at will? This is of course a key question. Apparently at German High Command nobody grasped the fact that the entire Flemish coast lay under the high water mark. However, along the German North Sea coast a similar topography existed, over an even larger tract of land. In spite of the proverbial *Deutsche Grundlichkeit* [German thoroughness] this blindness was certainly a failure on the part of German intelligence.

The Belgian Army had, in its recent history at least, not prepared for any flooding along the coast. Nevertheless the technical knowledge about floods was still taught at the Royal Military Academy, but solely in connection with the planned floods around the Fortified Place of Antwerp (for details see below).

The lack of such plans in this direction therefore might have fooled German High Command into thinking that the right conditions for such a project did not exist. But there is also a more scientific basis for the German ignorance. Since it has a little technical twist to it we are bound to engage in some explanation.

Originally ordnance maps in each European country were produced based on a national grid system. Besides the importance of knowing where you are, for the military planners it is also important to know the elevation of the land. For that purpose a general levelling was carried out, resulting in contour lines at certain intervals on each map. For the origin of this national levelling, that is the 'zero' of the system, each country started from its own reference point. In fact this 'zero' was arrived at through a mathematical formula after the observation of a series of high and low tides at a predetermined coastal location.

In 1875 the first Prussian General Levelling was started, strangely enough from a point in the Dutch city of Amsterdam, called *Nieuw Amsterdams Peil* (N.A.P.). This basis was agreed upon as cooperation between the Dutch and Prussian governments, but the Prussians would later come to call it *Normal Null* (N.N.). The original *Amsterdams Peil* (A.P.) had been determined in 1684 as being 'the average height of summer high tide on the IJ River near Amsterdam'.

In 1875 a general levelling was also carried out in Belgium. To arrive at its 'zero' (called zero Z) the Belgian Roads & Bridges Department started from a point in Ostend harbour determined before 1856 as, 'the average height of ebb tide at spring tide in Ostend'.

So, since each country started from a different reference point there was of course a difference in height between the two systems. In practical terms the German *Normal Null* was located 2.40 m above Belgian zero Z.

When the German Army invaded Belgium in 1914, the officers used German reprints of Belgian ordnance maps. For all purposes this should not have posed a problem. Elevation for instance is important to the artillery, but only as the difference between altitudes, like between gun emplacement and target. As long as the artillery calculates differences in elevation within the same levelling system, here meaning the same country, nobody will encounter any difficulty.

Regarding coastal floods, however, the story is totally different. Imagine a German officer standing close to the German seafront at a location indicated on his map as having an elevation of +1.00 m. We can then well imagine that at high tide his feet will still be dry since *Normal Null* measures from '0.00' at high tide. If, however, the same officer were in Ostend, holding a Belgian map, or its German reprint, and standing at a 'Belgian' elevation of +1.00 m he would actually be one metre above low water, or 1.40 m below his own *Normal Null*. The man would be swept off his feet by rising tide!

Accordingly, when the Germans arrived in the Belgian coastal region their (Belgian) maps showed contour lines with elevations that were, in regard to the German *Normal Null*, well above high water. They were unaware though that these lands were in reality polders situated between high and low water, thus prone to flooding at high tide.

By 1940 the Germans had definitely learned from their mistake in 1914. All German reprints of Belgian ordnance maps then carried a clear message: 'To adjust the Belgian elevation marks to the German *Normal Null* please subtract 2.4m.'

One typical feature – easily recognizable from the air – to determine if the land is lying lower than sea level is the existence of flood doors – four double mitre doors instead of two – in a canal entrance lock. It can only be attributed to the inexperience of the German aerial observers at the time that this fact went unnoticed, especially in Nieuport where three locks with this equipment were located practically side by side.

Why did the Germans, irrespective of the flood threat, not occupy the locks after the French had evacuated the Nieuport bridgehead on 26 October? According to Jos Vols, the Germans at the time were preparing for their assault on Ramscappelle the next day. This operation took so much of their attention that they never had the time or the manpower to force ahead on the Ostend-Nieuport road towards the locks.

The real reason is perhaps more complex. Certainly the menacing presence and lethal activities of the British flotilla offshore played a decisive role. The Germans had been heavily bombarded for so long that they had given up any hope of advancing along the coastal road to take Nieuport and subsequently Dunkirk. Irrespective of the possibilities to inundate, the Germans must have concluded that Nieuport and its waterways were of strategic importance to the French and that as such they would not let go easily of this advanced position to Dunkirk. The closer they would come to the locks the fiercer they expected the French resistance to be. That the French would simply abandon the bridgehead without a fight was for them definitely unthinkable.

For a combination of the above reasons the Germans concentrated all their efforts on a flanking manoeuvre by attacking Ramscappelle.

How was it that the Germans, evidently up to the last minute, never realized that a man-made flood was at hand? There are two generally accepted reasons on the German side for the sudden rise of the water level.

1. The Germans assumed that their heavy shelling of Nieuport and its drainage sluices

A wartime view from within the lock chamber of the Furnes Lock towards the tidal bay at low water. Across the bay we see part of the so-called Paling [Eel] Bridge. At the time it was the only remnant of the ancient fortifications around Nieuport. Today the area is an industrial zone and a sprawling marina.
Nieuport 1914-1918, R. Thys, 1922.

had somehow damaged the structures insofar as one or more gates had been destroyed with the result that the seawater had gained access to the polder accidentally. This does not in itself mean that the land could be permanently inundated by seawater.

2. As Otto Schwink wrote in *Ypres, 1914*: 'The rise of the waters was attributed to the torrential rain of the previous few days, and it was hoped that on approach of dry weather the excellent system of canals would soon drain it off.'

In this the Germans were partly right. With the weir on the Great Beaverdyke Vaart still in place and the North Vaart Gates closed since the departure of lockmaster Dingens a lot of rainwater had already collected in the polder.

From an historical point of view it would be interesting to set up a computer terrain model of the battle site and with the available data determine exactly how far the rainwater did actually contribute to the flood effort. We might then also be able to settle another old dispute: how much seawater actually passed through the Spanish Lock versus the North Vaart Gates?

Appendix V

Other Belgian Floods in 1914

Between the World Wars several authors have been rather critical concerning the knowledge of the Belgian military engineers in flood matters. Military authors like Bernard, Deguent and Greindl were the first to admit that the army, in 1914, was not acquainted with the complex hydraulic system that it encountered in the coastal area. But that did not mean that the officers were ignorant about flood techniques in general.

The principles and techniques of flooding as a means of defence against an advancing enemy were still taught at the Royal Military Academy. Proof of that can be found in the treatises of H. Girard and Victor Deguise. And it was not only a matter of theory. For example in November 1868, tests had been carried out at the Field Artillery College firing range to determine the resistance of dykes to heavy calibre bombardment.

The following are a few examples of other floods prepared and executed by separate engineer units prior to the arrival of the Belgian Army in the Furnes-Ambacht region. They demonstrate that the Belgian engineers were well aware of the possibilities and techniques of flooding, even in the midst of a field campaign. The historical research on the details of these – and other – hydraulic projects is still ongoing.

The Schyn flood

On 20 August 1914 the Military Governor of the Antwerp Fortified Place delivered a note to King Albert on the state of readiness of the Place. In it he wrote: 'Past Fort number 1 the fortification was to be extended [northward] by a continuous rampart; this only partially begun we had to set the flood of the Schyn [river] to finish off the fortification to the north'.

The Schyn River drains to a large extent the whole Antwerp metropolitan area. Centuries ago it ended in the Scheldt near the historical site of the city. With the growth of the urban area the downstream end of the Schyn river was diverted northward, finally circling around the new harbour in the north and ending in the Scheldt river some 13km downstream from the city centre. This northern section, through flat, open polder could easily be inundated by holding up the drainage water at the Twelve Sluices in the Scheldt dyke.

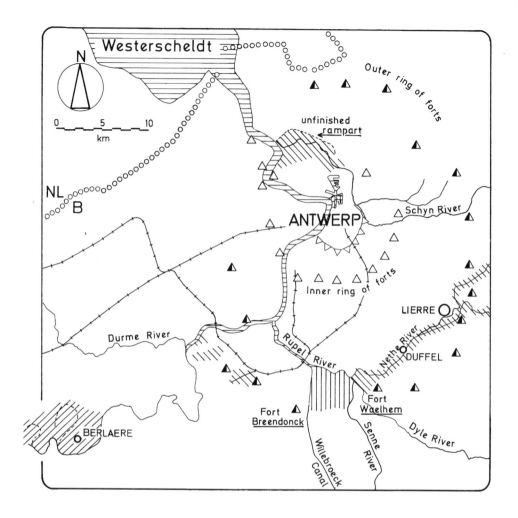

The Durme Flood

At the beginning of September 1914, German troops were already advancing south of Antwerp. On the 4th they attacked the town of Termonde on the Scheldt, halfway between Antwerp and Ghent. If the enemy succeeded in crossing the river the communication lines of the Antwerp Fortified Place with the coast would be in jeopardy. King Albert therefore ordered a flood to be set along the Durme river. This would provide for a second line of defence, five to six kilometres north of the Scheldt. Apparently the attempt failed mainly because of sabotage by local farmers.

The Senne Flood

The region of Brussels drains its water northward through the Senne River. In its 10km downstream section it runs parallel to the Willebroek Canal, also coming from Brussels

252

but 4 to 5km to the west of it. The land in between is low lying and drains at ebb tide through a multitude of small sluices in the Senne dyke. As there was an 8km gap between the Breendonck Fort to the west and the Waelhem Fort to the east this sector had been flooded over a width of 4km as part of the outer defence of the Antwerp Fortified Place.

The Nèthe Flood

Where the Senne river meets the Rupel from the south, another river also ends, coming from the east. It is the Nèthe, itself made up of the Large and Small Nèthe rivers that come from the higher sandy soils farther east. This river, together with the chain of outer fortresses, formed the backbone of the 1914 southern and eastern barrier around Antwerp. In preparation for the defence, its banks had been flooded all the way upstream past the town of Lierre. At that time a Lierre inhabitant, Frans Verschoren, wrote confidently: 'Behind the new modern fortifications the people were safe. Added to that the sluices that had been opened and the grasslands being flooded with water on the south side of town and the enemy, with his heavy guns could impossibly pass or get around. The people were sitting here pretty safe and free.'

The Berlaere Flood

With the threat of the enemy cutting off the Belgian Army's escape route to the coast a flood of the area around the town of Berlaere had been prepared by a detachment of *sapper-pontoneers cyclists* of the First Cavalry Division between 29 September and 6 October. This operation was carried out in order to prepare for a possible defence of the north bank of the Scheldt river east of Ghent. They had opened the drainage gates in the north dyke of the river between the towns of Wetteren and Berlaere.

We describe the procedure they used in some detail since it is quite typical for a chance flood.

Over the centuries the river here had built a wide flood plain and by 1914 had produced a few complicated meanders in this spot. Through human and natural activities these meanders had been cut off and the riverbed had been stabilized between artificial levees. As, at this location, the river is still subjected to tidal activity, the

The Kalken [Lime] Vaart east of van Ghent. Today a pumping station near the Scheldt River guarantees the drainage of the region. Close by, hidden in the dyke, a remnant from 1914 when drainage was accomplished by gravity through several small and manually operated lift gates. (next picture)
Author's photo archive.

253

This rusted gearbox of a small lift gate near the Kalken Vaart is all that remains of the hydraulic history of this waterlogged region. We estimate this archeological gem to date back to at least the end of the nineteenth century.
Author's photo archive.

adjacent land at the time was drained at low water through small gates with lift doors operated by a simple rack and pinion gear.

First the sappers evacuated all barges and boats from the river and the adjoining creek. Then, when the rising water level in the river equalled the level in the ditches, they raised the doors and let the water invade the drainage system. At high tide they closed the doors again until they could repeat the process with the next cycle. This they did until the Calcken Canal and the Old Scheldt arm had reached their highest level without overflowing. Once inundation would be decided on, it would only take one or two more operations to flood the polder.

Due to the rapidly changing tactical situation the actual flood never materialized but it is interesting to glance at the map and note that the result would have created an important obstacle for the enemy to cross. Over a front of some 13km a muddy lake would have been created with a width of up to 3km.

Bibliography

Books, Yser 1914 – 18

Brecard, Gen. C. T., *En Belgique auprès du Roi Albert. Souvenirs de 1914*, Paris, Calmann Levy, 1934

Galet, Lt. Gen. E. S.M., *Le Roi Albert, Commandant en Chef, devant l'Invasion Allemande*, Paris 6e, Librairie Plon, 1931

— *Le Roi Albert*, SGR/CHD Archives, copy with extensive anonymous comments

— *Albert, King of the Belgians, in the Great War*, Transl. E. Swinton, New York, Houghton Mifflin Co., 1931

Hans, A., *Het Bloedig IJzerland*, 1920

Leper, J., *Kunstmatige Inundaties in Maritiem Vlaanderen 1316 1945*, Tongeren: Michiels G., 1957

L'Hoist, André, *1914, La Vérité contre Tardieu*, n.d.

Mabire, Jean, *La Bataille de l'Yser, Les fusiliers marins à Dixmude*, Paris, Libr. Arthème Fayard, 1979

Ratinaud, Jean, *La Course à la Mer. De la Somme aux Flandres*, Paris 14e, Libr. Arthème Fayard, 1967

Ronarc'h, Vice Adm., *Les Fusiliers Marins au Combat, (Aout 1914 Sept.1915)*, Paris, Payot, 1921

Schwink, Cpt. Otto, *Ypres, 1914*, An official account published by order of the German General Staff, London: Constable & Co. Ltd., 1919

Schepens, Luc, *14/18 Een oorlog in Vlaanderen*, Tielt, Lannoo, 1984

Senesael, M., *De IJzerslag 1914*, Hoogstade, Senesael, 1958

Tardieu, André, *Avec Foch, Août Novembre 1914*, Paris, E. Flammarion, 1939

Thys, Cdt. R., *Nieuport 1914 1918. Les Inondations de l'Yser et la Cie des Sapeurs Pontonniers*, Liège, H. Desoer, 1922

Lut Ureel, ed., *Three generations of village schoolmasters in the front region*, (in Dutch), Lannoo, 1984

Documents and letters:

Annuaire Officiel de l'Armée Française pour 1914, Paris, Berger Levrault, 1934

Carnet des Officiers d'Ordonnance du 29 juillet 1914 au 31 décembre 1914,AKP # AE 530/1, Brussels, copies from 7 October to 2 November.

Compte Rendu des Operations 1914 17 des Chemins de Fer, Le Havre, Ministère Belge des Chemins de Fer, 1917

In memoriam Frans Cop, 1965

Journal Militaire Officiel 1914, pp184-201

Tableau synoptique des principaux événements de la Bataille de l'Yser , (18-31 octobre 1914). SGR/CHD, n.d.

Bernard, Prof. H., Letter to Lt-Col R. Thys. Introduction to Col Brustem, Head Hist. Sect. Dated 16/01/1960

Bourgoignie, L., Rapport de Mission. à Mr. Helleputte, Schaerbeek:11 p., 31/08/1922. 1923

Brecard, Gen Div C.-T., Gouv. Mil. de Strasbourg, letter to Lt Gen Dubois. On the French Yser involvement, 16 Oct. – 2 Nov. 1914. Dated 03/06/1931

Cogge, Clementine, Affidavit on events 25 Oct. 1914. (in Flemish): 1 p., 18 Jan. 1955

Cogge, Col C.A.C. Letter to Schoofs, ed. NSB. On article by T'Jaeckx, 2p., Dated 20/10/1954. Reminder on 13/11/1954

Cogge, Col C.A.C. Letter to Schoofs, ed. NSB. Reply to letter from 17 Nov.1954. Dated 14/12/1954. Reminder on 13/01/1955

Cogge, Col C.A.C. Quelques éclaircissements sur 'Les Inondations de l'Yser en octobre 1914. Etterbeek: 5p., 28 March 1955

Cogge, Karel, L. Rapport van Cogge: historisch dokument. First publ. 13/10/1951 in Het Wekelijks Nieuws 27/12/1968. Furnes, 1 July 1915

Cogge, Karel, L. Declaration on events 25 Oct. 1914. (in Flemish). 2p., 29 Aug. 1917

Cogge, Karel, L. Declaration on events 25-27 Oct. 1914. (in Flemish). Contactblad Vriendenkring Justitia (1973). Furnes: 3p., 11 March 1920

De Vos, Prof Dr L. Geschiedenis van Belgie van 1830 tot heden. Hist. course, p.108 – 111. Brussels: Royal Military Academy, 1990

Duvivier, Col, Hist. Sect. Belg. Army. Letter to A. De Ridder. Rectification on article by Recouly, 23-25 Oct. 1914. Dated 05/05/1931

François L., Henry J. et al. Statement: La légende des éclusiers de Nieuport. Bruxelles, 3p., 30 oct. 1920. Deposited at Hist. Sect. in 1960

François, Cpt L. Rapport du Cpt François Morlanwelz: 17 Dec. to Head Historical Section, 1921.

François L. Letter to Lt-Col R. Thys. Concerning Dingens. Dated 12/01/1960

François L. Letter to Lt-Col R. Thys. Agrees on the Dingens file. Dated 11/07/1960

Geerinckx, Col L. Journal de Campagne du 2A. 42p., n.d.

Hayois, Arch. Gaston (?). Comment l'Yser n'a pas été franchi. 1915

Lannoy, Gen Hon de. Idée première d'inonder les rives de l'Yser . . . SGR/CHD Archives, 1p., 1931

Maglinse, Maj. Rapport du 4 novembre sur le cpt cdt d'E.M. Nuyten. SGR/CHD Archives, 1p., 1914

Merzbach, Lt Col, Hist. Sect. Belg. Army. Letter to Lt L. François. Incl. 8 orders given to François betw. 20 & 26 Oct. 1914. Dated 09/09/1920

Nuyten, Col P.A. Inondations de l'Yser en 1914. to Head Hist. Sect. Belg. Army: 8p., 1927

Saccasyn ir. A., Public Works Ministry. Letter to Lt-Col R. Thys. On the 1914 Nieuport lockkeepers. Dated 24/03/1960

Schoofs, ed. NSB. Letter to Col C. Cogge. Reply on previous letters, 20 Oct. – 17 Nov. 1954. Dated 17/11/1954

Thys, R. Letter to L. François. Indications sur les inondations en octobre 1914. Dated 16/11/1921

Thys, Cpt R. Les inondations par la crique de Nieuwendam & par l'ancien canal de Furnes. Compte rendu, Bruxelles: 1921?

Thys, Cpt R. & François, SLt L. Les inondations par la crique de Nieuwendam & par l'ancien canal de Furnes. Compte rendu, Brux.: 1921?

Thys, Lt Col R. Letter to L. François. Enclosed copy to Prof H. Bernard. Dated 13/01/1960

Thys, Lt Col R. Letter to Prof. H. Bernard. On Slt François & Dingens, 15 – 20 Oct. 1914. Dated 13/01/1960

Thys, Lt-Col R. Reply to Ir. A. Saccasyn. Mocking thank-you letter. Dated 25/03/1960

Thys, Lt-Col R. Letter to L. François. On his planned questioning of the burgomaster of Nieuport. Dated 08/06/1960

Thys, Lt-Col R. Letter to L. François. Update. Dated 30/06/1960

Van Marcke G. Letter to A. Devèze, Min. of Nat. Def. 5p. incl. 2 hand-drawn maps. Dated 24/03/1923

Van Marcke G. Cover letter to L. Geerinckx. 2p. Dated 24/03/1923

Memoirs/Biographies:

Bridges, Lt Gen Sir Tom, *Alarms & Excursions, Reminiscences of a Soldier*, London, Longmans Green and Co., 1938

Cammaerts, Emile, *Albert of Belgium, Defender of Right*, London, Ivor Nicholson & Watson, 1935

Corti, E. C., *Maximilian & Charlotte of Mexico*, U.S.A. Archon Books, 1968

Foch, Marshal Ferdinand, *The Memoirs of Marchal Foch*, Transl. Bentley Mott, London, William Heinemann Ltd., 1931

French, Field Marshal J., *1914*, London, Constable & Co. Ltd., 1919

Gilbert, Martin, *The Challenge of War, W.S. Churchill, 1914-1916*, London, Minerva/Heinemann, Mandarin Paperback, 1990

Joffre, Marshal J., Mémoires du Marechal Joffre, 1910-1917, tome I. Paris, Librairie Plon, 1932

Marie José, Albert et Elisabeth de Belgique, mes parents, *Paris, ed. Plon, 1971*

Maurice, Maj Gen F., The Life of General Lord Rawlinson of Trent *London, Cassell & Co. Ltd., 1928*

Poincaré, Pres. R., The Memoirs of Raymond Poincaré, (1912). *Transl. Sir G. Arthur. New York, Doubleday, Page & Co., 1926*

— The Memoirs of Raymond Poincaré, (1913 1914). *New York, Doubleday, Doran & Co., 1928*

— The Memoirs of Raymond Poincaré. 1914, New York, Doubleday, Doran & Co., 1929

— *The Memoirs of Raymond Poincaré, 1915*. New York, Doubleday, Doran & Co., 1931

Rawlinson, Lt Col A., *Adventures on the Western Front, August 1914 – June 1915*, London & New York, Andrew Melrose Ltd., 1925

Smart, Charles Allen, *Viva Juarez!* London, Eyre & Spottiswoode, 1964

Weygand, Gen. M., *Idéal Vécu*, Paris, Ernest Flammarion, 1953

Williams, Jeffery, *Byng of Vimy*, London, Leo Cooper, Secker & Warburg., 1983

Books, The Great War:

— *14-18 De Eerste Wereldoorlog*, Band 1, Amsterdam, Amsterdamboek, 1975

Arthur, Capt. Sir G., *The Story of the Houshold Cavalry*, vol III, London, Wm. Heinemann Ltd., 1926

Bickersteth, Lt J.B., *History of the 6th Cavalry Brigade*, London, Baynard Press, n.d.

Buchan, John, *A History of the Great War*, Vol. 1. New York & London, Houghton Mifflin Co. & Th. Nelson Ltd., 1922

Cable, Boyd, et al., *Rolls Royce and the Great Victory*, Haworth, Bronte Hill Publ., 1972

Chatelle, Albert, *Dunkerque pendant la guerre 1914-1918*, Paris, Lib. Picart. 1925

Corbett, Sir Julian S., Naval Operations, *Vol I. History of the Great War based on Official Documents, London, Longmans, Green & Co., 1920*

Falls, Cyril, The Great War. 1914-1918, *New York,Capricorn, 1959*

French, Field Marshal Viscount, The Despatches of Lord French, *London, Chapman & Hall, Ltd., 1917*

Geffroy, G., et al, Les Eaux de l'Yser, *La France Héroique et ses Alliés, Tome I, 1914-1916, Paris, Libr. Larousse, 1916*

Gibson, Hugh, A journal from our Legation in Belgium, *New York, Grosset & Dunlap Publ., 1917*

Haythornthwaite, P.J., World War One: 1914, *London, Arms & Armour Press, 1989*

Holmes, Richard, The Little Field Marshal, Sir John French, *London, Jonathan Cape, 1981*

Miquel, Pierre, La Grande Guerre, *Paris, Lib. Arthème Fayard, 1983*

Mollo, A., Turner P., Army Uniforms of World War 1, *Poole, Blandford Press Ltd., 1977*

Simkins, Peter, World War 1, the Western Front, *Godalming, Colour Library Books Ltd. Mil. Press, 1991*

Studies:

Azan, Lt Col Paul, The War of Positions, *Cambridge, Mass. Harvard Univ. Press, 1917*

Broekmans, Gen Maj A., Eb en Vloed in Vlaanderland. 14-18, *band 1.pp.308, 313, Amsterdam, Amsterdamboek, 1975*

Casteels, R. & Vandegoor, G., 1914 in de regio Haacht. Kleine dorpen in de Grote Oorlog, *Brussels, HAGOK/CHD, 1993*

Deguise, V., La fortification passagère en liaison avec la tactique, *Tome I pp.96, 97. Bruxelles, Royal Military Academy, 1893*

Deguent, Maj R.H.A., *Les inondations du front belge (1914 1918)*, pp.1-35, Paris, Berger Levrault, 1929

Deroo, Frederic, *La Bataille de l'Yser ou le rôle de la géographie* Montpellier, Univ. Paul Valéry, 1989

Deseyne, Aleks, *Raversijde 1914-1918*, Batterij Aachen, Prov. W Vlaanderen, 1993

De Volder, Daniel, *Gesch. Overzicht v/h Openb. Vervoer Oostende/Veurne 1838/1914*, Brugge, Eigen Beheer, 1981

Duvivier, Maj BEM., *Bataille de l'Yser. Relation entre le commandement belge et les commandements alliés en octobre 1914.* 127p., 20 annexes. 1926. Russia Archive KML-MRA.

Girard, H., *Traité des applications tactiques de la fortification*, Tome II, pp.308-311, Bruxelles, Royal Military Academy, 1874

— *Traité des applications tactiques de la fortification*, Tome III, pp.262-273, Bruxelles, Royal Military Academy, 1875

Greindl, Lt Gen., *Les inondations au front belge (I)*, B.B.S.M.* Bruxelles, 1922

— *Les inondations au front belge (II)*, B.B.S.M.,Bruxelles, 1922

Haag, Prof Emer H., *Le comte Charles de Broqueville, Min. d' Etat, et les luttes pour le pouvoir (1910 1940)*, Bruxelles, Ed. Nauwelaerts, 1990

Janssens, Lt., *Le Lt Gen Nuyten. D' Ypres au Zoute*, Thesis prom. pp.15, 16 and 46. Bruxelles, Royal Military Academy, 1988

Nuyten, Lt Col P.A., *Les inondations sur le front belge*, B.B.S.M., Bruxelles, 1920

— *Les inondations sur le front belge*, Revue de Genie Militaire, XLIV, 1921

Parmentier, Lt W., *Historique du 1er Régiment de Guides*, 1928

Peteau, Maj A., *Aperçu Historique sur les Mouvements et Opérations des Corps et Div de Cavalerie*, Tome I 1914, Liege, Imp. Vaillant Carmanne, 1924

Schepens, Luc, *Koning Albert, Charles de Broqueville en de Vlaamse Beweging*, Tielt (B), Bussum (NL) Lannoo, 1983

Thielemans, M. R., *Albert I. Belgie en zijn Koningen*, Brussels, Alg. Rijksarchief, 1990

Thielemans, M. R., Vandewoude, E. *Le Roi Albert au travers de se lettres inédites 1882-1916*, Bruxelles, Office Int'l de Librairie, 1982

— ed. *Mémoires sur les ports d' Ostende et de Nieuport,1819-1821*, Handelingen v/h Genootschap voor Geschiedenis, Brugge, CXIII, Société d'Emulation, 1976

— ed. *Albert Ier, Carnets et Correspondance de Guerre 1914-1918*, Louvain la Neuve, Ed. Duculot, 1991

Truyens J., et al., *11 Geniebataljon 1948-1988*, Antwerpen, Verbroedering Genie, 1989

Umé, Maj F.P.J., *Les inondations sur le front belge*, B.B.S.M. Bruxelles,1920

Van Dam Van Isselt, Maj W.E., *De Onderwaterzettingen in het Ysergebied . . .* , Militaire Spectator, Den Haag, 1921

Van Overstraeten, R., ed., *The War Diaries of Albert I*, London, Wm. Kimber & Co. Ltd., 1954

Books, general:

Bernard, Lt Col H., *De Marathon à Hiroshima*, Tome I. pp.252-265, Bruxelles, Medische en Wetenschappelijke Bibliotheek, 1948

Caesar, Caius Julius, *Gallic War*, Transl. J. Pearl, Great Neck-NY, Barron's Educational Series, 1962

Chatelle A., Moreel L. *Dunkerque Libérée*, Imprimerie Silic., 1954

Kinder, H., Hilgemann W., *Atlas of World History*, Vol.II. New York, Penguin Books, 1978

McKnight, Hugh, *Shell Guide to the Inland Waterways*, 1975

Nelson, A., Nelson, K.D., *Dictionary of Water & Water Engineering*, Cleveland, The Chemical Rubber Co., 1973

Wawro, G., *The Franco-Prussian War. The German Conquest of France in 1870-1871*, Cambridge University Press, Cambridge, Mass. 2003

Wild, Alan, ed., *Russell's Soil Conditions & Plant Growth*, Longman Group UK Ltd., 1988

Articles:

De Overstrooming, Onze Helden, Brussel, S.A.B. d'Imp. 1922

Un ancien du genie à l'honneur, (Umé, Gen F.) Genie, # 7 1949

40 Jaar geleden werd IJzergebied onder water gezet, Het Volk (8 oct.1954)

Les sapeurs pontonniers maintinrent pendant quatre ans les inondations de l'Yser, Le Soir, Bruxelles, 1965

La compagnie des sapeurs pontonniers du genie belge, Manuscript for Le Soir, Bruxelles, 1965

Rapport van Cogge: historisch dokument, Het Wekelijks Nieuws (27 dec. 1968)

Revue du Touring Club de France, Aug./Sept 1919

Anciaux, L., *Les Inondations de l'Yser 1914*. Marine Academie, Mededelingen. deel XVI , 1964

Aston, Maj Gen Sir G., *Ostend in 1914 Cornhill Magazine* London, vol. XLV, 1918

Azan, Gen. Paul, *Il y a Quinze Ans., les Belges sur l'Yser* L'Illustration, Paris, numbers 4509 and 4510, 1929

Clairepée, Maurice, *L'Inondation des rives de l'Yser . . .* , Courrier de l'Armée, Nov. 1919

De Vos, Prof Dr L., *De carrière van Gen. P.A. Nuyten*, Brussels, Unpublished,1990

Dusart, R., *De Overstromingen aan de IJzer in 1914,* L'Union Eendracht, Brussels, Sep/Oct.1989

E.V.C., *Nieuw document over de rol van Cogge, Het Volk,* 28 Oct. 1964

E.V.C., *Getuigenis van Karel Cogge . . . , Het Volk,* 29 Oct. 1964

E.V.C., *Het verhaal van Karel Cogge . . . , Het Volk*30 Oct. 1964

E.V.C., *Tussenkomst van Karel Cogge . . . , Het Volk,* 1 Nov. 1964

Gils, R., *Militaire Inundaties tijdens de Slag aan de IJzer,* Simon Stevin – stichting, Mededelingenblad, number 2, zomer 1986

Hans, A., *Een Vlaamsch Gedenkteeken,* H.L.N., 17 juni 1920

— *De Onderwaterzetting van het IJzergebied,* (deel I, II & III). H.L.N., 18, 20 & 25 juni 1920

Jamotte, Maj Gen V., *Quel est l'auteur de l'inondation salvatrice? Pourquoi Pas?* Bruxelles, number 1045, 10 août 1934,

Leper, J., *Pas de gloire pour les modestes?,* Fidélité, number 10, 1952

Nevejans, M., *De Waarheid over K. Cogge,* Bachten de Kupe, 19, number 6, Nov. – Dec. 1977,

Nuyten, Lt Col P.A., *Rôle et Genèse des Inondations, Courrier de l'Armée,* 1919

Oehler, Dr Ing Th., *Aufgaben des Wasserbauing. in den Kampfen bei Nieuport 1914/18, Wehrtechnische Monatshefte,* April 1935

— *Aus der Geschichte der Wasserhindernisse, Wehrtechnische Monatshefte,* September 1935

Paquot, G., *La Légende des Eclusiers de Nieuport,* (partie I, II, III & IV). L.F.L., numbers 153, 156, 157 & 158, 1, 4, 5 & 6 juin 1920

— *La Légende des Eclusiers de Nieuport,* L.F.L., number168, 16 juin 1920

Tasnier, Maj., *De Slag aan den IJser,17-31 oct.1914,,* Onze Helden, Brussels, S.A.B.d' Imp., 1922

Tasnier, Maj L., *Cogge et les Inondations de l'Yser, Courrier de l'Armée,* 1926

Thys, Cdt Robert, *La Légende des Eclusiers de Nieuport,* (partie 1 & 2), L.F.L., numbers185 & 186, 3 & 4 juillet 1920

T'Jaeckx, R. E., *Hendrik Geeraert, Het Strijdersblad,*20 sep. 1954

Umé, Maj F., *La Légende des Eclusiers de Nieuport,* L.F.L., number17, 26 juin 1920,

Vols, Jos., *De Overstromingen in de IJzerstreek,* Bachten de Kupe, n.d.

Index

General Index

The names of hydraulic structures and waterways in western Belgium have not been included in the General Index. For them we refer to the Map Index.

Where we did not know a first name, a rank might have been substituted.

Only Belgian regiments have been included.

1st de Ligne Rgt: 67
1st Grenadiers Rgt: 193
1st Rgt Chasseurs à Cheval: 100
1st Rgt Chasseurs à pied: 134
2nd Rgt Guides: 67
2nd Rgt Chasseurs à pied: 152
3rd de Ligne Rgt: 212
4th de Ligne Rgt: 134, 193, 212
5th de Ligne Rgt: 219
6th de Ligne Rgt: 151, 219, 222
7th de Ligne Rgt: 27, 138
9th de Ligne Rgt: 134
10th de Ligne Rgt: 219
11th de Ligne Rgt: 152
12th de Ligne Rgt: 152
13th de Ligne Rgt: 219
14th de Ligne Rgt: 143, 151, 222, 227
Adam (Lt): 195, 199
Adventure (British light cruiser): 83
Albert I (King): xix, xx, xxi, 9, 13–14, 17, 22, 30, 34–35, 38–40, 45, 47–50, 55–56, 58, 65, 68–72, 79, 82, 84,
87, 89–93, 96, 109, 114–116, 120, 125, 135, 138, 163, 183–185, 207, 216, 226, 228, 230–232, 242, 246–247, 251–252
Albert II (King): xxi
All Saints' Day: 223
All Souls' Day: 226
Allewaerts: 170, 180
Amazon (British destroyer): 116, 120, 124
Ameland: 43
Amical (Belgian tugboat): 77
Amsterdams Peil: 248
Anciaux (Lt): 148
Aneca (G.): 161
Antwerp Roads: 5
Arch Bridge: 187–188, 207
Artillerie de Bruxelles: 33
Aspertagh: 78
Asquith (Lord): 7
Aston (Sir G.): 12, 44
Athlone (Prince A. of Teck, Lord): 145, 156
Attentive (British light cruiser): 83
Augagneur (V.): 79, 82
Avre River: 185

Baix (Gen): 141
Ballon (B.): 95, 128, 130, 214
Bamburgh Farm, Great: 115, 124, 134, 137, 146, 166
Bayern (Crown Prince R. von): 96, 103
Bayly (Sir L.): 43
Bazaine (A.F.): 14, 39
Beke: 78
Belgian Railway Company: 60
Belle (K. Van): 130, 214
Berchem, fortified barracks: 14
Bernard (H.): 143, 251
Beseler (H.H. von): 222

Bidon (Gen): 58, 113–114
Billemont (H.): 215
Biscay, Gulf of: 201
Biter (British aircaft carrier): 120
Blanpain (Cdr): 206
Blériot (L.): 65
Blokhuis Farm: 116
Blue House Farm: 113–114
Boelare House (Eecloo): 27–28
Bogaerde: 75
Bonaparte, (Emperor Napoleon): 6, 46
Borkum: 43
Borlon (Cdr): 84, 128, 148–149, 164, 210–212
Bornem, Fort: 2
Bourgeois: 196–198, 204, 243
Bourgoignie (L.): 165, 182, 197–198, 201, 204, 242–244
Brécard (Col): 62, 72, 81–82, 89, 90, 93, 114, 121, 135, 138, 140, 157, 166, 168, 178–179, 185, 192, 207
Breendonck, Fort: 2, 253
Brialmont (H.): 1, 2
Brichet: 182, 197
Bridges (T.): 8, 9, 67–69, 81–82, 121, 135, 143, 145, 156, 183
Brigade de Cavalerie Independante: 33, 50
Brilliant (British cruiser): 135, 138, 146
Broqueville (C. de): xx, 13, 20, 36, 38, 47, 49, 52, 55–56, 61, 79, 89, 90, 94, 143, 166, 182, 196–198, 204, 243
Bulthink (Cdr): 49
Bustard (British gunboat): 134, 146, 205

261

262

Map Index

The official Dutch name is in brackets.

R = river, C = city, T = town, V = village, H = hamlet, F = French name.